DAILY LIFE OF

THE JEWS IN THE MIDDLE AGES

The Greenwood Press "Daily Life Through History" Series

DAILY LIFE OF

THE JEWS IN THE MIDDLE AGES

NORMAN ROTH

The Greenwood Press "Daily Life Through History" Series

GREENWOOD PRESS
Westport, Connecticut • London

Library of Congress Cataloging-in-Publication Data

Roth, Norman, 1938–
   Daily life of the Jews in the Middle Ages / Norman Roth.
     p. cm. — (Greenwood Press "Daily life through history" series, ISSN 1080–4749)
   Includes bibliographical references and index.
   ISBN 0–313–32865–X
1. Jews—Social life and customs. 2. Jews—Intellectual life. 3. Jews—History—70–1789.
I. Title. II. Series.
DS112.R767   2005
305.892'4'00902—dc22   2005020790

British Library Cataloguing in Publication Data is available.

Library of Congress Catalog Card Number: 2005020790
ISBN: 0–313–32865–X
ISSN: 1080–4749

First published in 2005

Greenwood Press, 88 Post Road West, Westport, CT 06881
An imprint of Greenwood Publishing Group, Inc.
www.greenwood.com

Printed in the United States of America

The paper used in this book complies with the
Permanent Paper Standard issued by the National
Information Standards Organization (Z39.48–1984).

10 9 8 7 6 5 4 3 2 1

CONTENTS

INTRODUCTION

This book is not a history of the Jews in the medieval period (see "Bibliography" for some suggestions); rather, it focuses on aspects of Jewish culture and daily life. How did the Jews live? What was important to them, individually and as communities, during the medieval period? However, it is useful to provide here a very brief overall picture of the countries where Jews lived and what conditions were like for Jews in those lands.

For Jewish history, the term Middle Ages does not have the same meaning that it does generally. Arbitrary dates are set by historians for the beginning of the Middle Ages, some suggesting the fall of Rome (in the early fifth century, but what year? 410 is often agreed upon) and others even with the beginning of Christianity. The end of the period is also problematic. It was once assumed that a clear distinction could be made between the Middle Ages and the Renaissance, but then historians began talking about a Renaissance that began progressively earlier (eleventh century in some views, which surely is right in the middle of the Middle Ages). As for the Jews, the origins of Christianity meant very little to them, and even less the fall of Rome. Many Jewish writers of the nineteenth century, and even some today, thought that the Middle Ages for the Jews extended into modern times, at least the end of the seventeenth century, and some have suggested even later than that (this is due to a distorted interpretation of Jewish history according to which Jews were entirely without "culture" until the early modern period, which is, of course, false).

It would seem, however, that we can settle upon a period in Jewish history that marked a significant turning point, and that is the completion of the Babylonian Talmud, traditionally at the end of the fifth century (although in fact many additions were made after that), and the beginning of the geonic period. There seems to be a convenient and quite precise year for the end of the Jewish Middle Ages: 1492, the year of the expulsion of the Jews from Spain. That was such a cataclysmic event, not only for the Spanish Jews but for the whole Jewish world, that it clearly marks the end of an epoch.

Furthermore, most general histories of the medieval period focus exclusively, or at least primarily, on Christian Europe. This cannot be so with regard to Jewish history, for Jews lived in Muslim lands and the Byzantine Empire as well as in Christian Europe.

Jewish history begins with the "Holy Land," the country that medieval Christians called Palestine, after the old Roman name, and that for the Jews was *Erets Yisrael*, the Land of Israel, or simply "the Land." There were many conquests of the Land, by the Assyrians and Babylonians, the Hellenized Syrians, and the Romans. This had resulted in Jews being scattered in several lands, the Diaspora or dispersion (Hebrew *galut*), long before the final destruction of the Temple and the capital of Jerusalem by the Romans in 69–70 C.E.[1] (C.E. means Common Era, a term used by scholars to avoid the Christian designations B.C. and A.D.).

By the first century C.E. there was an enormous Jewish population scattered throughout the Roman empire and beyond, from Arabia to Asia Minor, Syria, Babylonia, and Egypt. Some of these countries (Syria, Asia Minor, Egypt, Babylonia) had at least one million Jews each. Over four million Jews lived in the Roman Empire, excluding Palestine. One out of five people in the Mediterranean world of the first century was a Jew. The Sibylline Oracles (part of the Pseudepigrapha, or books outside of the official canon of the Bible) observed: "And every land shall be full of [the Jews] and every sea; and everyone shall be incensed at your customs" (III. 271–72), which of course was true, as many in the Roman world despised the Jews. The Roman Strabo wrote that the Jews have "already gotten into all the cities, and it is hard to find a place in the habitable earth that has not admitted this tribe of men and is not possessed by them" (quoted by Josephus, *Antiquities* XIV.7.2).

The obvious question is, what happened to all of these Jews? When we come to the early Middle Ages, although there certainly are no reliable population figures, it is quite obvious that there were nowhere near a million Jews, much less several million as in the first and second centuries. There had been periods of persecution and killing of Jews in the Persian Empire, in the area that Jews continued to call Babylon, but these persecutions had been periodical and temporary, and it is impossible that vast numbers of Jews could have been killed. Some Jews in the Roman Empire, of course, had converted to Christianity, but the majority had simply assimilated and disappeared.

At the beginning of the sixth century, the largest Jewish population was still in "Babylonia" (Iraq), followed by the Byzantine Empire and then Egypt and North Africa. There were still very few Jews in Europe, mostly in Italy, parts of Spain, and certain towns in France (Gaul). The Land of Israel was never totally devoid of a Jewish population, but it was small. It had suffered further invasion by the Byzantines.

Jews in the *Byzantine Empire* and Asia Minor were severely persecuted by the Christians in the sixth and seventh centuries, and increasingly hostile legislation enacted in the theocratic state made life burdensome.[2] Jews were definitely "second-class citizens," and even their religious practices were subject to interference by the harsh laws. In spite of all this, at least some of them prospered economically, playing a significant role in international commerce, particularly the silk trade, and with a virtual monopoly on the manufacture of the royal purple dye used for the decoration of the cloaks of the emperors.

In the desert of Arabia, Muhammad (d. 632) had proclaimed a new religion, *Islam*, with himself as prophet. This religion was based in part on oral traditions he received from Jews and in part on similar traditions from Christians, but it was a definite reinterpretation of all these. At first, he appears to have believed that Jews in southern Arabia would flock to his new faith, but when he found that this was not to be, he turned his anger against them, making war on them and defeating and killing many. A curiosity was Yemen, where the ruler Dhu Nuwas, sometime after 516, converted to Judaism, along with most of his people. Christian Abyssinia several times invaded in an effort to wipe out these Jewish converts, who were rumored to have massacred some Christians, and at last they gained control of the country. The Jews, although persecuted and subject to discriminatory laws, continued to live in Yemen until modern times. In fact, there was a significant Jewish culture in Yemen in the medieval period and they were by no means cut off from the rest of the Jewish world, maintaining close ties with Jews in Egypt and Spain, for example.

The caliph Umar I in 634 drove all the Jews out of Arabia proper, expelling the last remaining ones in Khaibar in northern Arabia. He then began a series of conquests, starting with Palestine. When the Persians invaded that land in 614, the Jews joined in rebellion and raised an army in Jerusalem and Galilee to besiege Tyre. Their independence was short-lived, however, for in 640 the Arabs again invaded and conquered the land, and Jews were again banished from Jerusalem. Tiberias became the center of Jewish life until Jews were allowed again into Jerusalem in the eleventh century. With the conquest of the Persian empire by the Arabs in 637, followed by the conquests of Egypt and Mesopotamia (640–641), the majority of the Jews of the world came under Muslim domination. North Africa and Spain, as well as southern Italy, soon followed. The Muslim world now included territory, stretching to northern India, which was greater than the empire ruled by Alexander the Great.

At least until the end of the thirteenth century, the majority of the Jews in the world lived in these Muslim countries. Baghdad, the capital of the Abbasid caliphate, was established in 752, with the city being planned according to the astrological calculations of a Jew, the famous Masha'allah.[3] It was, coincidentally, right in the center of the area, marked by the joining of the Tigris and Euphrates rivers, where the ancient talmudic academies that had produced the Babylonian Talmud still flourished. Other important Jewish communities were soon established across the former Persian empire, some in cities that no longer exist.[4]

While Jewish settlement in the *Land of Israel* was confined mostly to Tiberias and a few other northern towns, there was a significant Jewish population in Syria, in towns all along the Nile in Egypt (where the chief center for the Jews was Fustat, a suburb of Cairo), and throughout North Africa and in Muslim Spain.[5] Enjoying generally cordial relations, if by no means full equality, with the newly converted Muslims of these lands (the Arabs remained, for the most part, in Arabia), Jews prospered economically and enjoyed the cultural advantages of the Muslim civilization, which we shall discuss in detail later.

Temporary setbacks included the persecution of Jews and Christians in *Egypt* and the Land of Israel (which was under Egyptian control) by the mad caliph al-Hakim, who imposed clothing and other restrictions (ca. 1005) and finally burned synagogues and churches (it was the rumor that he had destroyed the so-called Church of the Sepulcher in Jerusalem that launched the Crusades).[6] However, he rescinded some of his decrees and the situation returned to normal. In North Africa, the Almohads, a fanatical movement stressing strict religious practice, arose in the mid-twelfth century, and by 1147 they had captured most of North Africa, forcing Jews and Christians to convert or be killed. Numerous Jewish communities were destroyed. (They also conquered southern Spain, which will be discussed further on in this Introduction.)

Christian countries had an ambiguous policy toward the Jews. On the one hand, they were recognized as making an important economic contribution, particularly with their international commercial connections. On the other hand, many of the clergy hated them as "enemies" of Christianity. Synagogues were sometimes burned, and Jews were persecuted in other ways, while efforts were made to convince them to convert. But Christian theology and developing canon (Church) law also intervened to protect the Jews. St. Augustine (354–430), although no friend to the Jews, had argued that they must be preserved as "witnesses" to the truth of Christianity. More to the point, in practical terms, the first important pope, Gregory I (540–604), protected the status quo of the Jews and ordered the bishops of France to cease their efforts at compulsory baptism. He also ordered a stop to the burning of synagogues.

The privileged status, or "constitution," granted by him concerning the Jews was renewed by every pope in the Middle Ages, although by no means were all the popes friendly to the Jews. Hatred of them was more a theological than practical matter, however, and all the popes acted to protect the Jews in spite of often harsh expressions of feelings about them. It was the rulers of various countries, particularly France, England, and later Germany, who enacted discriminatory measures and expulsions against the Jews.

Jews lived in *Italy* from the time of the Roman Empire, but after its fall we have little or no information as to what became of the Jews.[7] There were some Jews in Rome itself after the fifth century, but there is no specific record of them until about 1000. Their tradition claimed that they were from the Land of Israel, as opposed to the majority of Jews elsewhere who were from Babylonia (however, Jews in Muslim Spain also made such claims, which may be merely propaganda). There were Jewish settlements in southern Italy, particularly the territory under Muslim control. In the twelfth and thirteenth centuries, the Jewish population in Italy increased, particularly in the papal states (the central part) where Jews were free from persecution. Jewish culture, particularly talmudic study, thrived in Italy from the earliest times, and there were important connections between the scholars of Italy and those of France and Germany. Later in the medieval period, Jews from Germany settled particularly in northern Italy and there were also immigrants from Spain in the fourteenth century, significantly increased after their expulsion from Spain, of course.

In *France* (Frankish Gaul), legends substitute for solid evidence as to the earliest settlement of Jews. In fact, nothing of certainty is known about them until the end of the sixth century.[8] Gregory of Tours condemned Cautinus, bishop of Clermont-Ferrand (ca. 551–571) for being on friendly terms with Jews, saying that this was not for their conversion, "which ought to be the preoccupation of a priest," but because he bought goods from them and was easily influenced by them. The next bishop, Avitus, indeed tried to convert the Jews, and one convert marched in the Easter procession in a white gown. Gregory wrote that "one of the Jews, no doubt put up to this by the devil, tipped some rancid oil on the head of this new convert." The infuriated mob destroyed the synagogue, and 500 Jews, reportedly, were forcibly baptized. It was this kind of activity that Pope Gregory I sought to end with his decree, but it had little practical effect at first.

In 582, King Chilperic also ordered that a large number of Jews be baptized, but many refused. A certain Priscus was especially obstinate and delayed receiving baptism until he could marry off his son to a Jewish woman in Marseilles. He had a quarrel with one of the converts, Phatyr, and on his way to the synagogue one Sabbath he was attacked and killed by Phatyr and some of his friends. Phatyr fled but was caught and killed by friends of Priscus. He was apparently the same Priscus whom Chilperic had befriended and from whom he bought goods. Once, in the presence of Gregory of Tours, he had tried to convince Priscus to believe in Christ, but Priscus replied "God has no need of a son, he has not provided himself with a son, and he does not brook any consort in his kingdom, for he said through the mouth of Moses: 'See now that I, even I, am he, and there is no god with me' (Deut. 32.39)." Gregory tried to argue using the usual Christian proof texts from the Bible, but "this wretched Jew" remained unconvinced.

In 585, King Guntram went to Orleans and was cheered there by the people, including Jews. Later at a banquet, the king reportedly said that the Jews had cheered him only so that he would order the rebuilding of their recently destroyed synagogue, but the king swore he would never do this, "for it is contrary to the Lord's will."[9]

In Carolingian France, we again have little information about Jews until the middle of the ninth century when Agobard, bishop of Lyons, and his disciple and successor Amulo, wrote and preached anti-Jewish propaganda, and the latter attempted to reinstate the Visigothic anti-Jewish legislation. Forced baptism of Jews, including children, was again practiced. In spite of this, Jews began to prosper in France in the tenth and eleventh centuries, largely through agriculture but also commerce to some extent. France was divided into counties, or territory under the independent control of counts, and the royal domain, or territory around Paris that belonged to the king. While there are no reliable figures, it has been estimated that few northern French Jewish communities had more than 100 families in the twelfth and thirteen centuries, and some had no more than 100 individuals. There were many more than this in the area around Paris.

In spite of the economic importance of the Jews, particularly in Paris itself, they were expelled from the royal domain by Philip II in 1182. They were ultimately recalled, but the situation became progressively worse, with a number of local expulsions from several cities throughout the thirteenth century, followed by another general expulsion from the country by order of Louis IX in 1250–1251. In spite of the fact that Jews were always recalled after a period of time, all of this greatly weakened their economic situation and therefore their usefulness to the king as contributors of taxes. In 1306, Philip IV decreed another general expulsion and seized all the property of the Jews.[10] They did not return to France (with the exception of Avignon in southern France) until the seventeenth century.

There was an increasing Jewish population in *Germany*[11](known as the Holy Roman Empire) throughout the eleventh and early twelfth centuries. This was due chiefly to the privileges granted them by lords of the cities and by the rulers themselves, urging them to settle in order to increase commercial activity and economic prosperity. Nevertheless, there was a recognized need to protect the Jews from potential enemies who might attack them. Thus, when the bishop of Speyer (Germany) in 1084 sought to attract Jews to his city, he provided a special place for them where they could be guarded by walls. His intention in bringing Jews there, he wrote, was that "the glory of the town would be increased a thousand times" by having Jews settle there. In 1157, the Jews of Worms received a general charter of privileges from Emperor Frederick I (Barbarossa), a ruler who was on good relations with "his" Jews and who was genuinely admired by them.[12] It should be noted, however, that these privileges were granted to specific Jews and in recognition of their actual or potential commercial benefit. It would not be until the thirteenth century, under the enlightened Frederick II, that Jews throughout the Holy Roman Empire would be granted a general privilege.

Much has been written about the so-called chamber serfdom of the Jews; that is, that they "belonged" to the imperial chamber. However, they were not serfs by any definition applicable in the Middle Ages, nor were they so called (the term *servi*, in *servi camera*, does not mean serfs). While they did not have absolute equality with Christians in many respects, neither were they feudal vassals, and, in fact, they had the right to move and live wherever they chose. That was a privilege enjoyed by very few Christians. Peasants were truly vassals, and even the nobles were tied to their overlords, and ultimately to the king, by feudal custom. Within their communities, Jews had full autonomy and freedom to observe their own laws.

The Jews suffered two major tragedies: the attack on several communities along the Rhine at the time of the First Crusade (1096), when some were killed and others forcibly baptized (although allowed to return to the Jewish fold), and again during the devastations of the Black Death, or plague, in 1348.[13] The situation in Germany grew worse throughout the fourteenth century, with numerous attacks and expulsions. The fifteenth century was even worse, including expulsions from towns and from entire territories.

In *England*, the Jews also received a charter of protection from Henry I (1100–1135), which was subsequently renewed by Henry II (1154–1189).[14] There was a small Jewish population, primarily in London, Norfolk, Oxford (part of the present university was built on land once owned by Jews), Lincoln, and York. The Jews survived mostly on moneylending, far more so than in the rest of Europe.

Edward I, after heavily taxing the Jews for years, finally expelled them in 1290, seizing all their property. Jews did not return to England until the time of Oliver Cromwell in the seventeenth century.

Jews had lived in *Spain* from at least 300 and probably earlier. However, the Germanic Visigoths conquered the Iberian Peninsula in the sixth century with the aid of the Byzantines, who controlled almost all of southern Spain until it was regained by the Visigoth King Swinthila (621–631). The Jews were then subjected to ever-increasing persecution and restrictions, including repeated efforts to convert all of them.[15] Some escaped to Gaul, but there in 629 King Dagobert decided to expel all Jews who would not accept Christianity. Although not all the Jews in Visigothic Spain converted, apparently most of them did. Finally, in 694, there was an order that all remaining Jews were to lose their property and become perpetual slaves. Only the invasion and conquest of nearly all of Spain by the Muslim Berbers of North Africa in 711 brought freedom to the Jews, and with it a substantial immigration of Jews from other Muslim lands.

The Jews thrived under Muslim rule, and although they had to pay taxes and did not enjoy the full benefits of equal status with the Muslims, they quickly adapted themselves to Muslim culture while at the same time preserving their own independent religion and ethnic tradition.[16] The Berber rebellion and civil war in 1010 brought the end of the independent caliphate of Muslim Spain, with a number of separate city-kingdoms (*taifas*) being established throughout Spain. Granada was the largest and most powerful, with a Jew, Samuel Ibn Naghrillah, serving as prime minister and commander of the army, fighting off attacks from jealous neighboring kingdoms and mercenary Christian soldiers in their service. Jews served as ministers also in other *taifas*, such as Zaragoza.

In the eleventh century, the Christians began the campaigns to reconquer land held by the Muslims. They won an important naval victory at Zallaqa in 1086, and the independent Muslim kingdoms ceased their warring against each other and invited the Almoravids from North Africa to help them fight against the Christians. In fact, the Almoravids took control of the entire Muslim part of Spain. However, the Jews were not persecuted under Almoravid rule, and with the exception of some incidents, such as a riot against the Jews in Córdoba in 1135, and some restrictions imposed locally, such as in Seville, the Jews prospered. This was, in fact, a period of great cultural development for the Jews.

The situation changed sharply when a fanatical Muslim religious group, the Almohads, took control of North Africa and in 1145 invaded southern Spain (al-Andalus), although they were not firmly established until 1163. Jews and Christians were persecuted, and many communities were destroyed. Jews were either forced to convert to Islam (many with secret reservations) or flee their homes. Maimonides and his family fled to Fez in North Africa, where, uniquely, Jews were not persecuted, and then to the Land of Israel, with Maimonides finally settling in Egypt after his father's death. Other Jews fled to Christian cities in northern Spain or Provence, bringing with them their knowledge of Arabic and of science, mathematics, and literature. Slowly the Christians were able to conquer more and more territory controlled by the Almohads, and by the middle of the thirteenth century almost all Muslim territory, except for the kingdom of Granada, had fallen to the Christians.

Neither Jews nor Muslims were persecuted by the Christians, who in fact needed both groups not only to maintain the newly conquered cities but also for their skill in agriculture and their knowledge of science, medicine, and other things. The newly conquered territory was divided between the kingdom of Aragon-Catalonia, under Jaime I (known as "the Conqueror," 1213–1276) and the united kingdom of Castile and Leon. Jewish legal rights were fully protected and their community autonomy was recognized. Jews served as officials, physicians, and advisors to Christian rulers much in the same way they had served Muslim kings. Alfonso X ("the Wise," 1252–1284) was the most famous of these rulers, under whom important scientific translation and original work was done by Jews.

Under subsequent rulers in both kingdoms, the situation of the Jews generally remained very good. There were periods of unrest and fluctuation in the overall pattern (as the present king of Spain, Juan Carlos, has aptly said, Jewish history in Spain was marked by "light and shadow"), but Spain's Jews never suffered the kinds of persecutions that happened with some frequency in France or Germany. Only in the summer of 1391, aroused by a fanatic archdeacon in Seville, did mobs throughout Spain attack Jewish communities. Many Jews were robbed or killed, in spite of the efforts by the kings to protect them, and many more were baptized. This time the baptisms were seldom forced but rather voluntary, from fear of what might yet happen to them. Thus, there arose a large group of *conversos*, or Jewish converts to Christianity, which was increased by the thousands due to the missionary campaign of Vicente Ferrer in the early fifteenth century.

In 1479, Fernando and Isabel united both kingdoms under their rule. They were as protective of their Jewish subjects as their predecessors had been. The problem was not the Jews, but the growing number of *conversos*, many of whom held positions of power in the government and in the church. This aroused jealousy and hatred on the part of many "Old Christians," which erupted in riots and civil war. The Inquisition, which had been in operation earlier, in the thirteenth century, to uproot heresy among Christians, was now revived in order to suppress the *conversos*, using the fiction that they were also heretics, although in fact they were good Christians. Thousands were burned at the stake and their property confiscated. The way was now open for the enemies of the Jews to demand their expulsion, on the pretext that they were influencing *conversos* (whom in fact they hated, since many were bitter enemies of the Jews). In 1492, the king and queen agreed to these demands and ordered the expulsion of all Jews from Spain, thus bringing to an end the oldest and most important Jewish civilization in the medieval world.[17]

Other lands in Christian Europe where Jews lived in the Middle Ages include Austria, Hungary, Bohemia (which included the modern Czech territories) and Poland.[18] Jews lived in Austria from at least the eighth century, but significant numbers appeared only in the thirteenth century. They had certain privileges and protection, but from the late thirteenth century on their situation worsened, until at last they were massacred in Vienna and expelled in 1420. There were some important rabbis who lived in Austria.

In Hungary, Jews originally were tolerated, but the thirteenth century brought increasing restrictions. However, the Tatar invasions in mid-century depopulated the country, and in order to resettle the cities, Jews were drawn back by the granting of new privileges. However, once again in the fourteenth century there were increased restrictions and heavy taxation imposed upon the Jews. The situation improved temporarily in the fifteenth century, but in 1490 there were ritual murder charges against Jews, resulting in riots.

Small groups of Jews settled in Poland from the tenth century on, but only in the thirteenth century was there a significant Jewish population in the Duchy of Lithuania and in Poland. Jews suffering persecution in Germany were attracted by the favorable conditions in Poland and Lithuania (which became united in the fourteenth century). The Jews enjoyed extensive privileges, particularly commercial, in the form of a royal charter from 1264, which was renewed and expanded in the fifteenth century.

While Jews indeed suffered periods of discrimination and persecution in the medieval world, this is not the whole of the story. Indeed, such persecution was not the norm and major incidents are separated by centuries and not just years. In the meanwhile, Jews generally enjoyed peace and prosperity, living in harmony if not always real friendship with their neighbors, whether Muslims or Christians. In many respects, the daily life of the Jew in the Middle Ages was not different from that of these neighbors. They shared a common language, economic situation, and style of life. The differences were, however, significant. Jewish culture was not simply a religion but rather included every aspect of personal and community life. Education was central to this, since knowledge not only of the Bible and of prayers was required but also of at least basic Jewish law.

In spite of the tensions that undeniably existed, the medieval Jew did not consider life intolerable or even particularly burdensome. Significant advances were made by Jews in all fields of knowledge, primarily in the Muslim world and in Spain but also in other lands. There was, as we shall see, also time for celebrations and enjoyment. There was, finally, a strong sense of belonging, to the family, the community and in a very real sense to the larger *am Yisrael* (people of Israel, the whole Jewish people).

NOTES

1. It is curious that terms that originally applied exclusively to the darkest aspects of Jewish history, such as *ghetto, diaspora,* or even *holocaust* have been appropriated and applied to other minority groups. This is not only historically and sociologically inaccurate, it dilutes and diminishes the original meaning of such concepts. Diaspora, for example, has a unique meaning in Jewish life, where it refers not only to the dispersion of Jews throughout the world, but also to the

continued existence of the Jews as a people and the centrality of their attachment to their ancestral land. These factors are absent entirely or in large part among other minorities. It goes without saying that to use the highly specific, and emotional, term holocaust to describe in any way the sufferings, however unjust, of African slaves, for example, is inaccurate.

2. See the article "Byzantium," with bibliographical references, in Norman Roth, ed., *Medieval Jewish Civilization: An Encyclopedia* (New York, 2003).

3. See the article on him in Roth, ibid.

4. Further information, and bibliography, on the Jews in the medieval Muslim world may be found in various articles in Roth, ibid.; for example, "Almohads," "Almoravids," "Islam," and "North Africa."

5. See "Palestine" in Roth, ibid.

6. See the article "Egypt," ibid.

7. It was, unfortunately, not possible to include a general article on Italy in *Medieval Jewish Civilization,* but see the index there and also the articles "Rome" and "Sicily."

8. Jews in France are discussed in various articles in Roth, ibid., especially the articles on individual kings; see also "Expulsion, France" and "French Law, Jews in." Particularly important is William Chester Jordan, *The French Monarchy and the Jews* (Philadelphia, 1989).

9. Gregory of Tours, *The History of the Franks,* translated Lewis Thorpe (Penguin Books, 1974) 207 (Book IV. 12), 265–67 (Book V. 11), 347–48 (Book VI. 17), 330–32 (Book VI. 5), 433 (Book VIII. 1).

10. See details in the article "Expulsion, France" in Roth, *Medieval Jewish Civilization.*

11. Several articles in Roth, ibid., deal with Jews in Germany; particularly "Germany," "German Law, Jews in" and articles on various rulers.

12. See the translation of some of these privileges in Robert Chazan, *Church, State, and Jew in the Middle Ages* (New York, 1980), 58 ff.

13. See "Black Death" and "Crusades" in Roth, *Medieval Jewish Civilization.* See further discussion of these here in Chapter 9.

14. See the article and bibliography in Roth, ibid.

15. See details in chapter one of Norman Roth, *Jews, Visigoths & Muslims in Medieval Spain* (Leiden, 1994). Various articles on Spain in Roth, *Medieval Jewish Civilization,* include "Andalucia," "Aragon-Catalonia," "Castile," "Expulsion, Spain," "Leon," "Provence, Spanish" and on various rulers.

16. For all of the following, see *Jews, Visigoths & Muslims in Medieval Spain.*

17. For details on all of these events, see Norman Roth, *Conversos, Inquisition, and the Expulsion of the Jews from Spain* (Madison, Wisc., 1995; revised paper ed., 2002).

18. See the excellent articles on Austria and Poland in Roth, *Medieval Jewish Civilization.* Unfortunately, it was not possible to find an author to write on Hungary; see now Nora Berend, *At the Gate of Christendom: Jews, Muslims, and "Pagans" in Medieval Hungary, c. 1000–c. 1300* (Cambridge Studies in Medieval Life and Thought, Fourth Series, vol. 50; Cambridge, 2001).

A NOTE TO THE READER

Hopefully this book is neither too technical for the general reader who knows little about the Jewish culture and Jews in the Middle Ages in particular, nor is it without interest even to the specialist in medieval Jewish history, since information will be found here that is not available readily, or at all, in other works. "There is no school (*beit midrash*) without innovation," as the old proverb states.

Every effort has been made to include as many aspects of what was important in the daily life of medieval Jews as possible. Due to technical restraints, certain things could not be dealt with here, such as clothing worn by Jews, details about agricultural activity, and some other things. The reader is advised to consult the appropriate articles on these items in Norman Roth, ed., *Medieval Jewish Civilization* (see the Bibliography at the end of this book).

Wherever possible, technical terms have been avoided, including most Hebrew terms. The few exceptions are such common words as Torah or Hagadah (there is no sound reason for the "doubling" of Hebrew letters in transliteration, so that has been avoided). There is a short Glossary at the end of the book. No diacritical marks or accent marks have been used for non-English words or names.

I have tried to keep notes to a minimum, but in some cases these could not be avoided. Wherever possible, except for some sources, bibliographical references are to works in English.

CHRONOLOGY

5th–6th centuries	Completion and additions to the Babylonian Talmud
6th–mid-11th centuries	Classical period of the *geonim*
620–630	Muhammad and the rise of Islam in Arabia
7th–8th centuries	Muslim conquests
711	Muslim invasion of Spain, end of Visigothic kingdom
882–942	Sa'adyah *Gaon* (in this period also al-Kindi, famous Muslim philosopher)
1000–1066	Samuel Ibn Naghrillah (Spain; 993–1056) Jews settle in England (1066), with William the Conqueror Solomon Ibn Gabirol (1021–ca. 1050?)
1096	First Crusade; Jews attacked in Germany and elsewhere
1040–1140	Rashi (1040–1105) Judah ha-Levy (1075–1141)
ca. 1092–1167	Abraham Ibn Ezra

1100–1200   Maimonides (1138–1204); in this period
                       "Averroes," great Muslim philosopher
                       Second Crusade (1150)

12th–13th centuries Christian "reconquest" of Muslim Spain
                       Great period of Hebrew poetry and biblical
                       commentary in Spain
                       Important Jewish contributions in science,
                       mathematics
                       Repeated expulsions of Jews from France
                       Burning of Talmud at Paris (1240)
                       Expulsion of Jews from England (1290)

14th century   Expulsion from France (1306)
                       "Shepherds' Uprising" (1320; Pope John
                       XXII ordered burning of Talmud throughout
                       France)
                       "Black Death" (1348)
                       Final Expulsion from France (1360)
                       Attacks on Jews throughout Spain (1391)

15th century   First Hebrew book printed (1475)
                       Expulsions from various countries
                       Expulsion from Spain (1492)

1

DEFINING THE MEDIEVAL JEW

It may seem peculiar to talk about defining the medieval Jew, since as a people the Jews have remained basically unchanged throughout their history. Well, yes and no. It is, first of all, crucial to understand that Judaism is not a religion but a civilization, a culture (this will be discussed further in Chapter 4). What is meant by civilization? Sociologists would no doubt offer many different definitions but would probably agree that it includes a common language, a common history, a variety of cultural manifestations (art, music, literature, and in more sophisticated cultures such things as philosophy and science), and a common identity or sense of being and belonging. This does not mean that there are not elements in Jewish life that may be classified as religious, but that this is not the *definition* of what it means to be a Jew.

However, as with all civilizations, Jewish culture has evolved and changed. Jewish life was quite different in the Hellenistic period from what it was in the biblical period, and again under Roman occupation of the Land of Israel. There were also significant differences in Jewish civilization in the Land and outside of it, in the Diaspora. The loss of the ancestral homeland, and the destruction of the Temple, in 70 C.E. brought about a cataclysmic change in the lives of Jews and in their national consciousness. These are issues that, in spite of all the many historical accounts that have been written, have not yet been carefully analyzed.

A major distinction that separates the medieval from modern and contemporary Jews is the strong sense belonging, of being part of a people that shared a common history, language, and cultural characteristics. Jews

Medieval Altar (twelfth century). The circumcision of Isaac. Abraham with a medieval Jewish hat. Nicolas of Verdun (c. 1150–1205). Klosterneuburg Abbey, Austria. Erich Lessing/Art Resource.

were unique in their sense of belonging to an ancient civilization that dates to biblical times. This was not true, for example, of Christians, who in spite of the theoretical claim of kinship with ancient Rome (the so-called Holy Roman Emperor, for example) really had neither an awareness of that culture and history nor even a common bond with Christians in lands other than their own. Christianity, in the end, is a religion and not a civilization. Jews everywhere had a sense of their common heritage, and their past was very much present in their daily lives and consciousness.

While these things survived to some extent in the early post-medieval period, for various reasons there were already divisions and even discord among Jews in various countries. The much-heralded "Enlightenment," actually a disaster for Jewish civilization, and "Emancipation" of the eighteenth and nineteenth centuries brought an end to whatever unity had still existed among Jews. For the first time in history, the vast majority of Jews (nearly all of those in central and western Europe, and ultimately in the United States and other American countries) no longer understood Hebrew, for example. The very existence of the Jews for centuries proved that they could survive without a national homeland, but no civilization can endure without its national language, which is the energizing force for creating and transmitting its culture.

Furthermore, beginning in the sixteenth century, there was for the first time a major division among Jews, between Sefardim (Jews descended from those expelled from Spain in 1492) and Ashkenazim, or European Jews. By the late eighteenth century these tensions had reached a serious level, and added to it was the growing division between western Jews, particularly Germany, and central and eastern European Jews, which climaxed in the nineteenth century.

Jews in the modern period began for the first time to define themselves, and so were defined by others, in terms of religion rather than as a people. "Reform Judaism" was created in Germany, quickly spreading to other western countries, and as a reaction first "Orthodox" and then "Conservative" Judaisms emerged, both also in Germany. In eastern Europe, where traditional adherence to Jewish law and custom (and to a larger extent than elsewhere, also Hebrew) continued, the reaction against these new divisions ironically caused Jews in those lands also to become increasingly defined in terms of religion. Most were "orthodox," a term they despised and never used, but there were distinctions between Hasidim and their opponents (*Mitnagdim*), which were at least as divisive as the distinctions between Ashkenazim and Sefardim, to be explained below.

Many Jews, both in western and eastern Europe, were not religious at all. Some were assimilated, some indeed converted to Christianity, and others sought various forms of secular Jewish identity, including Zionism. This latter phenomenon, which in fact has a much longer history than generally imagined (owing much, incidentally, to romantic Christian notions that predate the first Jewish champions of the modern movement), would have seemed most peculiar to the medieval Jew.

The attachment to "Zion," the almost mystical concept of the Land of Israel, very much was rooted in the Bible and in daily prayers and blessings after meals, which refer to the longing for the restoration of the Land. Nor was it mere longing, since in fact Jews had continued to live there even after the Roman conquest and destruction of the Temple, and throughout the Middle Ages many Jews settled there, engaging in *aliyah*, or "ascent," as it is known in Hebrew.

There has been, and is, a tendency on the part of Israeli historians to exaggerate medieval Zionism, however, and references to massive immigration of Jews or of a movement for return to the Land are not historically accurate or useful. For the pre-modern Jew, however, love of the

Land of Israel and the expectation of its restoration were a natural part of their daily life and thought, not something separated from that as a particular or even unique form of Jewish identity. The current way of life in Israel very seriously calls into question whether Zionism devoid of Jewish cultural roots and heritage is a viable option.

DIVISION AND UNITY AMONG MEDIEVAL JEWS

European Jews divided themselves into two general categories: *Ashkenazim* (from Hebrew *Ashkenaz*, the biblical name that came to be used for Germany) and *Sefardim* (also from biblical *Sefarad*, which came to mean Spain; the common spelling "Sephardim" is an antiquated form). The latter term, contrary to popular opinion, did not refer to Jews living in medieval Spain, but only to those who had left there and lived somewhere else (primarily North Africa or Egypt; following the Expulsion, also other countries, such as Italy, the Ottoman Empire, Amsterdam, and eventually the "New World").

In addition to these two major divisions, we may also distinguish other Jews in European countries, such as Italy, who were originally neither Ashkenazim nor Sefardim (historians refer to these as Italianate Jews, a peculiar term that would have had no meaning to them); in addition there were medieval Swedish and other Scandinavian Jews, largely forgotten today. Of course, the Jews of England could hardly be classified as Ashkenazim, except that after the expulsion from England (1290) they generally resettled primarily in France and Germany.

Jews in France also were not called Ashkenazim, but the Jews in central Europe were so called. Most of them had in fact settled in these various countries as immigrants from Germany. The distinctions between Ashkenazim and Sefardim were not merely due to countries of origin, but as we shall see, also significant cultural differences, including religious observance. In addition, there were, of course, the Jews who lived in the Muslim lands, distinct from either the Ashkenazim or Sefardim, as well as those in the Byzantine empire and in the Mediterranean islands.

Generally, however, there were more things Jews of different countries had in common than those that separated them. They had a common language, Hebrew, which even though rarely used for conversational purposes was still the language of prayer and of culture, in which most writing was done. When Jews from different countries came in contact, however, they often used Hebrew as the only common language of communication. They were guided by a complex system of laws that governed all aspects of personal and community life, and while there were growing differences in interpretation, the general foundation was universally the same. Most important, perhaps, was that they considered themselves to be not a religion but a *people*, a nation. This sense of history and destiny held the Jews of every country in bond with each other and provided the will to survive, in spite of intolerance and persecution.

But a will to survive is not in itself enough to ensure survival; there has to be also a *reason* to survive, the glue that holds the community together. For the Jew, this was provided by "tradition," particularly law, and by cultural development and creativity.

JEWISH LAW IN DAILY AND COMMUNITY LIFE

Traditionally, Jewish life is not compartmentalized into religious versus secular. There was, in fact, no specific word for religion in Hebrew until the medieval period, when it was necessary to find a term by which to designate Christian belief, for example. The notion of Judaism, that is, a religion, simply did not exist and would have been meaningless to a medieval Jew. However, all of life, for the individual and the community, was defined by law, beginning with the Bible and particularly the Pentateuch, in Hebrew *Torah* (which does not, as often thought, mean "law" but rather "teaching"). The commandments contained in it were understood to be of divine origin and obligatory upon all Jews.

Of course, not all the commandments apply to everyone or to every place or time. Some were intended only for the Temple and the priests, for instance, while others are to be observed only in the Land of Israel or only when the Temple was in existence. For that matter, while the number of commandments (613) was known by tradition, there was no agreement on what exactly all the commandments were. Maimonides, the greatest medieval legal authority, wrote (in Judeo-Arabic) a book, *Sefer ha-mitzvot* (Book of the Commandments) in its traditional Hebrew translation, in which he attempted to enumerate all the commandments and classify them according to "positive" and "negative." Not everyone agreed with his classification.[1] Finally, it did not really matter, since the observance of the commandments depended on rabbinic interpretation as contained in the Talmud.

Even a casual look at the biblical commandments makes it obvious that they are in need of clarification and detail in order to be observed. Tradition maintained that in addition to the written Torah there was an "oral" Torah, and that already Moses had passed on the explanation he had received about the observance of the commandments.[2] Each succeeding generation of leaders added to this tradition. Eventually, around 200 C.E., a kind of summary of these laws was compiled in writing and this became known as the *Mishnah* (teaching). In its present form, this is in a relatively pure and simple Hebrew, and divided according to major subject areas (known as Orders), with further subdivision into more specific topics. This became the basis for the Talmud, reflecting centuries of discussion and debate both in the Land of Israel and in Babylon (actually, there is both a "Jerusalem," or Israel Talmud and a "Babylonian," but the latter is the most complete and authoritative).

It became an obligation for every Jewish adult male to study not only the Torah but the Talmud as well, at least to the extent of his ability

Moses, from the tomb of Pope Julius II in San Pietro in Vincoli, Rome. The two horns have been symbolic of Moses since the Hebrew word for "rays of light" was mistranslated as "horns" in the Vulgata, the medieval Latin translation of the Old Testament. Michelangelo (1475–1564). S. Pietro in Vincoli, Rome, Italy. Erich Lessing/Art Resource, NY.

(see Chapter 2). However, many of the laws discussed in the Talmud are scattered throughout various tractates, or individual volumes, and it is far from obvious where these laws are to be found. For example, actually very few of the laws dealing with the Sabbath are found in the tractate of that name. Important laws and concepts dealing with civil matters, such as acquisition of property, are to be found in the treatise on marriage. Furthermore, the language of the Talmud is Aramaic, which was the spoken language in Babylon but no longer in the Diaspora in the medieval period.

Thus, it was often literally a foreign language for many Jews and beyond their comprehension. Thus, it became apparent that a simpler method of teaching the laws was necessary.

CODES OF JEWISH LAW

There were early efforts by some of the *geonim* (rabbinical heads of academies in Baghdad) and their pupils, in the eighth and ninth centuries, to arrange at least the most applicable laws into manageable form in various collections. Some of these had a lasting influence, particularly in the Jewish communities of Spain. Equally important, and in some respects more so, were the responsa, or written replies to questions received by the *geonim*. Such questions came from Jewish communities, and individuals, all over the world (Italy, Germany, Spain and the Muslim lands, in particular). They dealt with practical matters of daily life but also with more theoretical aspects of talmudic law and traditions. Hundreds of such responsa have survived to the present, and these decisions, together with the thousands written by other medieval authorities, became an integral part of Jewish law. The situation is roughly analogous to constitutional law and case law in modern times. The responsa are not "amendments" to the original law but rather interpretation and application to ever-changing conditions (this is discussed further at the end of this section).

The Jews of Spain were rapidly developing their own expertise in talmudic study, and their curiosity about talmudic law and traditions led them to inquire of the *geonim* concerning the history of the development of the Mishnah and Talmud, as well as a request for an explanation of the laws and of prayers and observances. This resulted in two important works, which remain of essential value to modern historians, the *Igeret* (meaning letter, actually a treatise) of Sherira *Gaon* (*gaon* is the singular form of the plural *geonim*), which not only detailed the historical developments mentioned but also of the *yeshivot* (schools) and the *geonim* in Babylon, and the *Sidur* (prayer book) of Amram *Gaon*.[3]

An important scholar of the eleventh century, Isaac b. Jacob al-Fasi, lived in North Africa, but in 1088 he was forced to flee and went to Cordoba in Muslim Spain. He was the author of a major work on Jewish law, known simply as *Halakhot* (laws). This is divided according to the sections of the Talmud, but includes only the laws applicable outside the Land of Israel. It became so popular that it threatened to replace the actual study of the Talmud. The work has frequently been published and is found appended to standard editions of the Talmud.

Other important Spanish scholars, such as Judah b. Barzilay in Barcelona, were composing their own works on Jewish law. Very important also were various sages in Provence, and of course "Rashi" (Rabbi Solomon b. Isaac, ca. 1040–1105) and his disciples in France, who not only explained the Talmud in a manner that made it more accessible but also wrote legal works and responsa that developed Jewish law in France and elsewhere. His sons-in-law and students wrote additional commentaries and discussions (known as *Tosafot*) on the Talmud, which also became influential throughout the Jewish world. Excerpts of these are printed in standard editions of the Talmud, together with the commentary of Rashi.

Great German rabbis, such as Gershom b. Judah (ca. 960–1028) and Meir b. Barukh of Rothenburg (ca. 1220–1288) and others, also wrote important responsa that became central to Jewish law throughout Europe and were studied even in Spain.[4] Indeed, by the thirteenth century, at least, German Jewish scholars had replaced those of France as the leading authorities, with the exception of the even more important ones in Christian Spain (in terms of responsa and Jewish law, that is; the innovative talmudic commentaries of the Spanish rabbis were not generally known outside of Spain, apparently, until much later).

In Muslim Spain, students of al-Fasi continued his tradition, and the responsa of several of these rabbis, most notably Joseph Ibn Megas, added to the growing body of legal literature. However, it was a particular student from Cordoba, who even in adolescence wrote a work on logic and began (at the age of 13) his extensive commentary on the entire Mishnah, Moses b. Maimon ("Maimonides," 1138–1204), who would become the most important authority for Jewish law.[5] His commentary on the Mishnah had already gained him a great reputation, but like his other works it was written in Arabic and thus accessible only to Jews fluent in that language. The same is true of his numerous responsa, although many of these were eventually translated into Hebrew (the commentary on the Mishnah was also translated in Spain, but only in the thirteenth century). Thus, he determined to write his major legal work not in Arabic but in Hebrew, and moreover in a clear and simple style similar to that of the Mishnah. This composition, *Mishneh Torah* (Repetition of the Torah), in 14 large volumes, covers the totality of Jewish law, including such extremely difficult topics as the intercalation of the calendar and other matters requiring a very sophisticated knowledge of astronomy, and also the sacrifices and laws relating to the Temple. This work immediately became accepted, in spite of some harsh criticism, as the definitive code of Jewish law throughout the world.

The merit of the work, in addition to its impeccable and innovative Hebrew style, is that it is methodically organized not according to talmudic tractates but by main topics and subtopics, making it very easy to find a particular law. He utilized not only both the Palestinian and the Babylonian Talmud but also all the writings of the *geonim*, the laws of al-Fasi, and the responsa up to his own time. However, the fact that he never cited his sources led to criticism. This has continued to be an area of research to modern times, and in fact sources have been found for virtually all of his laws.

The strictures of his opponents, particularly Abraham b. David of Posquières, as well as the constant search for the sources upon which he based his decisions, led to several commentaries on the work during the Middle Ages (and beyond). The author of one of these commentaries, Joseph Caro, would, following the expulsion from Spain (1492), go on to write the code of law that eventually became the final such work, accepted by all Jews (although with different customs and observances among Ashkenazim and Sefardim), the *Shulhan arukh* (prepared table).

Abraham bar Natan of Lunel (d. 1215), an important rabbi who lived also in Toledo, Spain, wrote *Sefer ha-manhig* (book of direction, or leading) on laws of prayer, Sabbath, holidays, and fasts. This is a practical book, intended for lay people, written in simple and clear Hebrew. His sources were primarily the Talmud, but also *midrashim* and writings of the *geonim*. Of interest are some of the current customs that he mentions.

Some minor works were written by rabbis in France (Moses b. Jacob of Coucy, thirteenth century, *Sefer mitzvot gadol*, on the commandments) and Germany or Austria. While such works were consulted, none carried the authority of legal codification. Other works dealt with specific areas of Jewish law, such as Aaron ha-Kohen of Lunel, who lived also in Majorca, where he wrote (1330) *Orhot hayim* (ways of life) on the practical daily laws and prayers, holidays, and the Sabbath.

The last major code of Jewish law in the medieval period was the *Arba'ah turim* (four rows, after the rows of stones on the breastplate of the high priest), simply known as "the *Tur*," by Jacob b. Asher of Toledo (d. ca. 1336). He was one of the sons of a renowned authority, Asher b. Yehiel, who came from Germany to Toledo where he was the chief rabbi and author of numerous important works, including commentaries on the Talmud and legal responsa. Unlike his father, Jacob was not actually a rabbi and lived an impoverished existence. His comprehensive knowledge not only of the Talmud and all its commentaries but of all legal writings from the period of the *geonim* to those of his father was without equal in his age. The massive four volumes of his code are each devoted to a separate category of law: *Orhot hayim* on daily life, prayers, holidays and Sabbath; *Yoreh de'ah* on slaughter of meat and laws dealing with food, as well as other matters; *Even ha-'ezer* on laws relating to women, marriage, and divorce; and *Hoshen mishpat* on civil law.

This work was so important that it soon replaced the *Mishneh Torah* as the definitive work on Jewish law. Joseph Caro, who as mentioned wrote an important commentary on the work of Maimonides, also did the same on this work, and he later used it (including the four divisions) for his own code of law, which actually only updates that work with the addition of subsequent legal opinions and interpretations.

RESPONSA, SOURCES OF LAW AND OF HISTORY

Mention has been made of responsa (in Hebrew, *she'elot u-teshuvot*, questions and answers), and they are referred to frequently in other chapters.

A major difference between Jewish law and general law is that the Jew is not allowed "ignorance of the law," nor may he rely upon lawyers (although in practice in medieval Spain Jews often took cases to a non-Jewish court and were represented by lawyers; sometimes Jews even acted as lawyers for non-Jews). The obligation for knowing the law rests with each individual, and not only is this of theoretical importance (see Chapter 2) but also practical, for each individual must daily decide matters pertaining to the law.

When an issue arose that was not clear in the available literature, or that perhaps was something not previously dealt with in the sources, an individual or a community would turn to an important authority for his opinion. Such an authority was not necessarily a rabbi but had to be expert in Jewish law (examples of those who were not rabbis include Maimonides, Nahmanides, and the aforementioned Jacob b. Asher—who nevertheless did not issue his own decisions). The written response to the question would include usually a careful analysis of the problem on the basis of talmudic and other sources and the decision that was reached. Such a decision was then binding upon the party who asked the question, but not necessarily on anyone else. However, the decisions of highly respected authorities were collected even during their lives and widely circulated, and such decisions were given careful consideration as legal precedent for future cases. The most important decisions by highly regarded authorities became, in fact, part of the codified law.

Such collections of responsa of the *geonim*, originally in Arabic but translated in Hebrew, were studied carefully, particularly in Spain and Italy. Others of importance included the decisions of early rabbis in Muslim Spain and in Provence. Very important were the rulings of the aforementioned Gershom b. Judah of Germany, although debate continues as to which of the attributed rulings are actually by him. One that certainly was his prohibited polygamy (actually, polygyny, marrying more than one wife), which was allowed by talmudic law; however, this prohibition was not accepted in Spain or in Muslim lands. It was known, but rejected, in Christian Spain but was probably not even known in Muslim countries. The responsa of Meir b. Barukh of Rothenburg, also mentioned previously, were extremely important and influenced opinion also in Spain.

As noted, the responsa of Maimonides, primarily because they were written in Arabic, appear to have had little impact in Christian Spain. We possess actually few responsa from some of the later Spanish authorities, such as Nissim b. Reuben of Gerona or Nahmanides, but they are of importance on a number of issues. It may be assumed that more responsa were written by them that have not survived. Particularly important are the responsa of Solomon Ibn Adret (ca. 1233–1310) of Barcelona, which number in the thousands (more existed at one time).[6] These deal with every possible aspect of Jewish personal and communal life, as well as many that are of a philosophical nature or discuss biblical or rabbinical traditions.

The modern historian is less interested in these collections as they relate to Jewish law than as a major source for understanding medieval life and problems. Carefully studied, they open for us a window into the world of the medieval Jew.

COMMUNITY ORDINANCES AND ENFORCING THE LAWS

In addition to the formal codes of law and the decisions recorded in the responsa, every local community, no matter the size, had the right to enact its own ordinances. While these could not, theoretically, contradict written sources of law and certainly not talmudic law, custom (*minhag*) often nullifies law, and the communities, through their elected councils, had broad discretionary powers. Such ordinances might deal with marriages or divorce, requirements for contributing to the salary of teachers or other officials, customs to be observed in synagogue services, and similar matters. The obligation to participate in taxes collected by the community, in addition to government taxes, was frequently a part of the ordinances.

Larger or more important communities had rabbis who usually were sufficiently expert in the law to oversee the enactment of ordinances so that they would be in conformity with legal principles. However, rabbis, no matter how important, often found that they were powerless to change or annul decrees already enacted before they came to the city (this was the case in Spain, for example, with such major scholars as Asher b. Yehiel in Toledo and Isaac bar Sheshet in Zaragoza and elsewhere).

The foundation of community life, just as personal or family life, was conformity to the laws and customs. Seldom were there problems of non-compliance, much less of serious crime, but such things are not unknown (see below on crimes). The larger communities had sitting courts (the *beit din*), which could judge infractions and require compliance or impose fines or other punishments. In all communities, such courts could be convened when necessary (see Chapter 4 for details about the composition of such courts).

In addition, the rabbis had the power to impose penalties on particularly rebellious individuals who either violated a rabbinical (or, more seriously, a biblical) law or community ordinance. Fines and bans or excommunication were the standard penalties in most countries. Bans were temporary, whereas excommunication was more serious and of longer duration. In either case, the offender was effectively cut off from the community and, denied the normal privileges of daily contact, would soon seek forgiveness. In Spain (Christian as well as Muslim), Jews had the right to impose not only corporal punishment (usually whipping) but also capital punishment. The latter was reserved exclusively for cases of informers against their fellow Jews, or against the community as a whole; that is, those who reported to Christian authorities things that, if true (usually they were not), could result in serious harm.

Not all Jews were observant of the laws, of course. There were also cases of crimes such as robbery, fighting, illicit sexual relations, and even murder. In Christian Spain, where Jews were allowed to carry and use swords (which had been allowed also in Germany but was ultimately prohibited), they sometimes also wore swords to the synagogue and we hear of fights breaking out; quarrels and fighting sometimes took place in synagogues in other lands as well.[7]

The more serious criminal cases were brought, or came on their own, to the attention of the governmental authorities and were dealt with by them. In Christian Spain, this was always done with consultation of important rabbinical scholars. Whenever possible, even serious crimes were dealt with by the local Jewish community. There were instances of Jews who lived in violation of Jewish law, or who repeatedly engaged in illicit sex, and their only hope was to move to a distant community where they were not known. We have far less, which is to say almost no, information about such things in other European communities, due to a lack of sources (and possibly even the suppression of the discussion of them by the Jewish authorities).

LAW IN THE DAILY LIFE OF THE JEWS

As mentioned, Jewish law incorporates all of life, both for the individual and the community. What did this mean in practice? The day began with a short prayer thanking God for restoring the soul after sleep. The hands had to be washed, and the complete morning blessings and prayers had to be recited before breakfast was eaten (after which, if bread was eaten, the grace following meals had to be said).

Also before eating, the *talit* (so-called prayer shawl) and *tefilin* (phylacteries) were put on by adult males and the entire morning prayer service was recited, either at home or in the synagogue. On Sabbaths and holidays, the *tefilin* were not worn (since the days themselves are considered a sufficient "sign," or remembrance), but the services were much longer. Nothing could be eaten on those days, in any case, until after the morning prayers, and for the Sabbath and holidays this was the main meal, which was served at noon.

There are numerous laws involving the preparation of food. The housewife also had to be expert in these laws, knowing about the separation of utensils used for meat and for dairy products, and inspecting the organs of chickens for signs of disease that rendered them unfit for eating (carcasses of animals were inspected by the slaughterer).[8] There were other specific laws that women needed to know, such as laws governing the menstrual period or ritual immersion following childbirth. As explained in Chapter 3, the woman was generally in charge of the home and all that went on there, maintaining strict observance of the applicable laws.

Even children, as we would understand the term, were bound by Jewish law, since a male was considered legally an adult at the age of 13 and a girl at the age of 12. From that time, they were obligated in the observance of all commandments and laws, and even prior to those ages they observed many of them as a form of education. Young boys would usually accompany their fathers to weekday services in the morning, afternoon, and evening (or at least one of these), and on Sabbaths and holidays they would often go to the synagogue with their mothers so as not to disturb the men in their longer prayers.

The men, usually, but often also women, engaged in business during the day. Every detail of such activity, including profit allowed, the nature of buying and selling, contracts and partnerships, was determined by the civil law sections of Jewish law.[9] Whether buying or selling, a small item or a house or field, the requirements of law had to be followed. In modern times, this important aspect of Jewish law has practically fallen into desuetude because of the requirements of state law, and the mistaken belief that Jewish law has little of relevance for modern life in these areas. In the medieval (and later) period, however, far more freedom was given to Jews to follow their own laws in regard to most such matters.

Contracts and partnerships between Jews and Christians also were made in accord with Jewish law, which in any case was usually more explicit than the generally customary Christian laws. It is interesting that we hear of no cases of objections by Christians to such conditions. On the contrary, just as Jews, at least in Spain, often took cases to Christian courts, so Christians sometimes sought out Jewish courts to resolve their own disputes.

As we shall see in later chapters, all other aspects of community and personal life, including study, marriage, Sabbath and holiday observances, requirements to visit the sick, and many other matters were done in accord with specific laws.

THE JEWS AND LAWS OF THE LAND

Of course, there were laws enacted either by kings or local officials (in Spain, also codes of law for each town or region), which Jews also had to follow. Jewish law provides for this already in the Talmud with the concept of *dina de-malkhuta dina* (the law of the kingdom is the law); that is, Jews must obey the laws of the government, unless such laws violate fundamental Jewish law or are enacted in an arbitrary and dictatorial way. Major Jewish legal authorities in Spain determined that this means that such governmental laws must be officially promulgated, made publicly known and enacted in accord with legal precedent and authority.

In reality, particularly in Spain, there was close cooperation between the Jewish communities and authorities and the governing officials. Famous Jewish scholars were advisors to the kings. Furthermore, the kings were themselves required to know Jewish law and to consult with Jewish authorities in all cases involving Jews. No other country had such requirements, of course, but there was often more cooperation than commonly imagined.

Even in France, where there were severe restrictions on Jews and frequent expulsions and seizure of their property, Jews were sometimes able to affect changes in discriminatory legislation by simply threatening to leave. Only twice in the entire history of the Jewish presence in Spain were there such concerns: in the thirteenth century, when there was fear that the church measure, enacted at the Fourth Lateran Council (1215), requiring all Jews to wear the "badge,"[10] or device on their clothing by which they could be instantly identified, would be enforced in Spain (it was not), and again in the fourteenth century in the kingdom of Aragon-Catalonia when there were rumors of planned violence against the Jews, which also turned out to be false. In the latter case, as mentioned elsewhere here, an extraordinary meeting of representatives of all the Jewish communities was held and certain measures were proposed to respond to the threat.[11]

There were definitely discriminatory actions and laws that affected the Jews everywhere, including Spain. Taxes, of course, had to be paid, and while it is far from true that the Jews were a "sponge to be squeezed dry" for the financial benefit of the kings, as earlier writers have suggested, the tax burden was a constant problem. In addition to regular taxes, there were also special imposts on various things sold or imported and exported, and also for the expenses of wars. But while in other lands the Jews had little or no recourse to paying taxes and simply paid what they were told, in Spain communities could and did appeal if in a certain year they were unable to meet the allotment, and these appeals were nearly always successful and the amount reduced.

Jews in Muslim countries were often required to wear special clothing, or particular items that would identify them (first in Egypt in the early eleventh century), particularly under the rule of the fanatical Almoravids and Almohads, even in Muslim Spain. Possibly these laws influenced certain church officials and others who wished to discriminate against Jews in Christian Europe. In England, France, Germany, Austria, and elsewhere (but not Spain, except for some rare instances), Jews were required to wear particular kinds of clothing and especially the so-called Jewish hat, a brimmed hat with a high conical peak.[12]

While there were no "ghettos" in the Middle Ages, in many cities Jews were required to live in special quarters, separate from Christians. Even in normally tolerant Spain there were attempts to enforce such restrictions, some successful and others not. Other discriminatory laws included such things as prohibitions on selling certain items to Christians, particularly portions of meat that were not permitted to Jews by the dietary laws (such as the hindquarters). Special restrictions were enacted in Germany and elsewhere about the sale of items taken in pledge for loans or purchased from Christians that might, in fact, be found to be stolen items (even if the thief was not a Jew).

Of course, there were constant regulations in all countries regarding the interest Jews were allowed to charge on loans. Few Jews made a living from lending money, contrary to popular belief; however, when they had money available it was profitable to make such loans, if the Christians repaid them.[13] In France and England, particularly, this was a constant source of tension and often resulted in violence against the Jews and as a pretext for their expulsion. Only in the later medieval period in Germany was this also the case. The expulsion of the Jews from Spain, however, had nothing to do with this, nor were there usually any serious problems involving money lending.

Generally, the medieval Jew, while living a life controlled both by Jewish and general law, found that life far from intolerable or burdensome and was able to make adjustments to live in harmony, albeit precariously, with the Gentile world.

BEYOND LAW: THE SPIRITUAL LIFE OF THE JEW

It is always difficult to discuss the operation and impact of law in Jewish life without making it sound like a burden. Few medieval Jews would have considered it as such, and this is not something about which we need to conjecture as we have sources (*e.g.*, the responsa) that demonstrate the extent to which ordinary Jews were deeply committed to the observance of even the most obscure of such laws. For example, a simple statement in the Talmud states the general rule that "seeing causes real damage," that is, one may not look into the windows of another person's house. The responsa from Spain reveal many questions dealing with this, such as when putting in a new window that would then be opposite the windows of a neighbor, or whether such a law applies when a Christian builds a house next door to the Jew (it does), and other such instances. These questions came not from rabbis but from ordinary Jews who were concerned with careful fulfillment of all the laws.

The extent to which it is possible to misunderstand the concept of law in Jewish life is demonstrated by the statements of a careful Christian scholar who was unusually well informed about Jewish law and practice, who wrote that the statement in the Talmud that he who would become pious should study *Neziqin* (Damages), while another rabbi said that he should study *Avot*, mean the same tractate (*i.e.*, the latter, or "Ethics of the Fathers"), since the Order of *Neziqin* contains tractates that are "purely juridical and in no way calculated to promote" piety.[14] This, however, is completely incorrect, since in the Jewish view it is precisely the careful observance of the civil law governing relations between people that is the foundation of true piety, and not just the ethical teachings, however inspiring, contained in *Avot*.

However, life was not entirely focused on what was or was not permitted. In addition to the daily and Sabbath prayers, whether in the synagogue or at home, and the observance of frequent holidays and joyous occasions such as betrothals, marriages, or the birth of a child, many sought comfort in a deeper analysis of their relationship, individually and as a people, with God. Such things as the study of the Bible, not as an academic exercise but in a spirit of belief and as a source of strength or solace in times of distress, played a major part in normal Jewish life.

Even the uniquely ascetic and sometimes excessive work of the thirteenth-century German pietist (*hasidei Ashkenaz*) movement known as *Sefer hasidim* incorporates some examples reflecting this spiritual element. One such is the charming story of a shepherd who was so ignorant that he did not know what to pray and a passing scholar heard him pray "Master of the world, it is known to You that if anyone gives me animals to tend I charge them, but if You were to give me an animal to watch I would do it for free because of my love for You." The scholar said to him, "Fool, that is not the way to pray," and taught him the correct prayers. But when the scholar left, the shepherd forgot all that he had taught him and also stopped saying his own simple prayers since he had been told they were wrong. That night the scholar had a dream in which he was told "You have stolen from Me one of My children." The next day he went and found the shepherd and told him to continue praying as he had been accustomed.[15]

One of the challenges Jews faced from Christian antagonists, and a matter of concern to them in any case, was the continued length of the "exile." Rabbinical tradition assured them that the loss of their homeland and their dispersion among the nations would not last forever, and that the awaited messiah would appear and restore them to their ancestral home. Nevertheless, over a thousand years had passed with no sign of such an event. It is not surprising, therefore, that we find constant calculations, even by great scholars and normally rational men, as to the exact year in which the messiah would come. The pious hope expressed in the closing words of the Passover *seder*, "Next year in Jerusalem!" must have been particularly poignant to the Jews who saw no real end in sight for the prolonged separation from their Land.

MYSTICISM, PIETISM, AND QABALAH

Mysticism in various forms was also an important part of medieval Jewish existence. Such traditions are found not only in the Talmud (and even the Bible) but in numerous early homiletical and exegetical writings, and in the responsa of the *geonim* (some of these references, to be sure, are forgeries, but by no means all of them).

The "pietists" (*hasidim*) of medieval Germany in the thirteenth century and later derived their mystical ideas from a variety of sources, including apparently Christian ones, and evolved an elaborate theology focusing on the divine nature and the problem of immanence and transcendence (see also Chapter 3 on mystical ideas of marriage). They stressed devotion and concentration in prayer and dedicated performance of the command-ments as a means of overcoming temptations and obstacles resulting from the "evil inclination," or natural urges, which seek to prevent such obser-vance.[16] Of course, none of this was actually new, being already found in talmudic teaching, statements in various *midrashim*, and in works like Judah ha-Levy's *Kuzari*. Asceticism and fasting, also very much stressed in their teachings, was not in accord with mainstream Jewish thought. Judah ha-Levy (ca. 1075–1141, Spain) also denounced it, in his general statement about the divine law:

Your contrition on a fast day does nothing [to bring you] nearer to God [more] than your joy on the Sabbath and holy days. Just as prayers demand devotion, so also is a pious mind necessary to find pleasure in God's commandments and law, that you should be pleased with the law itself from the love of the Lawgiver. You see how much He has distinguished you, as if you had been His guest invited to His festive board. You thank Him in mind and word, and if your joy lead you so far as to sing and dance, it becomes worship.[17]

In Provence and then sweeping throughout Spain, starting at the same period and intensifying in later centuries, was the movement known as Qabalah (tradition, but in this sense, mystical teaching). In large part, this was a reaction to the "dry" intellectualism of philosophy, particularly the Maimonidean tradition. While the exact nature of the development of the movement, influences, and so on (claims of Cathar influences are incorrect) are not clear, the main ideas emerged from earlier Jewish mysticism, although with some possible Christian mystical influences. In spite of the warnings of rational scholars against the forgeries and falsifications of some of these doctrines, the popularity of the new movement grew.

In the thirteenth century, the main center of the movement was in Catalonia, particularly Gerona and Barcelona, but it began to attract fol-lowers also in Castile. Scholarly work so far has focused almost exclusively on famous qabalists (including Nahmanides) and their writings, and to a lesser extent on some central ideas, although these ideas are not treated historically.[18] Just as important, and perhaps for the historian even more so, is the impact of these ideas upon the ordinary Jewish people in Spain.

What little we know of this is from the continuing "Maimonidean con-troversy," or the debate over philosophy in general. From these sources, it is apparent that there was a significant influence of qabalistic ideas, although as is often the case in a confused and distorted manner. People began to argue that the commandments themselves are not essentially

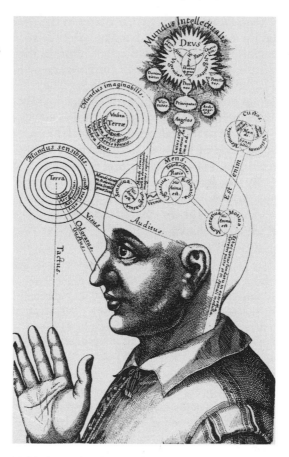

Kabbalistic analysis of the mind and sense attributing functions to the different regions of the brain. From Robert Fludd, Utriusque cosmi ... historia, Oppenheim, 1617–19. Image Select/ Art Resource, NY.

important, as long as the "secret" intention is understood. Nearly everything in the Bible became allegorized and there was growing emphasis on devotion and mystical "concentration" in prayer, on the various "secret names" of God, and so on. Strange mystics such as Abraham Abulafia (1240–after 1292), who severely condemned rabbis and talmudic teaching and even went to Rome in a futile effort to convert the pope to Judaism, did not help the reputation of the movement in the eyes of the orthodox.

The culmination of qabalah, and of Jewish mysticism generally, was the greatest forgery and one of the greatest hoaxes ever perpetrated, the large work known as the *Zohar*.[19] Written entirely (or nearly so) by Moses de Leon, a Spanish rabbi (d. 1305), in Aramaic—although with many errors—this literary masterpiece pretends to be a collection of mystical biblical exegesis and homily by talmudic sages, particularly the renowned Yohanan ben Zakai. It was known by careful scholars to be a forgery almost as soon as it was written, but it nevertheless had a profound impact throughout the Jewish world for centuries to come, with few ordinary Jews doubting its authenticity.

All of these mystical notions, rampant messianic speculation, the pietist movement in Germany, and qabalah in Spain (following the Expulsion there was a renewed upsurge of qabalistic activity in Safed in the Land of Israel, North Africa and elsewhere) can be seen as a response to the same general condition: the uncertainty of life for the Jews in the face of increasing hostility, and particularly in Spain in the fourteenth and fifteenth centuries despair over the massive conversions that took place. Certainly these movements did not dominate Jewish life, but such ideas did apparently fulfill a spiritual need for many.

NOTES

1. See the excellent discussion by Salo W. Baron, *A Social and Religious History of the Jews* (Philadelphia, New York, 1952–1983), 6: 97–98 and notes. The claim that the earlier homiletic work of Aha (not Ahai) of Shabha, *She'eltot,* was an explanation of the commandments is erroneous; see Baron, ibid., 38.

2. The simplest statement of the tradition of the handing down of the oral Torah from generation to generation is expressed in the opening chapter of the Mishnah known as *Avot* (Fathers), or *Pirkei Avot* (Chapters of the Fathers). See the excellent edition and translation by a Christian scholar, R. Travers Herford, *The Ethics of the Talmud: Sayings of the Fathers* (New York, 1945 and numerous editions, also paper, after that). This has a very good commentary and historical notes.

3. See for further information the article "Geonim" in Norman Roth, ed., *Medieval Jewish Civilization: An Encyclopedia* (New York, 2003) and the index there under the various names here mentioned. There was another prayer book written by Saadyah *Gaon,* but it was virtually unknown in the medieval period. Amram's *Sidur* is not actually a prayer book so much as a legal work, explaining the laws relating to prayers, the Sabbath, and festivals. In the eleventh century, Rashi (Solomon b. Isaac) in France, or his pupils, wrote another such prayer book.

4. See articles on the rabbis mentioned in Roth, ibid.

5. There is, of course, a vast literature on Maimonides. See briefly the article in Roth, ibid., and bibliography there. For his legal composition, see again the excellent summary by Baron, *A Social and Religious History*, 99–107.

6. Published in eight folio volumes, in several editions, and others in separate volumes. Many of his responsa nevertheless have been lost.

7. See examples cited by Joseph Shatzmiller, "An Aspect of Social Life of Provençal Jews," *AJS* (Association for Jewish Studies) *Review* 2 (1977): 228–30, with texts, 242–47. The specific incidents occurred in Manosque in the fourteenth century, but note the decision of "Rabbenu Tam" of France to impose a double fine on those who fought in a synagogue. Only a few brief articles have been written concerning crimes in other communities.

8. This inspection of chickens, until recently an important activity in the life of Jewish women, has now almost entirely been replaced by inspection at a slaughtering house or even factory, where packaged chickens are sold and even cut up into different parts. The first Ashkenazic chief rabbi of then Palestine, Abraham Isaac ha-Kohen Kook, known for his humility and other virtues, used to inspect chickens in the open market of Jerusalem on Friday afternoons. When he had to tell an obviously poor woman that the chicken she had bought was not fit, he gave her the money to buy another one.

9. There are few good works in English on Jewish law; see Bernard S. Jackson, *Jewish Law in Legal History and the Modern World* (Leiden, 1980). Menahem Elon, *Jewish law: History, Sources, Principles* (Philadelphia, 1994), 4 vols., translated from Hebrew, while considered authoritative, in fact contains many errors. More recent books are no better.

10. See the article "Badge, Jewish" in Roth, *Medieval Jewish Civilization.*

11. I have dealt with both these at length in Norman Roth, *Conversos, Inquisition, and the Expulsion of the Jews from Spain* (Madison, Wisc., 1995; revised paper ed., 2002).

12. For details, see the article "Clothing" in Roth, *Medieval Jewish Civilization.* Only one illustration was possible there, but some examples of Jewish clothing may be seen in Alfred Rubens, *A History of Jewish Costume* (New York, 1967).

13. See "Moneylending" in Roth, *Medieval Jewish Civilization.*

14. Herford, *The Ethics of the Talmud*, introduction, 4. *Neziqin* (Damages) is the name of the Order (*Seder,* or section) of the Talmud that contains the tractates dealing with what we might term civil law.

15. Judah b. Samuel, *Sefer hasidim* (Berlin, 1893), 6, Nos. 5 and 6.

16. See the excellent article of Joseph Dan, "Hasidism—Germany," in Roth, *Medieval Jewish Civilization*, and the bibliography.

17. *The Kuzari,* translated from the Arabic by Hartwig Hirschfeld (London, 1905), 113 (slightly modified).

18. Gershom Scholem, while certainly not the first scholar to investigate the topic, popularized it with many articles and books, the most accessible of which is his *Kabbalah* (New York, 1974), actually his collected articles from the *Encyclopedia Judaica.* The word is spelled in various ways, many libraries still using the most antiquated form: "cabala;" the correct transliteration is *qabalah,* or *qabbalah* for those insisting on keeping the doubling of certain letters. This book, like others, is primarily historical and biographical, although with many errors. An important contemporary scholar is Moshe Idel, whose general study, *Kabbalah: New Perspectives* (New Haven, 1988) is more thematic than historical and differs with Scholem in many points; however, its main fault is that it treats the whole development over centuries, and including modern Hasidism, as a unity with little or no awareness of historical differences. Moshe Hallamish, *An Introduction to the Kabbalah* (Albany, 1999), is perhaps the most readable and easily understood, although it has some of the same faults as Idel's book. There are numerous works in English that unfortunately are written by charlatans and should be avoided. Excerpts of some key texts in English translation may be found in *The Early Kabbalah,* translated by Ronald C. Kiener, with a good introduction by Joseph Dan (New York, 1986).

19. See briefly Roth, *Medieval Jewish Civilization*, 545–47. There is an English translation of the *Zohar* by H. Sperling and M. Simon (London, 1949; 2000), though it is not entirely reliable. See also the indices of the books listed in note 19.

RECOMMENDED READING

Baron, Salo W. *Social and Religious History of the Jews*. Philadelphia, New York, 1952–1983, vol. 6, chapter one.

Finkelstein, Louis. *Jewish Self-Government in the Middle Ages*. New York, 1964. Translation of some texts.

Roth, Norman, ed., *Medieval Jewish Civilization: An Encyclopedia*. New York, 2003. Articles cited in the notes here; see also the index, particularly for Maimonides.

2

EDUCATION

Perhaps the most important part of Jewish culture, without which nothing else would be possible, is education. Jewish life is based on the Bible and its further elaboration and explanation (not only of laws but also of beliefs and attitudes) in the Talmud. In addition to the Talmud, there are also collections of homiletic interpretation of the Bible, called *midrash* (plural *midrashim*), the compendia of laws mentioned in Chapter 1, which also were designed to make it easier to learn what is done in specific situations and in a sense serve also as commentaries on the Talmud, and numerous homiletical and ethical books, particularly in the later medieval period.

Throughout Jewish history, every Jew was expected to know enough Hebrew to read the prayers; but the desired norm was to be able to read at least the Torah (the Pentateuch). Beyond this, many boys studied the Talmud also, and this study was continued throughout adult life. Many also studied the various codes of law, beginning with that of Isaac *al-Fasi* in the eleventh century (a sort of summary of talmudic law), which was replaced in the twelfth century by the famous *Mishneh Torah* of Moses b. Maimon (Maimonides), which achieved almost universal acceptance. However, in the fourteenth century a new code was written, arranged in what was intended to be a more logical order and including only those laws applicable outside of the Land of Israel. This was the previously mentioned *Arba'ah Turim*, Four Rows, or *Tur* for short, by Jacob b. Asher of Toledo, son of the famous rabbi Asher b. Yehiel.

Study of the Torah meant memorization of the text, and study of either the Aramaic or, in Muslim lands, Arabic translation. From the eleventh century on, these were in effect replaced by the study of the commentary of Rashi. The Talmud was also learned with that rabbi's more important commentary on most of the tractates, and the additional commentaries of his students. In late medieval Spain, commentaries of other rabbis, particularly Asher b. Yehiel, were added or even substituted for those.

In addition to formal education, there was also the informal learning from such things as Jewish holidays. Passover, for example, includes the family meal (*seder,* which in fact means order) with the recital, in Hebrew, of the *Hagadah,* or telling, of the events associated with the exodus from Egypt, stories told by the rabbis, and so on. All of this, including the special symbolic food items present on the table before the actual meal was served, was intended to arouse the curiosity of the children, who in addition to asking the famous "four questions" (beginning with why this night differs from other nights) were encouraged to ask about each part of the *seder* and each incident related in the *Hagadah.* This created a sense of history, of connection to the Jewish people past, present, and future. Parents also took every opportunity to instruct their children in proper behavior and basic observance of Jewish laws and customs, although technically a boy under the age of 13 or a girl under the age of 12 was not responsible for such things.

Most Jewish holidays are, in fact, associated with some historical event. The delight, as well as curiosity, of the child was particularly aroused by the constructing of the *sukkah* or booth, a four-sided small outdoor enclosure, open to the sky but covered with branches from a tree, for the week-long holiday (Sukkot) commemorating the temporary structures in which the Israelites lived during their wanderings in the desert. The walls of the structures were elaborately decorated or painted, and ornaments hung from the ceiling and on the walls. In warmer climates, such as Spain and everywhere in the Mediterranean or in Muslim lands, all meals were eaten there and males often slept in them.

In a sense, everything in daily life and everything that happened in the home was part of the education of the child. As mentioned previously, children, particularly boys, were encouraged to observe some of the commandments and laws even though they were not legally required to do so, in order to educate them in the proper observance.

While all Jewish communities agreed that the basic requirements of education included mastery of the Hebrew letters (*alef-beit,* meaning alphabet), the prayers, and the Torah, and that advanced students should study the Talmud, there were major differences in education between the Jews in Muslim countries, including Spain, and those in Christian Europe, which here excludes Spain.

Preparations before the Exodus from Egypt. Luini, Bernardino (c. 1475–1532). Pinacoteca di Brera, Milan, Italy. Scala/Art Resource, NY.

JEWISH EDUCATION IN CHRISTIAN EUROPE

In European countries (and probably in Muslim lands, although we have less information), when a boy reached the age of five or six special celebrations were held to prepare him for beginning his education. Elaborate cakes, or festive bread, were prepared and given to the child to demonstrate the sweetness of the learning that he was to begin. The child would be dressed in special clothes and carried (by his father or often by an esteemed scholar) to the synagogue and given a tablet (of wood or slate) upon which would be inscribed the first and last four letters of

Elementary Education for Boys

the Hebrew alphabet and the passage "Moses commanded us the Torah, inheritance of the congregation of Jacob" (Numbers 11.12), which the teacher read and the boys repeated after him. Drops of honey were usually placed on the tablets, which the boys would taste (again, symbolic of the sweetness of learning). In some communities this would be a joint celebration, usually on the holiday of Shavu'ot, commemorating the giving of the Torah, and all the boys who had reached the age of five during the year would be brought together to partake in these rituals.

From this age, and even earlier in Muslim Spain, the boy was no longer a child in the sense of having absolute freedom to do as he pleased, but he was now a student who spent hours of every day (except Sabbaths and holidays) learning Hebrew reading and writing and the Bible. Most communities had schools and special teachers for this purpose. In villages too small to maintain such a school, private teachers would be hired or the fathers would be the teachers.

The school day was not short, nor interrupted for play and other activities. It began early in the morning and continued, interrupted only for a hasty noon meal, until late in the evening, six days a week. Older boys were expected to study on their own also on Sabbaths and holidays.

Education of Girls in Europe   Girls and women were exempt from formal education, since they had duties to perform at home that took most of their time. Nevertheless, in many cases at least the basic Hebrew prayers were taught by the father or mother, and some rabbis wrote that girls could be taught at least the Torah if the father wished (some rabbis specified in writing that their own daughters or granddaughters be so instructed). In many communities, girls had their own school, also usually a part of the synagogue.

Some women, indeed, were scholars sufficiently learned in Jewish law that their husbands (rabbis) consulted them on occasion, and others even taught the Bible or Talmud to men; for instance, the daughter of the *gaon* Samuel b. Ali (twelfth century), and Miriam, the daughter of Rabbi Solomon of Speyers and others as evident in medieval manuscript illuminations.[1] Miriam, the daughter of Rashi, was apparently quite learned, although the legend that she completed her father's talmudic commentary is false. Others include Hannah, the daughter of Rabbenu Tam, the grandson of Rashi. The wife of the rabbi of Vienna was mentioned by him in his legal decisions, and the daughters of a rabbi of Orleans were included in the quorum of three for reciting the blessing after meals, just like men.

One book of the Bible, the Psalms, was particularly studied and even memorized, and pious women often recited from it by heart while engaged in household duties.

Peter Abelard (d. 1141), head of a renowned school of philosophy in Paris and famous as the lover of Héloise, was no friend of the Jews; yet he grudgingly admitted their superiority in education when he (or one of his students) wrote that Christians only study for money to advance their careers and to please their families. The Jews, however, even if poor and with ten sons, send all of them to study letters (books), not for the sake of money like the Christians; and this is true not only of their sons but their daughters also.[2]

On the other hand, many women did not know Hebrew at all, so that rabbis ruled that they fulfilled their obligation of prayer by hearing the prayers recited. Even in Christian Spain, the custom in some communities was to read the book of Esther (called *Megilah* in Hebrew) on Purim in the vernacular to women who did not understand the simple Hebrew of that book.

In Muslim countries, and also in Christian Spain throughout the medieval period, most women were literate in the vernacular (Arabic or Spanish, sometimes both in Spain). As we shall see, women played a significant role in business in these lands and needed to read and understand contracts and other documents. There were a few examples of Jewish women who wrote

Saint Mary shows her breasts to her son and prays for mankind; Esther begs king Ahasuerus to save the Jewish people. From the "Speculum Humanae Salvations." Fourteenth century. Abbey, Kremsmuenster, Austria. Erich Lessing/Art Resource, NY.

Arabic poetry in Muslim Spain, but we have no complete literary compositions in the medieval period such as the famous Memoirs of Glückel of Hameln (Germany, 1646–1724) or the excellent poetry of Deborah Ascarelli (sixteenth century, Italy) or Sarah Coppio Sullam (seventeenth century, Italy).

**Education of
Boys: The Basics**
Only in the larger communities were there separate school buildings, sometimes attached to the synagogue. Usually, elementary education was in the home of a special teacher hired either by the community or by the fathers of the children. The quality of such teachers varied, but usually they were capable, and worked under special contract that specifically outlined their responsibilities. There were also private tutors sometimes hired by one or more fathers to teach their boys in their homes. Rarely, a father would teach his own sons if his occupation allowed him the time.

Class sizes were theoretically dictated by Jewish law, no more than 25 students per class (one French source set the maximum at ten). Considering the tender age of the pupils, it is obvious that little or no individual attention could be given in classes of as many as 25 students.

Actual learning began with the book of Leviticus, considered to be "pure" because it deals with offerings, and the child at that age is also "pure." Learning was done aloud with a special melody, the teacher chanting each verse and the children repeating it. Translation, at first in the vernacular and in later centuries in Yiddish (only in Europe), was also by memorization. It should be mentioned that translations of basic prayers were also learned at home, and the Passover Hagadah was also translated by the father, verse by verse.

Usually (almost always, in fact), the entire Bible was not taught, only the Torah. In the first place, the other biblical books are often extremely difficult, and lacking a proper knowledge of Hebrew grammar, few Jews in European countries (excluding Spain and southern Italy where such learning was routine) could understand them. In addition, scholars considered these books to be dangerous or even heretical, unless properly explained in the Talmud. This attitude persists to the present day among ultra-Orthodox, or extremely pious, Jews.

The life of a student was not easy. Even young boys of six and seven had to accustom themselves to study all day, until night fell, six days a week and with little or no outdoor recreation. A part of the Sabbath afternoon would be given to examination by their fathers on what they had learned during the week.

Once the boy had mastered his fundamental study of the Torah and attained a certain age (sometimes as early as 10, but usually 13), he would go on to study the Talmud. This also varied in different communities, but usually special instructors were hired for this purpose. Theoretically, while teachers of Torah to the younger boys were allowed to take a salary, many authorities did not permit this for teachers of the Talmud, since learning it was considered to be the free privilege (and responsibility) of every Jew. To get around this, such teachers were compensated for loss of time, that is, the neglect of their own studies while they were teaching students. In larger communities, a special school (*beit midrash qatan*, small house of study), usually attached to the synagogue, was used for the teaching of Talmud.

It should be mentioned that the Talmud is chiefly in Aramaic, with only some Hebrew, and as most students skipped the study of the Mishnah, which was written in post-biblical Hebrew, they again missed an opportunity to learn some fundamentals of Hebrew grammar. This situation was corrected only somewhat in a few communities in nineteenth-century Lithuania. Even today, few students learn the Mishnah prior to studying Talmud.

Students who showed particular promise, and in some cases even those who did not, were sent away to study in the more famous *yeshivot* (schools) of learned rabbis (in some communities, the *yeshivah* was a local one). There, they would spend years in study, seeing their parents only on holidays. Of course, the reality of life was that many students could not pursue such advanced study because they were needed to work the fields or help their parents in other businesses. One of the goals of marriage was to find a suitable father-in-law who would be able to financially support the groom while he continued his study of the Talmud for a number of years. In early modern eastern Europe, this often became a stipulated condition of marriage contracts. As we shall see in the following chapter, marriage took place at a very early age; however, the boy rarely began family life at that age but rather continued his study in the *yeshivah* for a number of years.

The main focus of education in all lands, including Italy and Spain and also throughout the Muslim world, was the **The Yeshivah** Talmud. This multi-volume work, created over centuries, embodies Jewish law in all its aspects: religious observances, personal conduct, marriage and divorce, civil law (buying and selling, property rights, and all related topics, as well as criminal law) and community law. But it is far more than a legal textbook; it also comments upon and explains statements in the Bible, provides historical accounts of life in the Land of Israel and in Babylon, and perhaps most importantly includes ethical teachings and insights from generations of the rabbinical sages whose ideas and teaching make up the collective work known as the Talmud.[3]

Manuscripts of the text came to Europe from Babylon (Iraq) and, by way of Italy, also from the Land of Israel (both the so-called Jerusalem Talmud and the Babylonian Talmud, but the former was studied only by advanced scholars). There were no printed books, of course, until the late fifteenth century, so that all study was done from manuscript copies. Obviously not every student could have such a copy, and they were shared or the text was learned by heart. Even today there are some who have memorized the entire Talmud. Memorization of at least parts of it is quite common.

Commentaries by Italian rabbis also made their way to Germany and then to France. Rashi (Solomon b. Isaac[4]), ca. 1040–1105, of Troyes (France) became the foremost authority on the Talmud, composing a commentary on nearly all of it, which offered a simple explanation of the often difficult text. He and his sons-in-law established important *yeshivot*, which became the centers of talmudic study and interpretation of law, and whose authority was acknowledged even in Spain. Rashi also wrote a commentary on the Bible, including even those books that were not generally studied by European Jews. This was less accepted in Spain, but in other countries it became required reading, particularly his commentary on the Torah. It had a significant impact on later Christian commentators, and even as notorious an anti-Semite as Martin Luther utilized it to an extent.

Important talmudic scholars in Spain wrote commentaries, including commentaries of Nahmanides, Ibn Adret, Yom Tov Ishbili, and others, which at once became standard and were studied not only throughout Spain but by Jews everywhere.[5] We have clear evidence that students and educated men, not just rabbis, studied these commentaries carefully.

When a boy completed his elementary education (Hebrew reading and writing, study of the Torah and basic laws), he usually would continue with the study of the Talmud. This was done either in a local *beit midrash* (house of study), as mentioned previously, or if the student showed sufficient promise he would be sent away to a *yeshivah*. This was an advanced school of study often headed by a famous scholar. Such schools attracted students even from far-off lands.

The most famous, until the end of the eleventh century, were those headed by the *geonim* in Iraq (Babylon as it was still called by the Jews). Students from Greece, Italy, Spain, and even Russia sometimes studied there. The *yeshivot* of France and Germany soon became famous, headed by the family and students of Rashi. There was developed a particular method of study and interpretation of the Talmud, intensive didactic analysis of virtually every statement in the text of a particular tractate, initiated by the students of Rashi and their students in turn, who came to be known as *ba'alei tosafot*, or masters of the additions (additional commentary on the Talmud). Many of these were French or German scholars, with some from other countries. Much of their teaching and interpretation was written down and eventually came to be required study, along with the basic commentary on the text by Rashi. Modern printed texts of the Talmud contain both the commentaries of Rashi and an abridged summary of the additional commentaries on every page. The far more extensive commentaries of the Spanish authorities are, for the most part, published in separate volumes, although some are included

Rothschild Miscellany (Northern Italy 1450–
1480). Rabbi studying. © The Israel Museum,
Jerusalem.

in more complete editions of the Talmud. There are also some later
commentaries by French and Provençal scholars.

The life of a *yeshivah* student was far from easy, in whatever country.
Study began at an early hour, immediately after the morning prayers
(usually at dawn) and continued until late at night. There is some evidence that a few *yeshivot* in Germany may have had sleeping quarters for
the students, but usually *yeshivah* students were lodged with families in
private homes.

There are, unfortunately, no diaries or other written records of their life,
as we have for students in the nineteenth century in Russia and Lithuania.
Undoubtedly, conditions changed little over the centuries, however.
Students were probably poorly fed and certainly lacked any form of
physical exercise, except perhaps a brief walk.

They were expected to master difficult talmudic tractates, attend
advanced lectures by their teachers and the head of the yeshivah, and

of course were subjected to intense oral examination on what they had learned. Learning was essentially rote memorization, just as was the case with young boys in learning the Bible. The talmudic text was recited at full voice in a special melody reserved for this purpose. The main hall of the *yeshivah* was filled with this loud chanting, accompanied by discussion and arguments over the interpretation of the text. Modern students accustomed to relative quiet in their studies would find such an atmosphere disturbing, if not frightening, and yet this method (still in use today) resulted in comprehension of difficult texts and the sharpening of the intellect through the challenge of heated debate with the companion, or fellow student with whom one spent days, months or even years in joint study and discussion.

These *yeshivot* were by no means rabbinical seminaries in the modern sense. Few of the students became rabbis, which title was granted only after years of intensive study not only of the Talmud but of the entire body of laws in codes such as that of Isaac *al-Fasi* and Maimonides. The majority of students went on to pursue jobs or professions. Their learning was entirely "for the sake of heaven," as it was called: to aid them in living in accordance to Jewish law and values.

Secular Learning in Europe   Secular learning of any kind (with the exception of basic arithmetic, which was necessary for business) was absolutely forbidden in European Jewish communities (even in Italy, until the late medieval period). In his commentary on Leviticus 18.4, Rashi warned that one should not think that since he has learned the Torah he may now also learn the wisdom of the nations. Later rabbis wrote even more strongly against the heresy of such things as philosophy and science. It is for this reason that no Jewish scholars of these subjects, nor even of medicine, are known to us from medieval France, Germany, Austria, or Poland. By contrast, as we shall see, there were hundreds in Muslim lands and in Spain, including Christian Spain. There were a few Jewish physicians in Italy, but they received their training elsewhere (in Sicily, for example, which was a separate country).

If the program of education in medieval European communities seems restrictive and unenlightened by our standards, it nevertheless had the advantage of cohesiveness and tradition. Jews from Italy to England to France and Germany, and later central and eastern Europe, shared a common background of a similar knowledge of the Talmud and the increasing number of commentaries. They shared a unity not only of observance of laws but of a common outlook and understanding of life. A medieval Jew could move easily from one community to another, from one country to another, and immediately feel at home.

There was little to challenge this way of thinking also in the general Christian world, where most people in any case were illiterate and the only alternative knowledge was to be found in the church and its theological teachings, which held no interest for the Jewish world. Universities were primarily for the training of church lawyers, theologians and government officials, carefully scrutinized as to their orthodoxy before being admitted. With the exception of some medical schools, these were anyway closed to Jews. The situation was quite different in Muslim lands and in Spain.

JEWISH EDUCATION IN MUSLIM LANDS AND IN SPAIN

The Arab conquest of the Persian Empire and of Egypt in the seventh century brought into the Muslim world a vast heritage of culture from ancient Babylon, Egypt, India, Greece, and Rome. This included mathematics, medicine, science, literature, and philosophy. Much of the enormous ancient knowledge of the world was translated, first into Syriac by Christians and then into Arabic, or directly from other ancient languages.

While the Arabs themselves had little interest in such things, and in fact returned to their desert, the newly converted Muslims, particularly of Persia (Iran), developed an impressive culture. Volumes of books were written in the subsequent centuries on every conceivable subject, some of them by Jewish mathematicians, scientists, and physicians.

Subjects of study, and of the thousands of books written, included all of mathematics (algebra, of course, was invented by the Muslims, but also studied were Euclidean and non-Euclidean geometry, trigonometry, and rudimentary calculus), physics, optics, astronomy, botany and zoology, Arabic grammar, and religious studies, Aristotelian and Neoplatonic philosophy and the major philosophical writings by Muslim authors such as al-Kindi, Ibn Sina and al-Farabi, to name a few, theory of music, and finally medicine. All of this was accomplished by the age of 18 or even earlier. To all of this, Jewish boys added the study of Bible and Talmud, of course.

Arabic became the standard language, spoken and written, for Jews in all Muslim lands. Even rabbinical scholars who were generally opposed to secular study, such as the *geonim* of "Babylon" (Iraq), and especially Saadiah *Gaon* (882–942), wrote their legal decisions and other works in Arabic (but written in Hebrew letters). Saadiah even found it necessary to translate the Bible into Arabic because many, perhaps most, Jews could not read the original Hebrew.

Education began in mosque schools with training in Arabic writing and reading of the *Qur'an*, followed by secular studies with private scholars for those so inclined. Jews were by no means excluded from all this, which began in local schools but soon required the advanced pupil (at the age of 16 or even younger) to travel for private study with the greatest authorities in these subjects. The student would receive a kind of diploma, signed by the scholar, which attested that he had successfully read (learned) certain books with him. This was a unique method of education, never since duplicated or even attempted. Imagine ordinary adolescent boys traveling throughout the world to study privately, or perhaps with one or two other students, with the greatest authorities mathematics, science, philosophy, and medicine. Not every Muslim or Jewish student could afford such a luxury, of course, but a great many did.

An identical system of education existed also in Muslim Spain, which included not only southern al-Andalus but the Muslim cities of northern Spain, such as Tudela and Zaragoza. The only difference was that there were no mosque schools in Muslim Spain; rather, instruction was either private or small groups of boys with one teacher, sometimes in the teacher's home or in the public market.

Jewish boys learned Arabic along with the Muslim students. Proficiency in both spoken and written Arabic was absolutely necessary for success in the Muslim world, and most of the private letters and documents preserved in the famous Cairo *Genizah*[6] are written in Arabic (usually, however, in Hebrew letters). Since we have proof that many Jews knew the *Qur'an* quite well, it is not unlikely that they also had studied this together with Muslim boys.

Learning Arabic meant not just the ability to read and write, but also calligraphy. The beauty of writing style was particularly stressed in al-Andalus, and we hear of Jews as well as Muslims who were praised for this. Samuel Ibn Naghrillah (993–1056), the prime minister and commander-in-chief of the Muslim kingdom of Granada and a scholar and poet, who had achieved his position at least in part due to his own eloquent Arabic style, took great care that his son (and successor) Yusuf should develop proper skills in Arabic.

In one poem that he sent to his young son, he wrote: "Your writing is elegant, like a sapphire it is clear/And its rows are straight like embroidery of a cloak." In yet another poem, the heading written by Yusuf indicates that Samuel wrote, or copied, some Arabic poems while awaiting a battle, and sent them to him "in order to accustom my tongue in them to speak fluently the Arabic language." The child was no more than eight or nine years old at the time.

Samuel himself was praised by contemporary Muslim writers for his excellence in Arabic style. He, like most educated Jews and Muslims, was able to compose Arabic verse extemporaneously.

The study of Arabic included also the study of poetry and learning both to write and produce extemporaneous Arabic verse of acceptable quality. We know of Jewish youth who learned poetry together with Muslim students, and excelled in their knowledge, some being praised by Muslims as better students than they were.

Eloquence in Hebrew writing was also considered an essential part of education for Jewish boys, made possible by the discovery of the basics of Hebrew grammar in al-Andalus in the eleventh and twelfth centuries. Boys actually studied Hebrew grammar, and there is evidence that both grammar and poetry were studied in some of the *yeshivot*. Later Hebrew translations of most of the important works on grammar and the Hebrew dictionaries (written in Arabic) brought this study to the Jews of Provence and, to a lesser extent, also to the rest of Aragon-Catalonia. While Hebrew was taught to younger boys in many cities there, it appears not to have been a part of the instruction in *yeshivot* as it had been in al-Andalus.

The study of Hebrew grammar, and such things as composition of Hebrew verse, quickly spread also to North Africa, Egypt, and Yemen. By the thirteenth century we have examples of Hebrew poetry from these lands, which, while hardly equal to the best in Spain, are generally quite good.

Jews, like Muslims, also learned advanced subjects from great Muslim scholars or specialists. Maimonides, who was born and **Secular** educated in Cordoba, learned physics and astronomy from the **Studies** greatest Muslim scholars in al-Andalus. He also studied mathematics and the other sciences, as well as philosophy, from Muslim scholars, and while still in his adolescence wrote his first book (in Arabic), an important treatise on logic. It is uncertain whether he learned medicine from Muslim or Jewish teachers, most likely the former. Important scholars, such as Solomon Ibn Gabirol and Abraham Ibn Ezra, certainly learned from Muslim teachers in their youth.

Many Jews who had this kind of education, such as the poet Judah ha-Levy and others, were able to earn their living when necessary as physicians. Others became full-time professional physicians, of course. Maimonides, who with his family fled al-Andalus due to the Almohad persecution,[7] went to Fez (where Jews were not persecuted, even though it was the Almohad capital) and continued his talmudic study. The family then went to the Land of Israel, where his father died, and afterwards he went to Egypt where in fact he earned his living as a physician.

Judah Ibn Tibbon, an important translator of Arabic works in Provence, but who had been born and educated in Granada, wrote in his "ethical testament" to his son Samuel, around 1190: "You know that the great ones among our people did not attain to positions of greatness and the highest levels except through [their expertise] in Arabic writing," citing as examples the aforementioned Samuel Ibn Naghrillah and others. He urged his son Samuel to study Arabic and reminded him that he had engaged special teachers for him.[8] He need not have feared, for in fact Samuel was to far exceed his father as an important translator of Arabic works by Muslim and Jewish authors.

As for the learning of Bible and Talmud in Muslim lands, the situation was very similar to that in Christian Europe. **Bible and** Boys began the study of the Hebrew alphabet and the Torah **Talmud** at a very early age, either with private tutors or, more usually, teachers hired by the community.

One document from the *Genizah* is an early "coloring book" for children. The Hebrew letters are given different colors, and the teacher wrote the outline of the letters, which the student filled in with the correct color.

Another such learning game had drawings of snakes with animal heads.[9] Papyrus, or later, paper, was still very expensive, however, and students usually used slates or wooden tablets.

The main difference was that throughout the Muslim world, and again particularly in Spain, pupils learned not only the Torah but the entire Hebrew Bible. Translation was, of course, in Arabic, but the translation of Saadiah does not appear to have been used in Spain. In faraway Yemen, however, it became standard almost from the time that it was written and remains to the present time highly regarded by Yemenite Jews. The Jews in medieval Yemen, incidentally, were also learned in secular subjects, and some grammatical and philosophical works were written there. They also greatly admired the secular Hebrew poetry, which was written in Spain by poets such as Ibn Gabirol, whose poems were received and circulated there soon after they were written; and so also in Egypt.

Yeshivot in Muslim Lands and Spain   Talmudic study was as important in the Muslim lands as in France or Germany. Not only the *yeshivot* of the *geonim*, but those of North Africa and, of course, Muslim Spain, were famous and drew students from many countries (including central and eastern Europe). The Land of Israel also had its *yeshivot*, at first in Jerusalem and later in Damascus (then part of the same Muslim territory), but they were headed by the "sectarian" Qaraites (who followed only the Bible, as they interpreted it) and had little impact on Jews elsewhere. North Africa, particularly Qayrawan (in modern Tunisia), also had some *yeshivot*.

Egypt was not famous for its scholars or *yeshivot*, with the notable exception of Maimonides and a few others (actually, the importance of Egypt as a center of learning grew in the later Middle Ages). In fact, it appears that Maimonides actually headed and taught in a *yeshivah* there, and may have been succeeded in this capacity by his son Abraham (who, like his more famous father, was also a notable physician). Descendants of Maimonides were important scholars for generations.

Two important *yeshivot* in al-Andalus were at Cordoba and Lucena. The great sage Isaac *al-Fasi* (from Fez in North Africa) was attracted to the latter, and taught many students who later became outstanding scholars, including Joseph Ibn Megas, who taught the father of Maimonides. Later in the eleventh century, a *yeshivah* was established also in Granada.

The tradition of learning the Talmud with the legal compendium written by Isaac spread throughout Spain and was only partly displaced by the more extensive Hebrew code of Maimonides (the *Mishneh Torah*).

In northern Christian Spain (the united kingdom of Aragon-Catalonia), talmudic learning was flourishing at least from the late twelfth century. The outstanding *yeshivot* were at Barcelona, Gerona, and Zaragoza, but there were several others. There was constant contact with the scholars of Provence, then a part of the kingdom, which brought also the influence of the French and German rabbis into the Spanish *yeshivot*. Solomon Ibn Adret (ca. 1233–1310) was the foremost scholar and head of the *yeshivah* of Barcelona, to which students came from throughout Europe to study with him.

Due to the persecution of Jews in Germany, Asher b. Yehiel (ca. 1250–1327), already a highly respected scholar, fled with his sons to Spain. He quickly was chosen as head of the Jewish community and the *yeshivah* of Toledo in Castile. Asher brought with him the methods of the German scholars, particularly the interpretations of the *ba'alei tosafot* (authors of the Tosafot). He also soon attracted students from distant lands, including eastern Europe. It should be noted that the language of instruction in these *yeshivot*, particularly Barcelona and Toledo, must have been in Hebrew because of this diversity of students. Nevertheless, the native spoken language of the Jews of Toledo remained Arabic, and Asher had some difficulties because he did not know this language.

Other scholars in the thirteenth through the fifteenth centuries established *yeshivot* throughout Spain, particularly in Castile in the later periods. Unquestionably Spain by that time was the outstanding center of talmudic learning in the world. Following the Expulsion of 1492, scholars brought that method of learning to their new homes in Italy, North Africa, Egypt, and eventually Turkey and the Land of Israel.

The education so far discussed was available only to boys, whether Muslim or Jewish. However, girls were not entirely excluded. Particularly in al-Andalus, many Muslim girls received instruction in reading and writing Arabic, including the *Qur'an*, and some women became accomplished poets. We know much less about the education of Jewish girls, but there were some who also became poets (Arabic poetry) and were recognized in Muslim literary circles.

Education of Girls in Muslim Lands

Certainly most Jewish girls received some training in reading and writing Arabic, which was essential for business. Both in Muslim and in Christian Spain, women often played a role in business, and in all legal transactions, such as purchases or sales of property owned jointly with their husbands, their consent and signatures were required on documents. There are, however, no examples of Jewish women who became scholars of Jewish law in Spain, as we have seen in Germany and some other countries. However, as we shall see, there were several women who formally studied medicine in Christian Spain and became licensed physicians and even surgeons.

BOOKS AND LEARNING IN JEWISH LIFE

Today we have the luxury of being able to find almost any work ever written in nicely bound and printed books, whether we own them ourselves or find them in a library. That, of course, was a luxury unknown in the medieval world (even after the invention of printing; in fact, early printed books were often more expensive than manuscripts). The medieval "book" was actually either a manuscript written on parchment or paper or a bound codex (individual pages, copied from a manuscript, and bound in a form similar to a modern book). These were, of course, tediously copied either by a professional scribe or an individual for his own use, and they often contained mistakes.

Christian libraries, both personal and the famous monastic and university libraries, had a surprisingly small number of manuscripts or codices. There were many Jews, particularly in Spain, who had larger libraries than some of the greatest medieval Christian libraries. However, there is no question that the Muslim libraries were the outstanding example of repositories of knowledge. Even considering the typical exaggeration, the main libraries of Baghdad, Alexandria, and Cordoba had enormous collections of at least several hundred thousand manuscripts and codices. Muslim scholars were prolific writers, frequently producing works which consisted of many volumes.

Jews valued books perhaps more than either Christians or Muslims, and in fact this was already proverbial in the Middle Ages. The Muslims referred to Jews as *ahl al-kitab,* "people of the book," and while originally this referred to the Scriptures, it came to include their general love for books. Famous in this regard is the statement of Judah Ibn Tibbon, the aforementioned translator in Provence, in his ethical testament to his son: "My son! make your books your companions, and your cases and shelves your orchards and gardens; graze in their gardens and gather their roses and pluck their fruit, spices and myrrh."[10] Earlier, the Hebrew poet and grammarian Dunash Ibn Labrat (tenth century) had written: "Let the garden of your delights be holy books/and your orchard Arabic books."

Not surprisingly, Jewish law contains statements about how books are to be treated, respect for what Dunash called holy books (the Bible, prayer books, and also the Talmud were considered in this category). Books could be, and indeed must be, loaned to others, but they must be treated with great care by the borrower. Some Jewish communities in Spain, and probably in other countries, had community libraries, and of course both *yeshivot* and synagogues had such libraries (for Spain we have, as usual, far more documentation, both from Jewish and non-Jewish sources). Lists of books owned by private individuals include also many secular works.

Yet manuscripts or codices were expensive, and particularly if they were copies carefully done by professional scribes. Theoretically, every adult Jewish male had to have a copy of the Torah, which according to Jewish law he should write himself. Few had the proficiency to do that, of course, but instead hired scribes either to make a Torah scroll, or more commonly a codex copy, for their personal use. In addition, there were prayer books for daily and holiday prayers, a Passover Hagadah (some of which were richly illustrated, but usually only for wealthy patrons), and copies of at least parts of the Talmud. Many individuals also had codes of Jewish law (either that of Isaac *al-Fasi* or Maimonides; sometimes both) and books on grammar, and often copies of philosophical works. Doctors also had medical treatises, in Arabic or Hebrew or both.

In spite of this, books were often scarce, and even important scholars sometimes complained that they could not find a copy of a particular talmudic tractate or other important book. Nevertheless, the rabbinic responsa (legal decisions and answers to various issues) show that not only the famous rabbis but their individual questioners had almost all of the standard works of Jewish law, commentaries, and other important sources. In fact, there is not a single Jewish classic known today that was not constantly cited by medieval authorities; but the opposite has happened; some of the sources they used are no longer exist.

ADULT EDUCATION

Education was not limited to children and youth. Jewish law requires constant study throughout life. The weekly Torah portion, read in the synagogue, had to be studied with the Aramaic translation, which was gradually replaced by the commentary of Rashi in European lands.

Also, in theory, every adult male (which in Jewish law means the age of 13 and over) must study the Talmud, knowledge of which was essential in order to understand Jewish laws and proper conduct. In reality, this was an ideal that was hard to realize for the reasons mentioned above: the scarcity of books and the high cost of obtaining correct manuscript copies. Nevertheless, there is considerable evidence that many adults did devote a portion of their day to talmudic study. In Spain, and certainly also in other countries, several men together sometimes hired a teacher to instruct them. Regular instruction in Talmud often took place in the synagogue. While clear evidence is lacking, it is probable that this also overcame the difficulty of acquiring individual copies of talmudic tractates and that such learning was by memorization, with the teacher reading the text and the students learning it by heart.

Many adult men undertook to complete the learning of a particular tractate in a year's time, either individually or together in a group. Upon the completion of this tractate, there would be a feast and community celebration. Similar celebrations were held when the copying of a new Torah scroll would be completed.

With the increasing interest in secular learning, only in Spain and Provence, many adults also began to learn at least the fundamentals of mathematics and the sciences. There was also significant interest in philosophy, as well as Hebrew poetry and literature. Ordinary letters and other "common" writings not by scholars show the influence particularly of the study of Hebrew grammar and of poetry. This was not limited to Spain, but was common also, as previously mentioned in Yemen and Egypt, as evidenced by letters in the Genizah, which sometimes contain quotations of poetry. There were also poets in those countries, although the quality of their work did not achieve the level of the Spanish Hebrew poets.

Jewish learning, again particularly or almost exclusively in Spain, was not confined to Jewish sources. We have examples of the influence of Latin and Spanish literature and even of medieval Christian theologians in Hebrew sources, whether literary or philosophical texts (and, indeed, translations). There are some few examples of such Christian influence, morality tales, and even sermons, in the thirteenth-century German Jewish pietist work *Sefer Hasidim,* and the Aesop fables and other popular folklore in the *Mishlei shu'alim* by Berakhyah b. Natronai in France at about the same time.[11] Other examples include the King Arthur legends and tales of Alexander the Great.

A specialized area of education was medicine. In Muslim lands, as mentioned previously, this was part of the standard education of boys, and many Jews were able to practice as physicians if they needed this as a temporary income. Others became professional physicians. In Christian Europe, there was no opportunity for Jews to formally learn medicine, and what medical help was available was mostly based on folk remedies. However, in Christian Spain (including, of course, Provence), Jews were able to study medicine at universities such as that of Montpellier or Lerida (in Catalonia). Others appear to have learned their trade from serving as apprentices to physicians. In any case, every doctor had to be examined and licensed, and these examinations included not only medical texts and practical knowledge but also texts of science and even philosophy.

With the exception of the study of medicine, however, Jews were not allowed to study in Christian universities, even in Spain (there is some possibility that in the fifteenth century the renowned astronomer and chronicler Abraham Zacut studied at the University of Salamanca).

Education certainly was a major factor in preserving the Jewish people and Jewish culture throughout the medieval period. The universal study of traditional texts resulted not only in a knowledge of law necessary both for private and communal life but also an outlook, or world view, which shaped the way Jews understood their relationship to God and to each other.

This does not mean that there was no room for individuality, nor that there were no dissenters, but such dissent was rare in the medieval period, when deviance from the norm was considered heresy and would lead to ostracism within the Jewish community everywhere. Even in Spain, for the most part, the secular knowledge acquired was reinterpreted, or integrated into the traditional Jewish system of belief. Aristotle and the Muslim philosophers, for example, were highly regarded, but at the point where some of these differed with fundamental Jewish beliefs, those differences were either overlooked or explained away.

Only some individuals succumbed to the conflict they saw in these views and evolved certain mystical doctrines that were a challenge to the traditional teaching. Rabbis such as Solomon Ibn Adret and others attacked such challenges with vigor, and ultimately triumphed.

The most serious challenge to Jewish tradition came from the enticements of Christianity, and mass conversions of Jews in Spain throughout the fourteenth and fifteenth centuries threatened to destroy the tradition. Many rabbis, in fact, converted, and *yeshivot* were closed, resulting in a serious decline of Jewish learning until the end of the fifteenth century when some *yeshivot* were again established. Secular learning also had nearly disappeared among the remaining Jews, and following the Expulsion of 1492, those Jews loyal to their tradition carried with them to their lands of refuge (Italy, North Africa, the Ottoman Empire) only the fundamentals of talmudic learning. The study of science, philosophy, and even literature was to remain dormant until being revived, in part, in the Renaissance.

NOTES

1. See further on this in the article "Education, Jewish" in Norman Roth, *Medieval Jewish Civilization: An Encyclopedia* (New York, 2003), 232.

2. Discussed, and translated, by Beryl Smalley, *The Study of the Bible in the Middle Ages* (Notre Dame, Ind., 1964 edition; reprinted 1970), 78. The statement was possibly by a student of Abelard.

3. There are a number of "introductions" to the Talmud and its teachings, such as Morris Adler, *The World of the Talmud* (Philadelphia, 1968) or Arthur Cohen, *Everyman's Talmud* (New York, 1948). A fairly good anthology of some of the ethical and religious teachings of the rabbis is C. G. Montefiore and H. Loewe, *A Rabbinic Anthology* (Philadelphia, 1960).

4. See the article "Rashi" in Roth, *Medieval Jewish Civilization.*

5. See articles on these and other rabbis in Roth, ibid. There is a vast bibliography on all of this, which need not be mentioned here.

6. See the article "Genizah" in Roth, ibid. For further details, see S. D Goitein, *A Mediterranean Society: The Jewish Communities of the Arab World as Portrayed in the Documents of the Cairo Geniza* (Berkeley, Calif., Los Angeles, London, 1967–1993).

7. On this, and all aspects of Jewish history in Muslim Spain, see Norman Roth, *Jews, Visigoths & Muslims: Cooperation & Conflict* (Leiden, 1994) (a revised Spanish translation is in preparation). For a brief summary of the life of Maimonides, excerpts from his writings, and so on, see Roth, *Maimonides: Essays and Texts* (Madison, Wisc., 1985).

8. *Hebrew Ethical Wills*, ed. and trans. Israel Abrahams (Philadelphia, 1948) 1: 59.

9. S. D. Goitein, *Seder ha-hinukh bi-mei ha-geonim* (Jerusalem, 1962, in Hebrew), 42, 43.

10. Abrahams, *Hebrew Ethical Wills* 1: 57, 63 (correcting the translation slightly).

11. See details on these in Roth, *Medieval Jewish Civilization,* 315–16 and 408–9 respectively, with bibliography.

RECOMMENDED READING

Goitein, S. D. *A Mediterranean Society: The Jewish Communities of the Arab World as Portrayed in the Documents of the Cairo Geniza.* Berkeley, Calif., Los Angeles, London, 1967–1993. Vol. 1.

Roth, Norman, ed. *Medieval Jewish Civilization: An Encyclopedia.* New York, 2003. Article on "Education."

3

MARRIAGE AND FAMILY LIFE

In Jewish law, marriage is not a sacrament or religious ceremony but a contractual obligation, or civil act. The Mishnah (*Qidushin* 1.1) originally prescribed that the acquisition of a wife may be by money, a document, or sexual intercourse. For modern sensibilities, this perhaps sounds very calculated and commercial, but it must be understood that this is a legal act and as such is discussed in the same technical terms used for all transactions.[1] As for ethical concerns, both the Talmud and later rabbinical literature detail quite specifically the husband's moral as well as legal responsibilities to his wife (for the latter, see the section that follows, "Status of Women"). The famous maxim of Proverbs (31.10–31) that describes a woman of valor, is still the constant guide for the Jewish husband and in fact is recited at the Friday night (Sabbath) dinner table, as it was also in the medieval period.

Over a period of time, the method of acquiring a wife was revised so that intercourse was no longer considered a valid method (in order to discourage sexual promiscuity) and "money" came to mean any object of value. In practice, this was usually a ring, but medieval authorities insisted that it be a plain ring with no precious stones so that the prospective bride's attention would not be distracted by the beauty of the stones (she must fully understand that the ring is being offered to her as a token of marriage and she must indicate consent).[2] It was customary, however, to give other jewelry to the prospective bride, and of course also after the marriage. Engagement rings were also given, in German lands only to the man (a gold ring, usually), but elsewhere either to the bride or to both of them. This was not, however, a universal custom.

The ambiguous "document" became, in fact, an elaborate promise of financial support, called *ketuvah* (Hebrew; Aramaic *ketubah*), written in Aramaic because originally this was the language spoken and understood. In medieval Spain, and some other lands, it became customary to also translate the document in the vernacular. Basic obligations of support were set by talmudic and rabbinical laws. In addition to the provisions of the *ketuvah*, the bridegroom had to pay a "bride price" (*mohar*) to the parents, and additional gifts were included as part of the betrothal (later, these were added to the *ketuvah* itself). Interestingly, a fourteenth-century authority stated that the Jews of Cologne were wealthier than those of Mainz and therefore specified twice the amount of money in their *ketuvot*, "as required by law."[3]

The bride also brought with her a dowry upon marriage. In addition to money, and in Muslim lands in the early medieval period instead of money, she also brought considerable amounts of personal property such as jewelry, clothing, copper and brass utensils (but not pottery, since the dowry had to consist of durable goods) and even serving girls. The jewelry often consisted not only of gold but many items with pearls (earrings, necklaces), while the clothing consisted of expensive linen and brocaded or silk robes and the like. Bedspreads and couches were also included. Of particular interest in one dowry list from Egypt (twelfth century) is a pen-box made in China, with two knives (for cutting quills), a sand-sprinkler for blotting the ink, and an ivory plate on which to sharpen the quills.[4]

The custom of the Land of Israel, continued after persecution compelled most of the Palestinian Jews to move to Egypt in the eleventh century, was a mutual obligation in which the wife also promised to serve and esteem her husband. The marriage was termed partnership (*shutafut*), although in reality such was the case with all Jewish marriages. However, a unique aspect of the Palestinian contract was the right of the wife to divorce her husband for any reason whatever, including simple hatred. Jews in Iraq (Babylon) followed this practice also.[5]

Other laws evolved in various countries, but especially in Babylon in the *yeshivot* of the *geonim*. Chief among these was the establishment of a formal engagement followed after a lengthy period (often a year) by betrothal (*'erusin*) and marriage (*nisu'in*, literally elevation). In some countries, these events were also separate, but in France and Germany it became customary to have the betrothal and marriage take place together in order to ease the burden of having two celebratory meals (one at the time of betrothal and another at the time of the wedding), with guests invited often from distant places. In some communities in Spain in the thirteenth century, the groom was required to provide a feast that would last for at least three days. Obviously not everyone could afford this, and no doubt community assistance was provided for those who could not manage this financially.

Neither the betrothal nor wedding could take place on the major holidays or during the intermediate days—the week between the beginning and end of the holiday—of Passover and Sukkot (this was because of a ruling that one rejoicing not be mixed with another; the holidays require their own celebrations), nor in the period between the end of Passover and the holiday of Shavu'ot (which was a period of mourning for the alleged death of students of Rabbi Aqiva[6]). In Germany, the custom was to have the betrothal on Friday, before the Sabbath, and the wedding on Saturday, at which the *ketuvah* was read. Elsewhere, Friday afternoon was the traditional time for the wedding itself. Weddings do not take place on fast days or days of mourning.

Medieval Jewish marriages, and indeed until the modern period, were almost always arranged between the parents of the prospective bride and groom and their families, or through the services of a professional *shadkhan* (matchmaker). Girls were often married while still minors, which means before the age of 12, although this custom appears to have prevailed more in Germany than elsewhere.[7] Nevertheless, boys, who became adults at the age of 13, were expected to marry soon after, and in any case not later than 18. Romantic love, of course, was not a factor at all, and rarely did the bride and groom even know each other before the marriage. However, as we shall see, a girl who had been married before attaining adulthood had the right of refusal once she reached that age.

There were many reasons for these young marriages. One explanation given by some French Jewish authorities was that because of frequent persecution, the father of the girl might fear that the dowry he had accumulated would be taken away from him any day.[8] A more plausible explanation is that with large families, often as many as ten children or more, the sooner they were married the less of an economic burden they were. Finally, the fact that these ages were established already in talmudic tradition was due to the quite sound and practical reason that sexual urges develop in adolescence and it is best to control these through early marriage. In general in the Middle Ages, also among non-Jews, marriages usually took place at such ages or even earlier.

MYSTICAL INTERPRETATIONS OF MARRIAGE

In medieval Germany, no doubt under the influence of the pietists (see Chapter 1), mystical explanations arose of marriage and of each aspect of the ceremony and customs involved in terms of the giving of the Torah or the commitment to the study of the Torah. Ten times was Israel called "bride" in scripture, symbolic of the Ten Commandments; and the fanciful counting of letters in words to deduce symbolic meaning was applied to demonstrate the "hidden" mystical meanings behind various words associated with marriage (as we learn from an important rabbi of the period).

Particularly interesting is the connection between the seven blessings recited at the wedding (discussed further on) and the "seven voices," which allegedly accompanied the revelation of the Torah at Mt. Sinai. The author refers, in an abbreviated manner, to Psalm 29, where in fact seven expressions using the word "voice of the Lord" do appear. However, no rabbinical (talmudic or midrashic) source, as far as I know, relates these either to the revelation or to marriage; in fact, it specifically ignores the Talmud (*Berakhot* 6b) which states that the Torah was given with "five voices," referring to Ex. 19.16.[9]

THE WEDDING

Weddings were usually held outdoors in a public place, seldom in a synagogue. In medieval Germany, there were special halls used for weddings in most Jewish communities, at least in larger towns and cities.[10]

It was customary to conduct the bride and bridegroom separately to the wedding hall, where dancing accompanied by singing and playing of instruments, took place. Originally, especially in Germany, it had been the practice to have weddings on Friday,[11] but the subsequent festivities that lasted through the Sabbath, including the use of Gentile musicians, aroused rabbinical opposition since even if there was no prohibition on Gentiles playing on the Sabbath, the idea of musical instruments on that day seemed inappropriate.

In many cases, in Germany as well as Spain, Hebrew poems celebrating the event were recited, some composed especially for the couple and in other instances traditional welcoming poems. Famous poets, such as Judah ha-Levy and Abraham Ibn Ezra, wrote several such poems. These celebrations could take place at the formal announcement of the betrothal and again at the actual wedding.[12]

Dancing and the playing of musical instruments was common at such celebrations, and also the wedding itself, in all lands. At times the rejoicing became excessive, including drunkenness. In Egypt there was a custom for women to put on veils (in Muslim lands at the time worn only by men) or men's hats and with swords dance in front of the men. Boys also were sometimes adorned with women's ornaments and their hands painted with henna (a dye used by women to paint designs on their hands). Maimonides and other scholars strongly objected to such practices.[13]

The *hupah* (canopy) originally was the ceremonial spreading of a prayer shawl (*talit*) over the bride and groom in order to symbolize a private enclosure, to avoid the unseemly appearance of marriage taking place in public, such as in a market place. Another reason given was that the bridegroom first put on a *talit* at the wedding, which only married men were accustomed to wear, and this symbolized a talmudic statement that the bridegroom "spread his *talit*" over the bride as an indication of marriage. Eventually this evolved into poles supporting the *talit*, and then the modern custom of a more elaborate canopy (although in traditional Jewish ceremonies the *talit* is still used). In some communities in Germany the custom instead was to spread the long end of the *zipfel* (a German word meaning mantle) of the groom over the head of the bride instead of the *talit*.[14]

The general custom everywhere was that the bride, and usually also the bridegroom, was carried on a special "throne" to the synagogue on the Sabbath prior to the wedding. This served as a public announcement of the intended marriage. The same was done at the actual wedding.

The actual ceremony had slightly different customs in various communities, but in general consisted of the placing of the ring on the bride's right hand, the recital of the "seven blessings" of marriage and of the bride and groom (which were said, or chanted, by the most distinguished person present; in modern times, the rabbi; see above on the mystical significance of these), and the drinking from a cup of wine by the groom, who then gave it to the bride to sip. This recitation of the blessings was the only "religious" aspect of marriage, and even this did not, of course, require a rabbi, although in some German communities the rabbi did officiate. Far more important than the rabbi are the two witnesses required (sometimes also separate witnesses who testified to the validity of the *ketuvah*). In modern Jewish weddings, the only reason that a rabbi officiates is because of the requirements of civil law that a clergyperson or other specified official conduct weddings. It is important to understand that in Jewish law it is not the ceremony that constitutes a marriage, but the legal acts outlined above.

In many communities, the bride wore a crown or diadem, or sometimes a garland of myrtles. In addition, the bride wore a veil to cover her face (possibly because of Genesis 24.65). The veil is lifted during the ceremony when the groom gives her the cup of wine to taste. In Germany, brides wore a special white cotton dress called, in German, a *sargenes*, the purpose of which was actually to reduce somewhat the rejoicing since this was also the garment worn on Yom Kippur (Jews are supposed to be in perpetual mourning over the destruction of the Temple in Jerusalem; thus, every celebration must be tempered by some reminder of this). The bridegroom also wore white and a special hat, worn by mourners, and placed dust on his forehead, all in memory of the destruction of Jerusalem.[15]

It was also perhaps for this reason that the custom began of breaking a glass at the conclusion of the wedding (there is some confusion about possible references to this in medieval sources; one source states that the glass used for the blessings was thrown against the wall by the bridegroom, but no reason is given).[16] At the conclusion of the wedding, and again during all of the celebratory meals during the first week of marriage, the "seven benedictions" were recited over a cup of wine (the celebration did not conclude with the wedding ceremony but in fact lasted for seven days of feasting and rejoicing). In some communities in Germany there was a special "wedding house" in which the bride and groom lived during the week.

The modern custom of throwing rice at the bride and groom, as a symbol of fertility, was of course unknown (rice being available only in Muslim lands), but in Germany grains of wheat were so used, to the shouts of "Be fruitful and multiply." At least in some German communities the custom was to throw wine from the glass used for the blessings on the house of the newly wed couple as a symbol of the blessings God would bring to them.[17]

Wedding gifts were customarily given and included things that might be expected, such as jewelry, dresses, and household items, but also richly illuminated manuscripts of the Passover Hagadah, or a Bible or prayer book.

DIFFERENCES IN CUSTOMS

In some lands, brides were frequently as young as eight or nine, and sometimes also the bridegroom; however, in general the custom everywhere was for girls to be married at the age of 12 or 13 and the boys often at 14. At this age neither the girl nor boy was considered to be a minor in Jewish law, but in the case where a marriage was arranged by the parents (or relatives or community officials if she was an orphan) of a minor girl she had the right of refusal when she reached majority (in fact, any bride had the right of refusal before the actual wedding). Obviously, this could be the cause of problems. Another potential problem was created by the requirement that the consent of relatives be obtained for such a marriage, and it sometimes happened that consent was given at the betrothal but withdrawn before the actual wedding. Partly to guard against such things, many communities (in Spain, all of them) enacted a law that no marriage could be entered into without the knowledge and consent either of a local sage or the elected representatives of the community. This substituted for the consent of relatives previously required.

In Muslim lands, marriages often were arranged as part of a social aristocracy or a business deal, even between people in different lands. There were cases of such arranged marriages for status or business also in Europe, but they appear to have been less frequent. Given the young age at which marriage usually took place, almost all marriages were arranged, of course, by the parents, usually with someone whom they knew or with whom they were related.

Of course, in the case of a promising young scholar, marriage was usually arranged with the daughter of a famous rabbi or someone financially able to support the young man while he continued his learning. Even less-outstanding students were often given this support, at least for a certain period, by the bride's parents. The fact that marriage took place at such a young age does not necessarily mean that the couple was actually living together; a period of some years might pass during which the bride continued to live with her parents and the bridegroom continued his studies. In post-medieval and modern Europe, this was almost always the practice, as it still is among some traditional Jews. In other cases, the young couple lived for a year or sometimes more with the parents of the bride.

Another significant difference between Muslim lands (and also Christian Spain) and Europe was that in the former countries Jewish men technically were allowed to have more than one wife. In Germany, a renowned **Polygyny (More Than One Wife)** rabbi, Gershom b. Judah (ca. 960–1028), issued a decree prohibiting polygyny and this was accepted throughout the Jewish communities of Europe, other than Spain. In practice, few could afford more than one wife, in addition to the obvious problems of jealousy that could arise; nevertheless, we hear of such cases even in Christian Spain in the later medieval period. There are several cases recorded in documents of the Genizah, indicating that the custom was much more common among Jews in Muslim lands than has been thought.[18]

However, the *geonim* had already enacted a law according to which a man could not take another wife without the consent of his first wife. This was reinforced in some later rulings, and sometimes a bridegroom would have to swear an oath to abide by this.

In Tunisia in the fourteenth century a case arose concerning a woman who refused to permit her husband his conjugal rights or to perform any duties for him and she also repeatedly cursed his father and mother, all because she had heard that he intended to take an additional wife. Simon Duran, an important rabbi formerly of Majorca, ruled that the Jewish court must send her a warning to stop, and announce this in the synagogue four consecutive Sabbaths, and if she persisted the court was to wait for a year (to see if she would change her behavior), after which time her husband could divorce her, giving her the settlement of her *ketuvah*.[19]

SEX IN AND OUT OF MARRIAGE

The issue of traditional Jewish attitudes to sex requires a book in itself.[20] In general, these attitudes were a strange mixture of liberal and extremely conservative, not to say repressive, concepts. On the one hand, according to Jewish law sex of any kind is strictly forbidden prior to marriage, and indeed this was one of the reasons for the early age of marriages (if a girl were found not to be a virgin, the marriage of course would be annulled and other, financial, penalties imposed).

However, marital sexual intercourse was not seen merely as a necessary evil whose only purpose was the production of children, although the obligation to have children is a biblical commandment. "Be fruitful and multiply" (Genesis 1.22) was interpreted as a requirement to have both male and female offspring, at least one of each. In reality, since birth control was not normally practiced, families tended to be quite large (ten children was not an unusual number). It was nevertheless an obligation of the husband to satisfy his wife sexually. There were certain restrictions, but in general a mutually satisfactory sex life was an essential part of marriage, the lack of which could be grounds for divorce. Strict medieval authorities imposed conditions that may arouse some skepticism as to their actual observance. These included a prohibition on sexual intercourse except on Friday night (the sacredness of the Sabbath was presumed to be beneficial) and then only in total darkness. Yet it was permitted to engage in any sort of sexual conduct with one's wife, and it was obligatory to show her affection. Nor must a husband engage in intercourse and think of another woman, nor while he is drunk or angry may he force himself upon his wife or have sex with her after he has determined to divorce her.[21]

Sexual activity of any kind outside of marriage also was generally prohibited; however, again in Muslim lands and in Spain throughout the medieval period, concubines were allowed and sanctioned by the most important rabbis. We know also of cases where Jews did not observe the prohibitions against adultery, and even instances of sexual relations between Jews and Gentiles were not that unusual (including Jewish men and Muslim or Christian women as well as Gentile men and Jewish women), in spite of government laws that theoretically required a death penalty for such offenses, even in normally tolerant medieval Spain (where in spite of this many such cases are known, including some kings who had Jewish mistresses). Official law, including royal decrees, was not always carried out in practice.

In Germany in the thirteenth century, a strict circle of pietists (*hasidim*) developed a moral code of conduct that included admonitions not only against any forbidden sexual conduct but even sexual thoughts or fantasies, particularly for unmarried young men. One means of overcoming such temptations was to roll naked in the snow, followed by fasting (what to do about such fantasies in months when there was no snow is not prescribed). If such strict advice was actually followed, there must have been many frostbitten and hungry young men. In spite of this extreme attitude, the same source relates the story of an old man who was told that a younger woman desired him and he was advised to dye his hair to make himself more attractive to her, to which he replied, "Forfend that I should deceive her, but she shall see that I am old and say what is in her heart if she desires me."[22]

Dyeing grey hair in order to appear more youthful was a common practice in Muslim lands, and perhaps also among Jews in Muslim Spain, where at least it is frequently found in the poetry. The attraction of males towards younger members of the opposite, or same, sex is by no means a modern phenomenon.

Yet even in pietistic Germany, there were cases of illicit sexual behavior. In one instance, an unmarried woman gave birth to a son and she presented him to a certain man whom she claimed was the father. He denied this, however. The baby was, of course, circumcised in the synagogue, but when the man performing the circumcision (the *mohel*) came to the part of the blessing that states "Give thanks to God for he is good" he omitted "for he is good," saying that since the infant was born illicitly it should not be said. A famous rabbi who was present became angry at this and ordered him to say it "for his law is like all who are born in sanctity."[23]

As we know from the poetry written in Muslim Spain, at least, both Jews and Muslims in reality had a very different view of sexual pleasure, which included attentions both to young women and boys, both in and out of the respective ethnic group. Other sources prove that this was more than a merely literary motif. However, strict moralists such as Maimonides were strongly opposed to such poetry, and of course to the passions it portrayed, and indeed he viewed even permitted sex as a necessary evil, to be controlled as much as possible; particularly for the philosopher or seeker after intellectual perfection. There is no evidence that the great sage's opinion was widely followed, however.

Illicit sexual activity was probably more frequent than the limited sources indicate. An amusing example from Muslim Spain was a Jewish merchant who made frequent trips and several times upon returning home found his wife in bed with his own brother. She once gave the excuse that she had lost her blanket during the night and thought it was her husband's blanket she was crawling under.[24]

Isaac b. Sheshet (1326–1408), an important rabbi in Spain, received a complaint from the community of Alcira in Valencia:

A Case of Sexual Misbehavior

I have seen your writing about the complaint which Aljuhar, wife of Jacob b. Joseph, brought before you against Isaac Cohen, that he went after her suddenly, saying to her that he loved her, to the point that he said to her, "If you do not do [as I request], give me a kiss so that I do not die because of my love for you." Another time he called her to go up to his house, saying that there is a "continual dripping" in his house [Proverbs 9. 13; the reference there is to a contentious wife], and she understood his intention that it was for evil and did not want to go, and then he spoke to her foul words; and he was accustomed to do this with other women. Isaac answered her complaint and sought to refute her by saying that never was his intention for evil, God forbid, but since they were neighbors they only played in a joking manner, as intimates play, and that never was he accustomed to this, for he is a Jew who lives in a presumption of propriety. The investigators asked the woman why she had not come to them before, on the many times which she said that this Isaac had pursued her, and she answered that she was afraid that her husband would quarrel with the man and one or the other might be killed.[25]

Thus we see that, contrary to the romantic notions of many writers who have tried to portray Jews as superior to the rest of mere mortals in their chastity and sexual morality, they were in fact very much like everyone else.[26] True, the ethical teachings both of the Bible and the Talmud may have set standards of near perfection, but in reality they often proved to be difficult to achieve. While a monogamous relationship and happy married life were the desired ideal, this did not prevent men, some of them eminent scholars and writers, from pursuing their passions in prohibited sexual liaisons.

STATUS OF WOMEN

A common assumption is that medieval Jewish society was patriarchal, with the woman being a mere chattel, or possession, first of her father and then of her husband. This is far from true, however. Women had specific rights guaranteed to them by Jewish law, as well as those provided in the law of the place where they lived.[27] As mentioned, a woman brought certain property, minimally a dowry, with her into marriage. The often substantial dowries of Jewish brides both indicated the esteem in which they were held and served as a guarantee of financial security for the newly married couple (although legally any property owned by the wife before marriage remained hers). Marriage contracts also often specifically ensured her interests in case of divorce and sometimes provided for other things, such as protection from being beaten or that her husband should not travel without her consent.

Generally, Jewish law requires that in every material way a woman's lot must improve after her marriage and not decline. One of the great rabbis of Spain, Solomon Ibn Adret (ca. 1233–1310), ruled that a man may be forced to erect a monument for his deceased wife's grave even against his will, for even after death she must benefit and not suffer harm. Additional clauses to the marriage contract sometimes specified such things as periodic purchase of new clothing, jewelry, and even household items. There are, indeed, parodies of such stipulations in secular Hebrew literature from Spain, and later Italy. The marriage contract was also used to specify particular behavior in which the husband must engage, or not engage, once married; for example, promises not to gamble or even in some cases not to make long business trips to far lands. Few limitations were imposed upon the bride, but in extreme cases she might be prohibited from visiting a certain relative with whom there were hard feelings on the part of the groom.

By law, the wife must live where the husband chooses. Often economic factors determined this, and the husband may decide to move to a different community where he can make a better living. However, in Germany there was a rule that a husband could not compel his wife to move to a worse place, or even to a better town in a different province. The exception to all of this was the decision to move to the Land of Israel, in itself considered to be a religious obligation, in which case the wife could compel her husband if it was her decision to go there. Refusal was grounds for divorce. While this was not a frequent occurrence, there were such cases.

Abuse of women was not tolerated, nor in practice do we hear of many instances of this. Jewish authorities imposed heavy fines on husbands who beat their wives, and later in the Middle Ages this could be a cause for compelling the husband to divorce his wife. A more serious, and frequent, problem was the abandoned wife. There were cases of men who simply moved to another city, or country, and left their wives and families.

More common was the man who went abroad on a business trip and never returned, either having drowned in one of the frequent storms at sea or else taken captive by pirates or killed. In such a case, if there was no reliable witness (even a Gentile may so testify) to prove that he had died, the wife could not remarry. In spite of centuries of the best efforts of rabbinical scholars, this remains a serious shortcoming in Jewish law. A simple means of avoiding this was sometimes used in the Middle Ages, nevertheless, and that was the obligation of the husband to give his wife a "conditional divorce" before leaving on any trip, so that if he did not return she would be considered divorced. Nearly as problematic would be the situation where a husband converted to another religion and refused to divorce his wife.[28] Efforts by the Jewish courts to compel him may have had no results, although in Christian Spain the kings or local authorities would often intervene.

Another decree of the aforementioned Gershom b. Judah was that no woman could be divorced against her will. Divorce by the husband was usually allowed only because of infidelity (some rabbis permitted it also if the wife was barren). If the wife wanted to be divorced for any reason whatever, she could compel her husband (through a court) to grant the divorce. If the wife was divorced and did not want to take any of the children from the marriage, her former husband was compelled to keep them. The single exception was an infant still dependant on the mother, but in that case he had to pay support for the infant.

Divorce did not normally require action by a Jewish (or other) court, with the exception mentioned above, but was accomplished in accord with biblical law by writing and giving to the wife a document (*get*) of divorce. Sources do reveal instances where this was ignored, and divorce was sought through a Muslim or Christian court.

As mentioned above, Jewish law insists that a woman's condition must be improved and not worsened after marriage. This was broadly interpreted, so that the basic law guaranteeing that she not be forced to move to another place against her will was extended to include not being forced to move from one residence to another, even a nicer one, since she must decide what in her view is nice.

In general, there were ten specific responsibilities of a husband to his wife. Three of these are biblical: provision of food and shelter, clothing, and sexual gratification (not merely having children). The others are rabbinical in origin: fulfilling the *ketuvah*, providing medicine and healing, redemption if captured, burial, providing for her in case she survives the husband, provision for daughters if she does not survive him (this was not required by biblical law only for the sons), and the right of her sons to inherit her *ketuvah* rights (in addition to their normal inheritance rights).

On the other hand, the husband has only four rights from his wife, all rabbinical: to profit from and have use of her property from before the marriage, to profit from her work (if she works), to benefit from anything she finds, and to inherit from her if he survives her. Any property (and possessions) that she had before marriage and any that she acquired while married belonged absolutely to her; although her husband has the right to benefit from it he may not sell it. Even "benefit" was restricted, since, for example, if he wished to use an item as security for a loan he had to have his wife's permission. Note that there is no specific inclusion of sexual rights for the husband, except that custom dictated this (of course, his obligation to sexually satisfy his wife presumes that he also benefited).

Again, in all Muslim lands, and in Christian as well as Muslim Spain, women had equality with men in all business transactions.[29] This meant that they could acquire goods and property in their own name, sell the same, and often engage in significant commercial transactions. In Christian Spain, at least, property was in joint ownership of husband and wife, and documents of purchase or sale bear the signatures of both. There were, both in Egypt and in Christian Spain, examples of women who achieved considerable success in commerce and became quite wealthy. In Europe generally, Jewish women often engaged in business, assisting in farm work or selling goods, and this helped the family finances, or in some cases was the sole means of support while the husband pursued his talmudic studies (that became far more customary in the early modern period in eastern Europe).

All women could sew, as well as spin wool or cotton and weave, and many also earned money this way (this was probably not the case with the more aristocratic women in Muslim lands). Young girls were taught these skills by their mothers. An interesting sidelight to this, and which should serve as a corrective to the common misconception of hostility between Christians and Jews, is that some Jewish women sewed crosses on the clothes of crusaders.[30]

CHILDREN

Children were normally the natural offspring of their parents. In the case of a widow or divorced woman who remarried, her minor children were provided for by her new husband as a special part of the marriage agreement. An innovation in Jewish law, introduced in Spain by Asher b. Yehiel (ca. 1250–1327), was that children born out of wedlock or contrary to marriages permitted by Jewish law were nevertheless considered natural children for the purpose of inheritance (indeed, the father had to provide for them). However, since Jewish law does not recognize adoption, such offspring were not considered real children of the father. As a matter of practicality, this meant that restrictions on physical contact (touching) with a female not one's wife applied in this situation with a girl, or contact between a boy and the woman of the house. These rules applied, however, only to children who reached an age near puberty. The same restrictions applied, of course, in the case of children from a previous marriage and a new husband or wife.

Children grew up with young parents. As mentioned, they were usually married at the age of 13 or 14. In any case, the husband would be at most a few years older than his wife. By the time the mother was in her early twenties, therefore, she would have several children and the oldest

The Birth of Samson, Manoah with a medieval Jewish hat. Verdun altar, begun 1181. Nicolas of Verdun (c. 1150–1205). Klosterneuburg Abbey, Austria. Erich Lessing/Art Resource, NY.

would already themselves be adults, since in Jewish law a girl becomes adult at the age of 12 and a boy at the age of 13. This meant that it was time to begin thinking of marrying off the daughter at that age. A boy was sent to learn at a *yeshivah* for a few years, if possible (during which time he may also have become married, although not living with his bride).

Children were not always safe in the medieval period. Even if they survived the numerous diseases and illnesses that were common, they might fall victim to attack and kidnapping by Gentiles. A poignant warning to this effect is the ruling, probably from Germany, that a mother must not walk in the public streets with her young son behind her lest the Gentiles take him and she might go to save him and herself be raped by them.[31]

Nevertheless, in Muslim lands even Jewish children were generally safe. As noted elsewhere, boys were routinely sent alone to study with various Muslim scholars in distant cities or even other countries. Children were often taken on business trips with their fathers, for instance from Spain to India, and in at least one case sent home alone via overland journey to Baghdad and thence to Egypt and back to Spain.

Boys in Muslim lands often enjoyed a more extended childhood, as previously mentioned, in that they received also a secular education. This education usually concluded by the age of 18. Certainly not every boy benefited from this, but by no means was it restricted to the aristocracy. Many Jewish poets and scholars in Spain who came from poor, or at least not wealthy, families benefited from this kind of education. Boys, exclusively, are mentioned because there is no evidence of such education for Jewish girls, although some certainly learned Arabic and even wrote poetry in that language. Girls, even at a very young age, were expected to help their mothers in household duties. They certainly had less freedom than boys, since it was considered desirable that they spend most of their time indoors and not be seen too much in public.

Thus, childhood was a much different thing than what we experience in modern society. Nor was this peculiar to Jewish life; a legal code from medieval Spain in the thirteenth century, for instance, provides that childhood is defined as up to the age of 7. When a boy reaches the age of 14, he is able to distinguish good from evil and is ready to marry. This was fairly standard for all of medieval Christian Europe.

Rights and Responsibilities

Jewish children were not totally without rights, and in fact they could acquire possessions on their own, as could women. Laws protected the rights of children, even beyond what the Talmud specified. In certain circumstances, minor boys could also be counted as part of the *minyan* (quorum of ten men required for public services) or even lead the congregation in prayer, although generally that was not considered proper. Theoretically, a father could marry his minor daughter to whomever he wished, but the Talmud had already prohibited this "until she grows up and says, I desire this man" (*Qidushin,* 41). As previously mentioned, a minor girl who had been married could refuse to remain married once she reached the age of majority.

Honoring one's parents is, of course, a fundamental biblical commandment. What this meant specifically was discussed in the Talmud. It was naturally assumed that a Jewish child spoke to and treated his or her parents respectfully. Among other things, a child had to rise when his father entered the room, could not sit in his chair, and generally had to assist him in all things possible and demonstrate respect for him in public. It was customary to refer to one's father as "my father and teacher," and some scholars also referred to their mothers thus. These rules and customs were not restricted to minor children, but were obligatory throughout the life of the parent.

Children, particularly boys, may have had to help their parents in their work, certainly in agricultural settings. **Work and Play** Throughout the medieval period, many Jews owned farms or vineyards, in Spain as well as in France or Germany. Yet the compulsory nature of education, accepted as a norm in all Jewish communities, certainly meant that such work was kept to a minimum. For Muslim lands, it has also been observed that there is little evidence of child labor.[32] This is true also for Jews in Christian as well as Muslim Spain.

If a boy did not go to study in a *yeshivah*, he would often be apprenticed to learn a craft or trade (in some cases in medieval Spain, Jewish boys, and some girls, were apprenticed also to Christian craftsmen and actually lived with them for a period of years, while faithfully observing Jewish traditions and eating only kosher food, as stipulated in the contracts). In Muslim lands, including Spain and Sicily when under Muslim control, apprenticeships were a standard practice and served not only to teach boys a trade but were also a part of the socialization process. Such agreements made between craftsmen or businessmen often served to strengthen commercial ties.

Children were not, however, "little adults" who merely imitated their elders in all things. They had their own lives, including play, which is an essential part of the physical and mental development of an individual. One great German rabbi wrote in response to a question about boys and girls playing with nuts on the Sabbath, a game in which they rolled the nuts down a board to see which one came to the bottom first, that it should be prohibited, but who is to prevent them? Better that they should be left alone.

Play involving balls is mentioned already by the *geonim*. Maimonides was also familiar with ball games, and used the analogy of a king who when he was a youth valued playing ball in the streets with other boys but now has found more valuable pursuits.[33] From the writings of other rabbis, such as the aforementioned Asher b. Yehiel of Toledo, we also know that boys played games with balls, even on the Sabbath (technically this would be allowed in Jewish quarters that were enclosed on the Sabbath, but the rabbi nevertheless frowned on the practice).

Small boys often had little wooden "horses," usually nothing more elaborate than a pole with a wooden head, and also often played with bows and arrows and wooden swords. We know also of more intellectual games, particularly in Spain where mathematical games were played in the streets, during which apparently the children would yell out answers to problems or orally compute various numerical combinations. Little is known about games played by girls, probably of a more domestic nature.

Children were exempt from the observation of biblical commandments and rabbinical laws, nor were they punishable (by God) for violations. The father was nevertheless responsible for guiding his children in proper conduct and teaching them the observance of those laws that were possible for them (excluding, for example, observances of fasts, which might endanger their health).

Adolescence Adolescence, as we think of it, did not really exist, since both boys and girls legally and socially became adults with the onset of puberty. Again, however, the situation was different in more affluent cultures such as many Muslim cities. Documents from Egypt and North Africa attest to Jewish adolescents with too much time on their hands who congregated in groups outside the synagogue on Sabbaths (we hear of a similar complaint in Barcelona), and sometimes organized themselves into "communities," which often caused dissent with their elders.

In Alexandria (Egypt), and doubtless other communities, Jewish adolescents and young men sometimes became drunk and engaged in brawls. Curiously "modern" is the story of one such boy who fled his father and joined up with a group of other youths who spent their time playing music and drinking.[34] However, we hear of nothing similar to the wild street fighting of Christian adolescent gangs in Renaissance Italy.

FAMILY STATUS AND CONFORMITY

Individuality and independent thinking or behavior were not encouraged in medieval Jewish life, no more than they were in Muslim or Christian families. Particularly in villages and small towns, to be thought in any way different from other individuals or families was to invite ridicule at the least and social ostracism at the extreme. Of course, any deviation from observance of laws or even customs could bring excommunication, either temporary or of a permanent nature. This meant that one could not pray with the congregation in the synagogue, nor would anyone speak with the offending party or transact any business with them until the ban was lifted. Conformity was thus a major part of life. One dressed as the neighbors did, had the same kind and quality of furnishings (allowances being made only for wealthier people), shared the same education, and ate the same kind of food. In larger cities, there may have been room for more individual expression, certainly in the privacy of the home, but conformity was also a controlling factor even in larger cities.

Family status was important, but apparently less so in Europe, including Spain, than in Egypt and other Muslim lands, where there seems to have been a hierarchy of aristocratic or wealthy families who also controlled business. This was much less the case in Europe. In Christian Spain in the high Middle Ages (fourteenth and fifteenth centuries), we do find such families, particularly in Aragon and Catalonia. However, family status was far less important generally among medieval Jews than it was in later centuries. Even the sons and sons-in-law of famous rabbis, including those who themselves became rabbis, did not boast of their descent nor did they enjoy any special privileges because of this.

There is no doubt, on the other hand, that certain families achieved prominence in the community either because of their special piety and scholarly achievements or because of their wealth and business accomplishments. In Spain, there were also those who had government connections, officials of local government or even of the kings, and in some cases dynasties of such officials were established. There is evidence in the late medieval period of growing resentment of the privileged status of such individuals.

For many of the above reasons, divorce was rare in medieval Jewish life, although not unknown. In such cases, the divorced wife and her children were guaranteed financial security by the terms of her marriage contract and the supervision of the Jewish court. Every effort was made to assist a divorced woman in remarrying. Sometimes more precarious was the situation of a widow, particularly if she still had young children to care for. Almost every Jewish community had special funds to provide for needy widows and orphans, if there were no other family members to take care of them. Trustees, appointed by the Jewish court, supervised the inheritance and needs of orphans who had property.

FAMILY LIFE

Many have written that the synagogue was, or is, the center of Jewish life, to the point that this has become a cliché. However, it is not correct. If any institution could be said to be the center of Jewish life, surely it is the family. Even from the point of view of religious observances, the family and not the synagogue takes precedence. All prayers begin at home, as soon as one arises, and indeed most prayers that may be said in the synagogue may be said at home, there being no obligation to pray in a synagogue.

The Sabbath and all holidays are initiated in the home, with the wife lighting the candles (in medieval times oil lamps were usually used) and reciting the blessing that inaugurates the Sabbath or holiday. If the family, or at least the males, then went to the synagogue for evening services,

Presentation of Christ in the temple. Bonaccorso, Nic-
colo' di (fourteenth century). Uffizi, Florence, Italy.
Scala/Art Resource, NY.

upon their return the father would recite the *qidush* (sanctification) over a
glass of wine before the meal was served, but in fact it was the woman's
blessing of the lamp that signaled the beginning of the Sabbath or holiday.

The wife and daughters, from an early age, were responsible for cleaning the home and preparing it for Sabbaths and holidays, as well as cooking and serving the meals. Wealthy families lived in relative luxury, often
with Christian servants or (in Spain and parts of southern Italy) even
Muslim slaves.[35] Their duties included cleaning, cooking of meals (supervised by the Jewish woman) and serving at table. Technically, slaves
could only be kept for a limited period, after which they must be freed,
or converted if they so desired. In practice, this was not always observed.
Slaves were never to be mistreated, and on the contrary often were virtual
members of the family. Spanish sources reveal slaves eating at the table

on Passover, receiving gifts on Purim and other holidays, and even being taken to the synagogue.

There were problems inherent in having servants or slaves, however, in addition to the cost. For example, it was necessary to ensure that they did not touch open containers of wine, which would render it unfit for Jewish consumption, and for similar reasons all cooking had to be constantly supervised. Sexual problems also arose, with not a few instances of intercourse between the Jewish man and a female servant or slave (we know of few such cases involving Jewish women, but it is not impossible that this happened without coming to the attention of the authorities; in Spain, at least, there were some Jewish mistresses of kings and probably of some nobles).

Other important obligations were carried out only in the home. Among these, also performed by the woman, was the separation of *halah*, or a small portion of the dough from which bread was baked (in memory of the giving of priestly and levitical gifts in the time of the Temple). Some marriage contracts specified that the woman was to be trusted in all matters relating to the house and the preparation of food. The Jewish wife had to have a not inconsiderable knowledge of laws concerning such things.

Holidays necessitated more work in the home. The holiday of Passover required a thorough cleaning of the house for the removal of all leaven products, with a final inspection before the holiday actually began. Of course, the central focus of the holiday was the evening meal (*seder*), centered entirely around the family, the preparation of which was an elaborate procedure. The holiday of *Sukkot* required the building of a special booth (*sukkah*) in which meals were eaten, and if possible at least the male members of the family also slept there. The rabbinical holiday of Hanukkah required the lighting of candles, or oil, in a menorah displayed in the window (or entrance to the home). Purim had no particular home celebration, but gifts, usually food, were sent to friends, including Gentiles.

THE FAMILY AND EDUCATION

Education was also an essential part of family life, and another religious obligation. Infants were entirely in the care of their mother, who was responsible for nurturing them and also for instilling in them a proper respect for religious observances. She would teach them their first simple prayers (learned by heart), see to it that they washed their hands immediately upon awakening as required by law, and they would also learn from her what was to be done in the home. They would also observe, in most cases, her own piety in such things as the recitation of special blessings when required and her recitation of Psalms (also usually by heart).

The Talmud already recognized this central role of the mother in the education of children, and prescribed that at the Passover *seder* the father was to distribute the *matsah* (unleavened bread) to the children so that they would learn that their sustenance came also from him. On that night, even the youngest infant was involved in the educational experience of the Hagadah, which instructs that the father explain the story to the child who is too young to ask. Other Jewish holidays also involved significant educational aspects, since each is connected with an historical event. Such things as giving gifts not only to Jews but also Gentiles on Purim also were used as a means of teaching children moral lessons.

As we have seen, once the boys were old enough to begin formal schooling (by the age of five or earlier), the father became responsible for their education. Again, the initiating ceremony was in the home, and only after that was the child carried to the school and his actual training begun. The involvement of the father was henceforth limited to examination of what the boy had learned during the week, although he could challenge the teacher if he thought the instruction inadequate. When there was no such school, such as in small towns (particularly in Spain), the father, or several together, would hire a private teacher. In rare cases, particularly when the father was a scholar of note, he would teach his sons himself.

On Sabbaths and holidays, the meal would conclude with the discussion of an aspect of Jewish law or reading from the Bible or Talmud, at least among the more learned. It was also customary, particularly in Europe, to examine the older boys on Sabbath afternoons on what they had learned during the week.

THE FAMILY AT HOME

Modern sociologists distinguish the nuclear from the extended family. This would not have been a meaningful distinction to a medieval Jew. Most people in the Middle Ages were born and grew up and married in the same community, where their parents and grandparents and other family members also lived. In such a situation, the entire family was more or less one unit. Grandparents, aunts, and uncles, also played a part in the raising and education of children. Unfortunately, we do not have sufficient evidence to determine to what extent, if at all, other family members may have shared a house with the nuclear family of husband, wife, and children.

It is certain that there were no old age homes or retirement communities, where aged parents were shut away and forgotten except for an occasional visit. If an elderly family member became incapacitated to a greater or smaller degree, they certainly would be brought into the home to live out their days. Respect for parents and respect for elders in general was also a biblical commandment, and one that was scrupulously observed in all Jewish communities.

HOUSES AND FURNISHINGS

The conditions of family life were dependent on economic status. In larger cities, in whatever country, houses were generally larger and more massive (built of stone, for instance, instead of wood) than in small towns or villages. It has been suggested that Jews built stone houses for protection, and indeed we read in the sources that in times of attacks (in England or Germany, particularly) that Jews took refuge in stone houses. These did not always protect them, since the roofs were set afire. However, another more likely explanation is that stone offers much better insulation both from cold and heat than does wood, and of course such houses generally were safer from fires.

Only in Spain have medieval Jewish houses survived in any number, and of these only a few relatively unchanged. They range from small homes of two or three rooms to larger ones of two or more stories, with patios and courtyards.

In crowded medieval cities such as Toledo, Barcelona, or Gerona, houses were usually of more than one story. Medieval Jewish homes of this sort survive in Gerona and Toledo. Often, a shop would occupy the first floor, with the family living above it. In contrast to this, homes in Muslim cities such as Cordoba, Seville, or Granada had courtyards, fountains, and gardens, often several of these. Some homes of wealthier Jews in Toledo also had courtyards and gardens. These homes, of course, continued to be used after the Christian conquest of these cities, and surviving examples may be seen today.

In Muslim lands (except Muslim Spain, where cities were less crowded), houses were often several stories high; in Fez, for example, often six or seven. Houses were cooled by use of a large canvas or linen cloth hung from the ceiling on which water was sprinkled to create a kind of "air conditioning." In others, and generally in Muslim Spain, houses were cooled by fountains in the courtyard and by channels of running water that led into the main rooms of the house. Many homes had elaborate gardens and several fountains. Large open windows, covered with elaborate lattice work, also provided cooling.

Only in more affluent homes did children have their own room, and certainly not the luxury of a separate room for every child (many Jewish families had five or more children). In many homes, the family slept together, converting the sleeping space into other purposes during the day. Such conditions still prevail today in parts of the ultra-Orthodox sections of Jerusalem.

Bedrooms, at least for the father and mother, were, however, important and the furnishings surprisingly modern. However, in Muslim Egypt, at least, there were no separate bedrooms; rather, people slept in small heated cubicles in the winter and large open rooms, used also for other purposes, in the summer.[36] Homes in Muslim Spain, however, did usually have separate sleeping rooms.

While in Muslim countries, and probably also southern Spain, the custom was to sleep on the floor on cushions or couches, with only light linen coverings, beds in Jewish homes in Europe and northern Spain were either of wooden frames or solid box-like platforms, with the mattress (if any) supported by leather straps. Large bolsters, or in some countries pillows quite similar to modern pillows, supported the head; these were often covered with colored cloths. Covering included sheets and cloth or fur blankets, and in Muslim lands also fine linen coverings.

Other furnishings were chests or larger standing cabinets for clothing and one or more chairs. Often a sturdy locked chest containing valuables would be kept at the foot of the bed. A small table near the bed would hold the bowl and small pitcher, or metal container, containing water with which the hands were washed immediately upon awakening. Towels were used for drying the hands.

Water had to be drawn from wells in the courtyard, where there was one, or even from communal wells. Toilets were also outside the house or were shared by several families (in German cities, and sometimes also in other lands, they were on the city walls or over a river)[37], and in cold winter temperatures both carrying water (sometimes frozen) and relieving oneself must have been a hardship. Water used in cooking, and for washing dishes and utensils, was stored in very large tapered tubs, probably made of metal, which can be seen in some Spanish manuscript illuminations. Possibly these tubs were heated by fire or coals.

Bathing was in general not common among Christians in Europe, except for the nobility (and even then strictly limited); this remained the case until at least the eighteenth century. In Spain and in Muslim lands, however, public baths were to be found in every town and city (some Jewish communal baths, not ritual baths, have also been discovered). Some wealthy homes had private baths.

Even in other European countries, Jews bathed more regularly than Christians, and the pious custom of men also going to the ritual bath (*miqveh*) on the eve of Sabbaths and holidays was beneficial in lands where there were no private or communal bath houses. In Jewish homes in Germany in the later Middle Ages, large wooden tubs for bathing were often to be found in the house. Water for these would be laboriously heated on the stove. The quite modern showers that were common in ancient Greece and Rome were unknown in medieval Europe, as also were the flush toilets of the ancient Babylonians.

Every home, as well as public buildings, such as the schools or synagogues, had a *mezuzah* affixed to the right doorpost as one entered the building and each room. This was a scroll on which were inscribed the words of Deuteronomy 6.4–9 and 11.13–21, in accord with that commandment to "write these words on the doorposts of your house and on your gates." These scrolls were written by a trained scribe, exactly as a Torah scroll would be written. In some wealthy homes, elaborately decorated covers of silver or other metal would encase and protect the scroll, but often the scroll itself would simply be affixed to the doorpost or placed in a cut-out niche. A few such medieval scrolls and cases have survived.

Daily living in a medieval home was generally not very pleasant. Particularly in colder climates, including northern Spain, houses were notoriously cold in the winter. Few had fireplaces but relied on heat from stoves. In Spain, on the other hand, most homes at least in the cities did have fireplaces, either open hearth with large chimneys or (particularly in northern Spain) enclosed furnaces covered with ceramic tile or brick. The intense heat of summer in southern Spain must have been even more of a discomfort. Thick walls and white plastering on the outside, such as still seen in houses in the region today, helped, as did the cooling effect from the fountains previously mentioned.

Some Jewish homes in Germany had a winter and a summer house, actually not separate houses but rather separate parts of the house. The winter house contained the stove that heated the room, or rooms,[38] and the summer house was an attached area, either outside the main house or as a kind of open upper gallery, which was at least open on the sides to permit the circulation of air. Wealthier homes in southern Spain and in Muslim lands sometimes actually had two such separate houses.

Lighting was also poor and inadequate, with crude candles predominating in Europe, sometimes supplemented by oil lamps suspended from the ceiling; these were the rule in Spain and Muslim countries (however, poorer people also used cheaper candles). Again, only the wealthier families could afford glass for these suspended lamps, which somewhat increased the amount of light.

In homes that did not have oil lamps, candles would be lit from the large synagogue lamps at the end of Sabbaths or Yom Kippur (when no light could be kindled) and carried to the home in order to renew the light there. Again, the danger of fires is obvious, particularly in homes left unattended while candles or lamps were burning.

Windows were either open to the outside, perhaps covered with a grate, or in European countries sometimes covered with oiled parchment or paper or scraped hides. Only wealthy homes, particularly in Spain and Italy, had glass windows. At least one medieval synagogue in Germany had glass windows. Of course, covering the windows at all prevented them being used for ventilation, and in fact very few homes had window coverings. Again, very commonly in Spain can still be seen the heavy wooden shutters on windows, which open usually to the inside of the house. These would be closed at night (night air being considered dangerous) or when the house was left unattended.

Clocks were not known in German homes until the fifteenth century and were either mechanical devices with weights or simple hour-glasses using sand. However, in Spain clocks of various kinds were quite common at least by the thirteenth century and in some cases earlier. Some were quite elaborate, including water clocks. Treatises were written, also by Jews, on the making and running of clocks, and some Jewish artisans were even clockmakers to the kings.

FOOD: PREPARATION AND EATING

The kitchen was always removed from the main living quarters, in a separate room outside the house, in Muslim lands and Spain, both because of the danger of fire and as protection from the heat generated in cooking (in Christian Spain, judging from the few houses that have survived, the kitchen was in the home but removed as far as possible from the living area). In European lands, we have little information, but apparently kitchens were actually part of the home. In Germany in the thirteenth century some were accustomed to eat outdoors even on Friday nights (the Sabbath meal); however, this was because they ate that meal early, before nightfall, but the French rabbis objected to this and ruled that the meal should be after nightfall and eaten in the house where the Sabbath lights are.[39]

Every home had at least a small wood-burning kitchen stove, and more affluent homes also had baking and spit-roasting ovens, in which game and large sections of beef would be laboriously turned by hand on a spit that rotated the meat in front of a fire. In some cases, cooking was done in pots hung in the fireplace. Some cities had communal roasting ovens, and most baking was done in communal ovens or by professional bakers; again, both the danger of fire and the extreme heat made baking in private kitchens a rarity.

Rabbinical law required the eating of a hot meal on the Sabbath day, and in order to avoid the danger of fire such dishes were often sealed in pots and kept warm in the communal ovens and then brought home for the mid-day meal. In Muslim lands and in Spain, this special dish (*adafina*) was prepared of vegetables and chickpeas, sometimes also with meat, and kept warm either in the family oven or a communal oven overnight to be eaten at noon. In European countries the equivalent, commonly known as *cholent* (probably derived from the French word *chaud*), was a sort of stew prepared with chicken, or beef if possible, and in later centuries also beans and potatoes.

In smaller European homes, eating took place in the kitchen. In more affluent homes, and in most homes in Spain, there would be a separate dining room, or tables (often on trestles, so that when not in use the table could be stored) would be put in the main room when meals were eaten. Tablecloths were probably used only on Sabbaths and holidays (our only source of information is from manuscript illuminations, usually of Passover scenes). Often such cloths were elaborately embroidered with floral or animal designs. Women also displayed their considerable ability in needlepoint or embroidery for such things as cloths to cover the special loaves of bread eaten at Sabbath and holiday meals and for decorative cloths or tapestries hung on the wall.

The family sat on benches, with only the father and perhaps an honored guest seated in armchairs. In Muslim lands, there were generally no chairs; instead, everyone sat on the floor on cushions and small individual tables were placed before each person. No separate dining room was necessary, and the main living room would serve for this purpose. Poorer homes, of course, had only one or two rooms, used for all purposes.

Dishes and other vessels, such as cups and glasses and wine decanters, as well as linens, were stored in cabinets or cupboards. In poorer homes, such utensils were often made of wood, but most families managed to have at least one silver or gold cup for reciting the *qidush* (sanctification, the blessing over wine) to inaugurate the Sabbaths and holidays. For some reason not immediately apparent, copper was more common for all such utensils in Egypt, even in wealthy families. Laws requiring separation of meat and dairy foods meant that two sets of dishes and cooking utensils were needed, and many homes had complete separate sets for the Passover. In wealthier families, gold and silver utensils were common.

The kinds and quality of food varied also according to the country and even region where one lived. In northern Europe generally there was little variety of vegetables. Fruits, with the exception of apples, pears, and grapes, were virtually unknown. Meat, while eaten regularly, was probably expensive. A prized delicacy among German Jews was *pastete*,[40] apparently a kind of pie or pastry (the modern German meaning) but with meat rather than fruit. The most common form of meat for Christians, pork, was of course not allowed to Jews, and cows were raised primarily for milk. The few beef cattle raised or bought live on the open market must have made the cost of beef too high for daily consumption for the average person.

Varieties of Food

As in early modern eastern Europe, chicken and fish were undoubtedly the staple foods. However, wealthier Jews were able to afford such luxuries as goose, especially for holiday meals. Cakes and pastries of various kinds were popular, and in some communities special cakes were baked for the Sabbath and holidays.

The situation was quite different in Muslim lands, Spain, and southern Italy. Meat of various kinds was abundant, including beef, lamb, and goat (according to Ibn Ezra, goat meat was eaten in the Muslim lands, including Spain, and "all doctors agree that there is no better [healthier] meat," which even the sick are permitted to eat.[41] Medieval recipes survive from Muslim countries, as well as Christian Spain, and are surprisingly elaborate and varied. In Spain, at least, many Jewish farmers raised herds of cattle, or more often sheep and goats, and live animals were purchased also at special markets. In Italy as well, most food items were widely available and various kinds of fowl (pheasants, quail, partridges, ducks, and other fowl) were consumed, as also in Spain.

Fish, popular everywhere as previously mentioned, was of course a staple in the diet in Spain, as today, blessed with an abundance and variety of fresh- and salt-water fish. In few, if any, other places in the world is it possible to catch fish in the rivers flowing through the center of cities such as is true in Gerona or Burgos.

Fruits and vegetables of all kinds were also widely available in Muslim lands and throughout Spain. Among the common fruits mentioned by Maimonides ("Treatise on Asthma," ch. 3), for example, were apricots, watermelon, peaches, mulberries, dates, grapes, figs, apple, quince, and raisins. Of course, citrus fruits of all kinds were very popular (both the words *lemon* and *orange*, among others, derive from the Arabic). Vegetables mentioned by Maimonides include leeks, beets, asparagus, fennel, parsley, mint, pennyroyal, summer savory, watercress, radish, lettuce, pumpkin (*Coloquinte*), "Swedish turnip" (*Brassica napus*), cauliflower, eggplant, regular turnip, and cucumber (listed as a fruit!). Of course tomatoes were not yet known.

Maimonides provides some interesting recipes, personal favorites such as chicken with fennel or a lamb dish with an almond sauce, all of which are actually quite good, and a detailed recipe for making mustard. He reports that he himself only ate one full meal a day, however, sometimes supplemented with chicken soup or a confection made of several egg yolks and cane sugar (which sounds very much like modern Spanish *yemas*, an extremely sweet but very popular candy). He drank only one cup of wine a day, but also an interesting drink of honey, vinegar, lemon, and water which was supposed to be healthy.

Few other Jews, except perhaps for the ascetics in later medieval Germany, followed such a strict diet, and two or even three meals were common. The Spanish custom of serving two enormous "plates," or entrees, at the noon and dinner meals derives from a late medieval prohibition on eating *more* than that. Surviving menus from medieval Spanish Christian aristocracy would challenge the most skilled French chef of today.

From the point of view of health, also, differences in diet are important. Maimonides, a physician, was not writing a cookbook, but recommendations concerning diet that he believed were beneficial to health (such statements, indeed, appear throughout his works). There is no doubt that Jews in those lands with an abundance of fruits and vegetables lived longer and healthier lives than those in European countries, to which are to be added the custom of frequent bathing and the availability of fresh and wholesome water throughout the year.

Family life for the average Jew in the Middle Ages was not markedly different from that in later centuries. The most significant difference, in comparison perhaps with modern life, is that both the family and the home played a much more central role.

NOTES

1. S. D. Goitein, *A Mediterranean Society: The Jewish Communities of the Arab World as Portrayed in the Documents of the Cairo Geniza* (Berkeley, Calif., Los Angeles, London, 1967–1993), 3, The Family: 441 note 2, claimed that "the [Hebrew] root

qdsh means 'holy,' that is, belonging exclusively to God." This is completely incorrect; the root has nothing to do with "holy" but rather means "set apart" and its original usage in the Bible in no way relates to God. Land, for example, is said to be "set aside" and prostitutes were referred to either as *qadeshah* (female) or *qadesh* (male). The Aramaic term *qidushin* applied to the act of marriage, therefore, refers to the particular woman being set aside for a particular man. The tractate Qidushin deals very briefly with marriage and much more significantly with numerous aspects of civil law: acquisition of goods and property and other matters.

2. Abraham b. Natan of Lunel, *Sefer ha-manhig*, ed. Yitzhak Raphael (Jerusalem, 1978) 2: 536 and corresponding sources cited in the notes there.

3. Jacob b. Moses Mölln (or Molin), *Sefer Mahari"l*, ed. Shlomo Spitzer (Jerusalem, 1989), 472, No. 13; cf. *Ketubot* 12 (those who have more money must specify a larger amount than those who have less).

4. Shelomo Dov Goitein, "Three Trousseaux of Jewish Brides from the Fatimid Period," in *AJS* (Association for Jewish Studies) *Review* 2 (1977):77–110, with texts and translations (see 94 for the Chinese pen-box, line 24).

5. Mordechai A. Friedman, "Marriage as an Institution: Jewry under Islam," in David Kraemer, ed., *The Jewish Family. Metaphor and Memory* (New York, Oxford, 1989), 33–34. The author is a recognized authority on medieval marriage customs as found in the Cairo Genizah documents.

6. See Chapter 5, on the holiday of Shavu'ot, on this legend.

7. Goitein, "Three Trousseaux," 76–78, gives the impression that medieval authorities simply disregarded the talmudic injunction against fathers marrying off their minor daughters without their consent, which simply is not true. Such marriages, even though legal, were not generally condoned. Nor did he mention at all the absolute right of the girl to refuse to continue being married once she attained majority.

8. *Tosafot* ("additional" commentaries on the Talmud) to *Qidushin* 41A.

9. Samson bar Tsadok, *Sefer Tashbats* (Warsaw, 1875), No. 464, the longest section in the book. The author was a student of the renowned Meir b. Barukh of Rothenburg. Rashi makes no mention of any of this in his commentary on the Psalm cited. This passage has apparently been overlooked by Gershom Scholem and other authorities on Jewish mysticism. This needs to be added also to the detailed study that hopefully will be written about the mystical and allegorical significance of the number seven generally and in Jewish sources.

10. However, in Mainz it was the practice to have the wedding actually in the synagogue, after the morning prayers; see *Sefer Mahari"l*, 465, and the detailed description of the wedding celebrations there, 464–66 (that rabbi, 1365–1427, was an important authority).

11. See, for example, the statement about leaving the synagogue while it was still light when marriages took place in order to eat the wedding meal, which served also as the Sabbath night meal, in Samson bar Tsadok, *Sefer Tashbats*, before section No. 1.

12. The most thorough study of the use of dance halls/wedding halls in medieval Germany is Zvi Friedhaber, "The *Tanzhaus* in the life of Ashkenazi Jewry during the Middle Ages," (Heb.) in *Jerusalem Studies in Jewish Folklore* 7 (1984): 49–60. These are discussed also by Abraham Berliner, *Hayei ha-yehudim be-Ashkenaz* (Warsaw, 1900; photo reprint Jerusalem, 1969).

13. The so-called "*Hidushei ha-Rambam*," actually excerpts from a writing by his son Abraham that records either actual additions to the code of law by Maimonides

or statements reported in his name, in Moses b. Maimon, *Qovets teshuvot ha-Rambam* (Leipzig, 1859; photo rpt. Westmead, England, 1969), part 1, 51a.

14. Jacob Mölln, *Sefer Mahari"l*, 466. I have seen that custom mentioned elsewhere also but cannot now recall where.

15. Berliner, *Hayei ha-yehudim*, 77. It was customary for both bride and bridegroom to wear white gown-like garments, and at least in some places dust on the foreheads of both bride and bridegroom as a sign of mourning for Jerusalem; *Kol bo* (an anonymous medieval collection of laws), no. 75 (there are numerous editions of this work and thus I do not cite a page number; I used the Lemberg, 1860 edition). Jacob Mölln does not mention the custom of wearing white.

16. Jacob Mölln *Sefer Mahari"l*, 467. See there n. 9 for other sources on this custom.

17. See on this Samson bar Tsadok, *Sefer Tashbats*, No. 465. It is apparently this custom that has been confused by some with the later custom of breaking a glass; see Joseph Gutmann, "Jewish Medieval Marriage Customs in Art: Creativity and Adaptation," in Kraemer, *The Jewish Family*, 50, citing a thirteenth-century German rabbi; but "desecrating the wine by spilling it" clearly refers to the custom mentioned here, not breaking the (empty) glass.

18. Previous writers, usually for apologetic reasons, have tried to deny the reality of such marriages even in Muslim lands and have ignored altogether the examples from Spain. Thus, even Goitein (*Mediterranean Society* 1: 73–74) tried to deny or minimize the existence of such marriages, but recent research has revealed extensive examples; see Friedman, "Marriage as an Institution," 38–39, and his "Polygyny in Jewish Tradition and Practice: New Sources from the Cairo Geniza," American Academy for Jewish Research, *Proceedings* 49 (1982): 33–68. Spanish examples will be detailed in my forthcoming book on Spanish Jewish culture.

19. Simon b. Semah Duran, *Sefer ha-tashbetz* (Lemberg, 1891; photo reprint Tel Aviv, s.a.) part 2, no. 175. This work, by a fourteenth-century Spanish rabbi, is not to be confused with the work of a similar title by the previously mentioned German rabbi Samson bar Tsadok. The title of that work is formed from his name (*Teshuvot Shimshon bar Tsadok*), whereas the title of Duran's book is the biblical word for "embroidered coat" (according to the translation of Saadyah *Gaon*).

20. For a concise summary and bibliography, see Roth, "A Note on Research into Jewish Sexuality in the Medieval Period," in Vern L. Bullough and James A. Brundage, eds., *Handbook of Medieval Sexuality* (New York, 1996), 309–17. Note that both the "treatise on sexual intercourse" attributed to Maimonides and the "Holy letter" on the same, attributed to Nahmanides, are forgeries, in spite of which they continue to be discussed by many as if they were authentic.

21. The previously cited *Kol Bo*.

22. Judah b. Samuel (thirteenth century), *Sefer hasidim* (Berlin, 1891), 281, no. 1106.

23. Jacob Mölln, *Sefer Mahari"l*, 484, No. 19. Nevertheless, the same rabbi was far more strict with regard to an actual bastard, an illegitimate son of a married woman; see there, No. 20.

24. Isaac al-Fasi, *She'elot u-teshuvot* (Livorno, 1781; reprinted Warsaw, 1884), No. 73 (I related this story in *Jews, Visigoths & Muslims in Medieval Spain: Cooperation & Conflict* (Leiden, 1994), 149.

25. Isaac b. Sheshet, *She'elot u-teshuvot* (Jerusalem, 1968), no. 265.

26. Once at a conference in Israel when I mentioned some examples of boy love in medieval Hebrew poetry, a certain scholar turned and whispered to me that "we don't talk about that." This was years after the eminent Israeli authority Hayyim Schirmann had first cautiously revealed the existence of such poetry, and years after I had written my initial study of the subject, "'Deal Gently with the Young Man'–Love of Boys in Medieval Hebrew Poetry of Spain," *Speculum* 57 (1982): 20–51. Since then, I have written numerous articles on this and related themes.

27. See the excellent article "Women," by Judith Baskin, in Norman Roth, ed., *Medieval Jewish Civilization: An Encyclopedia* (New York, 2003), and the bibliography there.

28. For instances of these things in Muslim Spain, see the section "Abandoned Wives and Apostate Husbands" in Roth, *Jews, Visigoths & Muslims*, 187 ff. Note there particularly the case in which the renowned Isaac *al-Fasi* ruled in favor of a woman who converted to Islam, after which her former Jewish husband remarried and gave the house he had promised her to his new wife. The great rabbi stated that her conversion could not remove property from her possession. The "conditional divorce" was apparently a virtual requirement in Jewish communities in Muslim lands; see Goitein, *Mediterranean Society*, 3. The Family, 189 ff.

29. See, for example, S. D. Goitein, "A Jewish Business Woman of the Eleventh Century," in Abraham A. Neuman and Solomon Zeitlin, eds., *The Seventy-Fifth Anniversary Volume of the Jewish Quarterly Review* (Philadelphia, 1967), 225–42. There are many similar examples from medieval Spain.

30. See "Christian-Jewish Relations" in Roth, *Medieval Jewish Civilization*, 153.

31. The aforementioned anonymous collection *Kol Bo*, at end of section 75.

32. Goitein, *Mediterranean Society* 1: 98–99.

33. From his commentary on the Mishnah, introduction to *Sanhedrin* 10.1; see the translation of the original Arabic text in Norman Roth, *Maimonides: Essays and Texts* (Madison, Wisc., 1985), 51.

34. See Miriam Frenkel, "Adolescence in Jewish Medieval Society under Islam," *Continuity and Change* 16 (2001): 263–81, particularly 269–71.

35. There is still no good study of slaves in medieval Jewish life. For Muslim Egypt, see Goitein, *Mediterranean Society* 1: 130–47; however, there are some erroneous statements there: manumission did not automatically confer the status of a Jew upon a slave; intercourse with a slave was not punishable by death; slaves were not "baptized," the ritual immersion was an issue of purification identical to that performed by Jews on various occasions. On slaves in Muslim Spain, see Roth, *Jews, Visigoths & Muslims*, particularly 153–62, where also some of Goitein's erroneous statements are corrected.

36. Goitein, "Three Trousseaux of Jewish Brides," 100.

37. Samson bar Tsadoq, *Sefer Tashbats*, No. 38.

38. It was permitted on the Sabbath to touch the furnace, or stove, which heated the rooms, for additional warmth apparently, since there was no danger of stirring the fire in an enclosed furnace; see Samson bar Tsadoq, *Sefer Tashbats*, No. 32.

39. Samson bar Tsadoq, ibid., No. 3 and see note there.

40. Samson bar Tsadoq, ibid., 30b.

41. "Long" commentary on Ex. 23.19; *Ibn Ezra peirushei ha-Torah*, ed. A. Weiser (Jerusalem, 1976) vol. 2, p. 161.

RECOMMENDED READING

Friemann, Abraham H. *Seder qidushin ve-nisuin.* Jerusalem, 1964.

Goitein, S.D. *A Mediterranean Society: The Jewish Communities of the Arab World as Portrayed in the Documents of the Cairo Geniza.* Berkeley, Calif., Los Angeles, London, 1967–1993.Vol. 3: The Family.

"Marriage" and "Food," in Roth, ed., *Medieval Jewish Civilization.*

Moses b. Maimon (Maimonides), *Treatise on Asthma,* trans. S. Munter. Philadelphia, 1963. Unfortunately, not an accurate translation.

4

THE COMMUNITY

After the family, the most important institution in medieval Jewish life was the community itself. Just as "family" in the larger sense meant the totality of one's relatives, so "community" ultimately included all Jews everywhere. In this almost mystical sense, rabbinical tradition speaks of *am Yisrael*, "the people Israel," *klal Yisrael* "the totality of Israel" or *keneset Yisrael*, "the assembly, or community, of Israel."[1] All Jews are united as one people, in whatever country they live and whatever languages they may speak.

Since "Judaism" (an anachronistic term, actually "being Jewish") is not a religion but rather a civilization, there is no functional equivalency of "Synagogue" and "Church," as some writers have tried to maintain. However, there was in the medieval period a very close similarity between this Jewish concept of the unity of Israel and the Christian theological notion of *Res publica Christiana*, the totality of the body of Christians.[2] On the other hand, that was never more than a somewhat obscure theoretical notion, whereas the sense of Jewish unity, of being one people, was very real and a constant factor in Jewish life.

Throughout history, this was more than a theoretical concept, it was a reality that enabled Jews to rely upon assured hospitality and whatever assistance they may require when traveling from one land to another. In the medieval period, Jews, particularly on business, made constant journeys to other countries. In fact, one of the characteristics that marked the special, privileged, status that Jews enjoyed in the Middle Ages was the freedom to travel wherever and whenever they chose. Jews from

Hungary and Russia arrived in Germany, students from Russia and other countries went to study in Toledo, and Jewish merchants from Spain traveled to Egypt and India.

The sense of kinship with Jews in different lands was possible because of common cultural and religious ties, as well as a knowledge of different languages that many Jews acquired. And if all else failed, it was always possible to communicate in Hebrew.[3] This does not mean, of course, that any Jew was always welcomed in every Jewish community. Laws of hospitality could be strained if someone overstayed the welcome, as a later Hebrew ditty put it succinctly: "The first day a guest, the second a burden, and the third he flees" (or is asked to leave).

In the more restrictive sense, community meant the group of Jews with which one was in most frequent contact. Usually this was a group that lived together in a quarter of a town or city, and such a community is called *qahal* or *qehilah*; in Spain the term *aljama*, derived from Arabic, was used to refer to either a Jewish or Muslim community (in Catalan, the word *call* was used for a Jewish community). Jews who lived more or less isolated, for example as farmers, were part of a community only as they related to other nearby Jewish families or towns; for instance, going to a town to make purchases or possibly to celebrate holidays. One of the unique features of Jewish life in medieval Spain was the fact that many Jews lived in small towns and tiny villages or sometimes as isolated farmers or grape growers.

This situation exists even in contemporary life, where individual Jewish families living in a rural community may go to the nearest larger city to spend the holidays. There are also still Jewish farm families in the United States (and in other countries). Inevitably, there is a loss of interaction with other Jews and a diminished sense of communal ties in such a situation.

There is another way in which the community was similar to the family. Few aspects of Jewish life are focused on the individual. Sabbath and holiday observances, synagogue worship, even the study of Talmud, all these and more presuppose sharing with family and close friends. This is no less true of the personal life celebrations, such as the birth of a new child, attaining legal adulthood (13 for a boy, 12 for a girl), or death and mourning. The community also supports this, where all members of the community are living essentially the same kind of life, and joys and sorrows, weddings and funerals, and holiday observances are all shared within the larger community. Each one is part of a whole, and just as the child learns by example from his family what it means to live as a Jew, so the individual learns within the community what are these larger responsibilities.

THE SMALL COMMUNITY, PART OF THE LARGE COMMUNITY

The community with which one was most familiar was usually that into which he or she was born. Unlike modern times, people in the

Middle Ages tended to stay in the same community most or all of their lives. The entire family, nuclear and extended, was likely to be in the same community.

Only conditions of persecution, such as in Germany or France, sometimes caused people to move to a different town or city, and even then not only entire families but sometimes even entire communities would move together. In Spain, there was considerably more movement of individuals or families from one community to another, usually seeking better economic conditions. Expulsions of the entire Jewish population, such as occurred in France several times, in England (1290), in later medieval Germany frequently, and in fifteenth-century Spain and other countries, of course disrupted these Jewish communities completely.[4] As individuals and families settled in new lands, they brought with them their own customs and culture to the extent that was possible, but new ties inevitably had to be established.

The local Jewish community was autonomous, with its own customs, regulations, and institutions, as we shall see. However, it was also part of a larger community composed of several such local communities. In Germany, particularly, the larger cities (Worms, Mainz, Speyer, Cologne, and others) were the centers for a number of nearby smaller communities. Rabbinic leadership, as well as a certain degree of regulation, came from these central communities (see further on this in the section on "Structure of the Community"). This sort of formal organization was not typical in other countries; however, in medieval Christian Spain various smaller communities were associated with larger towns or cities for tax purposes. Of course, important rabbis in major communities (Mainz in Germany, Troyes and later Paris in France, Barcelona, Zaragoza, and Toledo in Spain, to name but a few) became the recognized leaders for the entire region and often for the entire country.

There was another important sense in which communities felt themselves bound with others; for example, when rumors of the impending attacks during the First Crusade (1096) reached the Jews of Germany, they immediately informed their fellow Jews in France so that they could prepare themselves (in the end, no attacks occurred there). In Aragon-Catalonia in the early fourteenth century, there was great concern about impending persecution (the fears were groundless), and extraordinary measures were taken to organize all the Jewish communities of the kingdom to plan proper responses. Sadly, when actual attacks came in the summer of 1391, there was no longer the possibility of such organized response, given the loss of leadership due to massive conversions earlier.[5]

There were also tensions and conflicts between communities. Jews from both the Land of Israel and Iraq living in Egypt carefully guarded their autonomy, just as Jewish communities in North Africa (in the ninth through eleventh centuries) resisted the efforts of the academy in Jerusalem to impose its will upon them. Also, already in the medieval period began the division between Ashkenazim (originally, Jews of

Jewish Procession in 1417. Foto Marburg/Art Resource, NY.

Germany, but eventually the term came to include all the Jews of northern, central, and eastern Europe) and Sefardim (Jews of Spain and their descendants in Italy, North Africa, Egypt, and the Ottoman Empire). This was due to differences in legal and religious observances, as well as different customs and language.

Nevertheless, there was never the kind of antagonism and open hostility that was typical between Christian communities and countries in the medieval period, with the growing sense of nationalism that divided people and led to such things as bitter quarrels and boastful claims of superiority in church councils, reflected also in literary sources.[6]

THE PHYSICAL NATURE OF THE COMMUNITY

There were no ghettos in the medieval period; the notion of Jewish quarters with narrow streets enclosed behind walls is generally incorrect.

However, in some German cities, and even in a few places in northern Spain in the later medieval period, it is true that there were gates to the Jewish quarter that had to be locked at night. This was as much for the protection of the Jews from possible attack as it was, undeniably, an attempt to separate them from their Christian neighbors. However, in many towns Jews and Christians (or Muslims) lived together, literally as neighbors. This does not mean there was always peace and harmony, but generally this was the case. Neighbors need not love each other, but it is after all easier to get along than not.

In Germany in the early medieval period, Jews were not only welcomed but were eagerly sought as residents who could bring increased prosperity to the cities through trade and other economic activity. Special charters or privileges were granted, at first, in the very early periods, to individual Jews and their families, and then to all Jews. By the thirteenth century, these privileges were granted by rulers for the entire kingdom. According to the terms of these privileges, Jews were granted freedom to settle and to travel, something denied to the average Christian in the Middle Ages, as well as other benefits.

By the early eleventh century, Jews had settled in all the major towns along the Rhine river in Germany, and in some smaller communities elsewhere. In each of these towns, Jews lived in a special quarter or neighborhood, but there was usually no physical barrier until after the attacks on Jews at the outset of the First Crusade.

In France and England, the situation in general was similar to that in Germany. Jews lived in larger towns (relatively, for especially in England all towns, including London, were quite small), but many also were farmers or lived in small rural areas. In France, there were large counties (Normandy, Champagne, and others), over which the kings had no control; only a small territory around Paris belonged to the rulers. Many Jews would leave this territory if conditions became oppressive, as they often did, and negotiate better conditions with one of the neighboring counties. Frequent charges made by the kings were that neighboring counts or countesses were harboring "their" (the king's) Jews. This, of course, was not because of any love of Jews but rather their perceived economic benefits.

In Muslim lands, including Muslim Spain, Jews did not necessarily live in special quarters or neighborhoods apart from Muslims. In Cordoba, for example, aristocratic Jewish families, including that of Maimonides, lived in the fashionable suburb in the western part of the city together with wealthy Muslims (including, interestingly, the family of Ibn Rushd, "Averroes," whose ideas later were so similar to those of Maimonides but yet unknown to him). The situation was the same in other cities, such as Granada.

Jews lived also in towns and cities in northern Spain under Muslim control, including Zaragoza and Tudela, and of course in all the towns and cities after the Christian reconquest. Life and cultural activity in these Muslim cities was virtually identical to that in the southern cities, such as Lucena, Cordoba, and Toledo. Jews traveled frequently between all of these cities, often living in several different ones at various times.

In the early medieval period, some cities in al-Andalus were called by the Muslims "Jewish cities," with the claim being made that they were entirely populated by Jews, or nearly so. This is certainly an exaggeration, with the possible exception of Lucena, but it does indicate that there was a substantial Jewish population in these cities. Granada, for example, had its own Jewish section, called Jewish Granada, as was the case in North Africa and Egypt.

Fez in North Africa, for example, had a separate Jewish quarter or suburb, but so also did Muslims from Spain (Andalus) who settled there. These were thus not segregated areas but reflected the desire of the inhabitants to live together and maintain their own distinctive communities. In Egypt, Jews lived in a number of small towns, but chiefly in the cities of Alexandria and Fustat, a suburb of Cairo (unlike North Africa or al-Andalus, Jews were not allowed to live in the capital itself).

Particularly in Egypt, there was a great diversity of Jewish population, with Jews from the Land of Israel (including the heretical Qaraite sect), from "Babylon" (Iraq), North Africa, and Spain. Each of these had its own communities, customs, synagogues, and other institutions. There were also business travelers and others who arrived from Italy and other countries.

In Iraq, there were always a large number of Jews living in Baghdad, but others were in the nearby small towns along the Tigris and Euphrates rivers where the Talmud had evolved and where in the early medieval period the *geonim* had their *yeshivot*. Community life was lived strictly in conformity with the laws and customs set down by these leaders, but with remnants of more ancient talmudic traditions. Jews in the former Persian Empire were another important population, with communities stretching to southern Russia and the frontier of India. Aside from a considerable amount of detail about economic factors, unfortunately little is known about life in these communities.

In Christian Spain, including the former Muslim cities conquered by the Christians in the twelfth and thirteenth centuries, Jews lived in nearly every village, town, and city. Only in some of the cities in Catalonia (Barcelona, Tarragona, and Gerona) were there special Jewish quarters, or more or less segregated areas. In later medieval Castile, attempts were made to create such separate quarters, with limited success.

In Barcelona and Tarragona, as well as many other cities throughout Spain, the Jews were given castles, in which some of them lived, and which they had to defend against possible attacks on the city. Such attacks were not directed against Jews, however, but came from invading armies from another kingdom. Remnants of some of these Jewish castles may still be seen in Spain.

The narrow cobblestoned main street of the Jewish quarter (*call*) of Gerona is also still to be seen and provides an example of what other such Jewish quarters in the kingdom probably were like. On both sides of such streets rose buildings two or more stories tall, which housed different families on each level (except for very wealthy ones who may have owned an entire building or more).

Elsewhere in Spain, such as Aragon and Castile and Leon, Jews did not normally live in special quarters protected by walls. Nevertheless, in larger towns and cities there were Jewish neighborhoods clustered around one or more synagogues. These were not segregated, and some Christians or Muslims may also have lived there; such was the case in Toledo, for example, and in Zaragoza and even in smaller towns in Aragon, where Muslims also continued to live. Many of the Jewish quarters of Spanish towns and cities survive today.

Christians and Jews generally enjoyed favorable relations, often living not only next door to each other but in the same courtyards. An amusing example of how lack of first-hand knowledge of Spanish cities can distort understanding was the claim by one writer that because the Jews of Toledo customarily wore the prayer shawl (*talit*) in the streets on their way to and from the synagogue on the Sabbath, this is "proof" that they lived separated from Christians. On the contrary, there was (and still is) a church in the very center of the main Jewish quarter, and the cathedral is not far away. The fact is that Jews had no reason to fear their Christian neighbors. We read in the sources about Christian neighbors visiting in Jewish homes or vice versa. Of course, this was the case in France and Germany as well, but perhaps not as frequently (or the sources do not reveal as much information).

STRUCTURE OF THE COMMUNITY

Whatever the physical similarities or differences between Jewish neighborhoods, or quarters, the Jewish community structure was basically the same in every country, much of it derived from talmudic law and custom but also with some local variation influenced by Christian or Muslim custom.

Every adult male, was automatically a member of the *qahal* (official community). Women were considered to be represented by their husbands, or fathers if they were unmarried, and while they perhaps may have had a voice in certain public discussions (there is no evidence one way or the other), they had no vote. This was probably true even in Spain, where women had greater legal privileges than in other countries. However, we hear of rare cases where a woman served in an honorary position as "head" of the synagogue, most likely in charge of the women's section of the synagogue.

**Community
Councils**

The striking thing about the community structure is that
the rabbi was usually not the head of the governing body
of the community, which had an elected council. Elections
were annual, except in some cities, like Worms in Germany,
where members served for life. This council in turn chose one of its members as official head of the community. There were some exceptions to this,
where particularly great scholars were actually the heads of the community
as long as they remained there. Even so, they were assisted by the elected
council, whose opinion they consulted. While the Talmud advocated that
such councils be composed of "seven good men of the city," in practice,
especially in the early medieval period, many councils consisted only of
three men. Later, important rabbis in Germany and elsewhere attempted
to enforce literally the talmudic requirement of seven.[7] The situation in
Spanish Jewish communities will be discussed separately.

Meetings of the community council usually took place in the synagogue,
unless there was a separate hall for that and other purposes (as in some
German cities). Important announcements were also made in the synagogue, including betrothals, weddings, circumcisions, announcement of
lost articles, official government proclamations, excommunication of an
offender, and sometimes debts that were outstanding and even property
for sale. These frequent announcements interrupted the Sabbath services
and were a constant source of annoyance to rabbis, who protested usually
in vain against such practices.

In Germany, there was also a synod composed of the rabbis and leaders
of the three most important communities, Worms, Mainz, and Speyer, which
made decisions that ultimately were accepted by all the Jews of Germany.

**Governing the
Community**

The right of community councils to enact regulations
(*taqanot*) was established already in talmudic law, and
every resident of the community had to abide by these
regulations. Usually, the executive council (the "seven
good men," although in practice the number was sometimes more)
enacted these rules, but in extraordinary matters, and especially for new
communal taxes, the entire community council (in Spanish Jewish communities, usually 40 men) would meet. In certain matters, the consent
of a rabbinical scholar was required for enacting any new regulation
that concerned such things as marriage or divorce. However, established
custom was everywhere recognized as authoritative, even against the
technical law. Some rabbis objected strenuously to customs of which they
disapproved or felt were contrary to law, but they seldom had the power
to get these customs changed.

COMMUNITY OFFICIALS

Special community officials, often called by the talmudic term *parnasim*,
were in charge of charitable organizations. Sometimes this term was used

for the members of the council themselves; in Spain, they were known as *muqadamin* (an Arabic term). If not the members of the council, these officials also were elected for annual terms. In addition to these, there was also the *gabai*, sometimes more than one, who was responsible for the collection and disbursal of internal (that is, Jewish) taxes for such things as the maintenance of charitable institutions and other community needs.

These communal taxes, also in other lands, were collected from all male adults (over the age of 13) and on such things as the sale of meat or of wine. In some countries, particularly Germany in the late medieval period, the government interfered and seized the money collected on such things.

There also was the *shamash*, technically "servant," or beadle of the synagogue. His job was to supervise the synagogue and everything that went on there, including the important issue of assigning seats or places in the synagogue. He, or in German communities an assistant called *Schulkopfer* (literally, "synagogue-knocker"), would go from house to house knocking on doors to call people to services or to announce the beginning of Sabbaths or holidays. He also made important announcements in the synagogue during services. In addition, he sometimes was appointed to carry out or see to enforcement of the decisions of the Jewish court. So important was the *shamash* that his term of office often extended beyond the annual term of the council, sometimes for his lifetime.

The community rabbi was, of course, the most important official, even when he was not the head of the community.[8]   **The Rabbi** Unlike a modern rabbi, his duties were not ceremonial but rather educational and judicial. He did not preside over services, rarely if ever preached a sermon, and only in some instances performed marriages. Any of this could be done by any adult male (once again, over the age of 13; however, many communities enacted rules that only a more mature adult should lead public services, out of respect for the congregation).

The chief duty of the rabbi was to interpret Jewish law for the community as a whole and for individuals who asked him questions, and secondarily to teach Talmud to advanced students or male heads of households. Originally, rabbis were not paid a salary, and there was tremendous opposition by many authorities to the idea of salaried rabbis. By the thirteenth century, however, the custom of paying rabbis was common at least in Castile, and by the following century was spreading to other parts of Spain and finally to other lands, including North Africa.

The legal justification for this change was that rabbis were being paid (as were teachers) as compensation for the loss of their own study time while engaged in community responsibilities. In reality, communities found that it was increasingly difficult to get learned rabbis, and also teachers, unless they paid them a respectable salary. There was sometimes keen competition between cities to hire a particularly important rabbi, whose presence enhanced the status of the community.

Maimonides on Why Rabbis Should Not be Paid

Know that what is said "Do not make the Torah a spade to dig with" means do not consider it a vessel for income, and all who benefit in this world from the honor of Torah cut off their soul from the life of the world to come. [But] people observed this clear language and cast it behind their backs [ignored it] because they do not understand, and so I will explain it. They [the sages] apportioned a claim on individuals and communities, and made the offering of the Torah a law of taxes. They misled people by complete deception concerning this obligation, that they must aid scholars and students and people engaged in the study of Torah, whose Torah is their occupation. All this is an error without foundation in the Torah and without legs to rest upon at all.[9]

Although there were challenges to this opinion, it was not until the end of the fourteenth century that it was finally set aside by Simon b. Tsemah Duran, a rabbi of Majorca who fled the riots of 1391 there and went to North Africa. He wrote several reasons why rabbis should be salaried, concluding:

Everyone whose craft is the "craft of heaven" [religious profession] and his Torah is his trade and all his activity is study, and he has reached the level of teaching and is important in his generation such that he is appointed an official and a judge and teacher and he preaches in public is worthy of receiving a salary and other benefits.[10]

It should be mentioned that there often was more than one rabbi, particularly in larger communities. This was not determined by how many synagogues there were, for quite often there were several even in smaller towns. The rabbi was rarely dependent on any particular synagogue; rather, different groups of Jews in a community might engage their own rabbi, or else there might be more than one *yeshivah* that needed rabbis as their teachers. On matters of law, usually the foremost scholar would be considered the authority, but there were often disputes among local rabbis.

While we have surprisingly little, or almost no, evidence about the ordinary rabbis of communities in other lands, there is considerable information about those in Christian Spain. Some were incompetent and denounced for their lack of learning and in some cases for giving rulings that were clearly contradicted by talmudic law. However, most had at least the fundamental qualifications and performed their duties ably, and some were in fact excellent scholars and even maintained *yeshivot*, although they are not among the famous rabbis.

On a different level were those who achieved a great reputation because of their learning, in every country. In Italy, France, Germany, and England, and in most cases also in Muslim lands these were actual rabbis (Rashi, his sons-in-law and grandson; Meir b. Barukh of Rothenburg and many others; in Spain, Meir Abulafia, Nissim b. Reuben Gerundi, Solomon Ibn

Miniature from Moses Maimonides, Mishne Torah (Jewish religious code drafted in 1180). Southern European, ca. 1351. National & University Library, Jerusalem, Israel. Bridgeman-Giraudon/Art Resource, NY.

Adret, Asher b. Yehiel and his son Judah and others). However, in Spain there were also great scholars who were not actually rabbis (the most important of these was "Nahmanides," Moses b. Nahman; ca. 1194–ca. 1270), but who because of their reputation were recognized as heads of their communities.[11]

The outstanding example of this was Maimonides (Moses b. Maimon); born and educated in Cordoba, he moved eventually to Egypt where he was the recognized head of the community and also a famous physician. Through his great knowledge of Jewish law, and especially his code of law, *Mishneh Torah*, he became the acknowledged authority in nearly every Jewish community in the world.

There was at least one woman rabbi in the Middle Ages, the wife of Joseph b. Yohanan, father of Matityahu, chief rabbi of France in the late fourteenth century. She was a learned scholar whose opinion on a difficult talmudic passage was cited by later authorities.[12]

Other Officials   Other salaried officials were the *hazan*, a term that has continued to the present as cantor, or one who sings certain prayers in the Sabbath and holiday services (in popular understanding, leads the services). However, in the medieval period this was not always the case. In Muslim countries and throughout Spain, the *hazan* usually was a teacher and reader of the Torah in the synagogue and only rarely, or incidentally, a leader of prayer. The talmudic term *shaliah tsibur* (literally, messenger of the congregation) was used for someone appointed, temporarily or on a regular basis, to read the prayers. This may have been the case in some other countries as well, at least in the early medieval period. Only in late medieval sources is there evidence of the *hazan* exclusively being one who sang Sabbath and holiday prayers.

This position was perhaps more important in German and French communities than in Muslim countries or Christian Spain. While there were salaried cantors even in Muslim Spain, there are more references to this as a profession in the northern European sources. There were often controversies about the appointment of a cantor, and in some cases government officials and even a bishop intervened to appoint someone to the position. Rabbis objected to this, and the important communities of Speyer, Worms, and Mainz imposed a ban against anyone who sought such intervention.[13]

The slaughterer (*shokhet*) was a permanent salaried official, knowledgeable in the complex laws concerning the slaughter of meat and fowl. So complicated are these laws that not every community could find, or afford, such an individual and in some cases two or more small communities would share in the services of a slaughterer. Lacking even this, an individual with only basic skills, and even a Gentile, could perform the slaughter as long as a learned Jew who knew the laws supervised. Any questions arising about the fitness (*kashrut*) of slaughtered meat had to be resolved by a scholar.

Teachers were extremely important, as we have seen in Chapter 1, and normally a community was obligated to hire teachers for elementary school children. If the community was too small for this, the responsibility would be shared by the fathers of children old enough to begin their education. The number of teachers hired was determined by the size of the classes, set by rabbinical law (usually a maximum of 25 students per teacher). As with other salaried officials, their contract was for one year and could be renewed for satisfactory performance. Larger communities also had a *yeshivah* that they had to maintain, since there was no tuition charged to students. Charitable donations also helped to support these schools and their rabbis. In fact, we know very little about the system of maintenance of these important institutions.

The scribe (*sofer*) was another important official, at least in larger communities. His duties included the preparation and writing of Torah scrolls in accord with strict laws that governed the form of every letter, and the kind of parchment, ink, and quill used. He therefore had to be learned in these laws, and a man of good character. He also wrote the parchment segments that contained certain biblical passages and were inserted into the *tefilin* (phylacteries), small black leather boxes worn on the forehead and arm by adult males during weekday morning prayer, and also in the *mezuzah*, a small case affixed to the doorpost of every room in houses or public buildings, in accord with the biblical commandment.

The scribe also wrote biblical codices; that is, manuscripts of the Torah or of the entire Bible that were used for private study, and also large manuscripts of prayers for use by wealthy patrons or by synagogues. Some scribes, particularly in Spain, were renowned experts, whose services were sought from many different communities or private individuals. These were often richly illuminated with pictures and designs, by specially trained artists who were also paid for their work.

COMMUNITY INSTITUTIONS AND BUILDINGS

Among the institutions that every Jewish community had to maintain was the *miqveh* (so-called ritual bath), required **Bath-Houses** for women for immersion after the menstrual period and after childbirth, and also customarily used by men for immersion on the eve of Sabbaths and holidays. It was also used for the required immersion of new glass or metal vessels and utensils before they could be used and for some utensils that thus could be made fit for use during Passover.

Some smaller towns did not have a special building for this, and a local river or lake would be used, but the obligation to build a *miqveh* takes precedence over even a synagogue.

A dispute arose in one community in Germany in the fifteenth century between those who wanted to build a new *miqveh* that would be closer to their homes so that women would not be afraid to walk home, especially at night. Others objected, saying that their wives were already too old to need a *miqveh*. The rabbi who was consulted, an important authority, cited the earlier ruling of the renowned Meir b. Barukh of Rothenburg (ca. 1220–1293) that the majority opinion always prevails in any community decision, to which he added that in any case everyone uses the *miqveh* at least on the eve of Rosh ha-Shannah and Yom Kippur, including men, and indeed so prevalent is this custom that some mistakenly believed it was a commandment and recited a blessing for it.[14]

A special supervisor was appointed to oversee the proper maintenance of the water as required by Jewish law. Obviously, one or more women were in charge of the actual supervision of the immersion of women according to their requirements (before marriage, after every menstrual period, and after childbirth). Remains of some medieval ritual bathhouses have been discovered in Spain, France, and Germany.

Public baths were also part of the larger communities. Although bathing was not popular among medieval Christians (even considered dangerous to health), it was necessary for Jews, particularly prior to immersion in the *miqveh* and for men and women prior to Sabbaths and holidays. In Muslim lands, including Spain, public baths were established at government expense, often more than one in a city. This custom spread throughout Spain. However, in most towns and cities there were separate days when Jews were allowed to use the public baths. Very wealthy people, primarily in al-Andalus, had private baths in their homes.

Schools
The second most important physical institution, after the *miqveh*, was the school, which has been discussed in Chapter 1. This also took precedence over a synagogue, when defined as a building whose only purpose was for prayer (called *beit keneset*). However, few smaller communities had such specific buildings; rather, a *beit midrash* (school) served both as a school and a place for services. According to Jewish law, one may pray anywhere, and private houses often served a dual function as a place for prayers. Synagogues as such usually existed only in larger towns (further details on the synagogue will be discussed in Chapter 5). Small communities that could not afford a separate building for a school, or did not have a sufficient population, had classes in the home of the teacher.

Libraries
Some communities, again particularly larger ones, also had libraries for the use of their members. These could either be maintained in the *beit midrash* or, as was frequently the case in Spanish cities, in a special building. In some cities in Spain, one or more librarians were hired by the community. While we know their names and salaries, we know nothing about their actual duties, which certainly included keeping a record of books borrowed.

Courts
The Jewish court (*beit din*) was a more complex institution than others in the community. Established, standing courts of three or more scholars were rare, only in large cities where major rabbis constituted such courts as they were needed. The usual practice, following talmudic law, was to compose a court of three men (not necessarily rabbis) to judge particular cases as they arose.

Nevertheless, in cities in Spain during the Muslim era, and sometimes in Christian cities, there was a professional *dayan*, or judge, who was a salaried official (actual judges of a *beit din* were never salaried, which would violate Jewish law). His function was to supervise any appointed court and ensure that Jewish law was correctly administered, but he did not judge cases. In theory, this should have been the job of the rabbi, and it is not altogether clear why a separate official was needed for this purpose.

The courts did not have a special building but met in the *beit midrash* or perhaps even in private houses.

Cases came before courts, or courts were called into being, for a variety of reasons. Jewish communities in the medieval period, everywhere and not just in Spain, were granted autonomy with regard to their own laws in criminal and civil matters. Nevertheless, and in spite of strict talmudic prohibition, some Jews in Muslim lands and in Christian Spain took their cases to Gentile courts. For the historian, at least, it is a good thing that it was a common practice to go to Gentile courts, since in that way many important records have been preserved. In the aforementioned ruling of Meir of Rothenburg, he also stated that members of the community may compel each other to follow the majority ruling, whether by Jewish law or if necessary by Gentile courts.

In Germany, rabbis ruled that one may choose to go to another city to be judged by the *beit din* there. Some cases arose that involved the local rabbi or else an important man in the community, and there was fear on the part of the litigants that the court could be influenced by this.[15]

Disputes could arise over property, debts, something loaned and either not returned or not properly taken care of, insults, or the adjudication of documents, particularly a *ketuvah* or *get* (see Chapter 3). In relatively simple disputes, in accord with talmudic law each litigant could choose anyone he wanted to act as judge and the two judges would then choose the third. Rarely do we hear of this in practice, however. Usually, all matters were brought before the regular *beit din* of the community, or the nearest town if the litigants were isolated farmers or lived in small villages. More serious cases, such as crimes including murder, were always judged by the *beit din*, and sometimes the opinions of great scholars were sought. Of course, in many instances, such serious crimes in fact came before the secular authorities.

In Spain, where the king was the ultimate arbiter, he often appointed famous scholars to judge particularly important cases. It is important to note that individual rabbis could give legal opinions in response to particular questions but they could not alone render judgment in any case. The individual who consulted a rabbi for an official opinion was obligated to abide by his opinion, and if the rabbi was a renowned scholar, his written opinion would serve as precedent, although not legally binding, for decisions elsewhere. Since Jews, like Christians, had the right of appeal in Spain, they could and often did take their cases finally to the king himself for justice. Amazingly, the kings were required to be informed about Jewish law (some actually were, but most often they relied on Jewish advisers).

Some larger cities, such as Cologne in Germany, had a special building for a community bakery. Many towns had smaller communal bakeries or ovens. There were also community bakeries in some towns in Spain and **Bakeries and Butcher Shops** elsewhere. It was also necessary to have a bakery, or at the minimum special ovens, for the baking of *matzot* (unleavened bread) for Passover.

Stores, or sometimes merely tables in an open market, sold meat and fowl to Jewish customers, and in spite of the frequent suspicion that attached to the custom, that part of the carcass that cannot be consumed according to Jewish law (the hindquarters) was sold to Christians.

Some communities also had special kitchens for roasting **Communal** of large carcasses and preparation of meals for festive occa- **Kitchens** sions, such as weddings or holidays. In Germany, especially, such kitchens were also used for making large quantities of soup. The large cauldrons for these purposes were also used for boiling water for the purification of all metal utensils and vessels that were to be used during Passover. It has been conjectured that a manuscript illumination from Spain (ca. 1330) depicts a communal kitchen and dining hall with 11 men and women (but no children) seated at the Passover meal, quite reminiscent of Christian portrayals of the Last Supper. However, it is not impossible that this is meant rather to illustrate a private home with an extended family or invited guests. No written sources confirm such a custom of a communal Passover meal.

Many German communities, large and small, had a dance **Dance Halls** hall, which was also used for weddings or other communal celebrations. The aforementioned ruling of Judah Mintz (fifteenth century), citing Meir of Rothenburg, mentions also wedding halls as one of the buildings that a community may decide to purchase, build, or alter, and members of the community must follow the majority decision on this. There is no record of such halls in Spain or other countries. Nevertheless, extremely large weddings, with guests coming from all over Spain, as we find in the sources, must have required some kind of public facility for the celebrations.

The needs of travelers had to be met. In many European **Hospices** communities, this was one of the duties of the *shamash* of **and Inns** the synagogue, who discovered if there were any visitors or strangers and would then see that they were lodged and fed with local families. However, the Christian hospice, providing both rudimentary health care for the ill and very primitive lodging for travelers, was imitated by a number of Jewish communities. The hospice may itself have been influenced by the far more elaborate system of inns maintained at government expense throughout the Muslim world. Such community inns existed also in many Jewish communities both in Muslim and Christian Spain. While these also were somewhat spartan, at least they provided food. Most of them charged money, however, both for lodging and food, in accord with the ability of the guest to pay.

Actual hospitals, as opposed to the hospices previously **Hospitals** mentioned in other countries, existed in Jewish communities only in Spain and some Muslim countries, Egypt and Syria, for instance. This was primarily because only these countries had trained and qualified physicians and surgeons (see the following chapter). Even in these countries, not every community had a hospital, of course, but the larger cities did. While we have some information about these, unfortunately there is lacking the complete detail we would like. It is certain that quality care was provided and that operations, even of the most serious kind (eye and brain surgery, for example), were performed.

Maimonides, a physician renowned not only among Jews but Muslims as well, may or may not have performed operations, but it is certain that his son Abraham was a highly skilled surgeon and famous Muslim doctors came from far lands to observe his surgical skill.

Cemeteries, of course, were necessary for the burial of the dead according to Jewish law. Of necessity, these were usu- **Cemeteries** ally outside the town or city, often at some distance; although in some towns they were close to the Jewish quarter. Several medieval Jewish cemeteries have survived, in whole or in part, and the tombstone inscriptions have provided valuable historical information.

The obligation of every individual Jew to assist someone in need is not charity but precisely an obligation, the fulfill- **Charitable** ment of a biblical commandment to "pursue justice" (*tsedeq*), **Institutions** from which the word *tsedaqah* comes, but it is not charity, as usually translated. Rather, the concept is that when something is not right, or out of order, it must be set right. One who does this, for instance feeding someone in need of food, is not doing some special kind act or good deed, but rather fulfilling a commandment. With respect to the Jewish community, however, it is proper to speak of charitable institutions, which were established and maintained at community expense (taxes and contributions) to provide for special circumstances beyond the ability of any one person to satisfy.

Examples would be the needs of widows and orphans. While nothing prevented a widow from working, or remarrying, in reality her time was devoted to the raising of her children and she usually was unable to work. Marriage also did not come easily, since as we have seen most marriages took place at an early age. The community had to provide for the financial needs of widows. True orphans, who had lost both parents, were perhaps a rarity, but there certainly were such cases. If there was not immediate family to take them in, communities (at least the larger ones) had special homes for orphans, where they lived and were educated. Orphan girls also had to have the expense of their wedding, however minimal, provided.

Ransom of captives was a particularly important obligation. Frequently Jewish travelers, especially at sea, were captured by Christians or Muslims and held for ransom (the alternative being slavery or death). There are many records of the raising of funds for such purposes, again particularly in Spain where famous scholars involved themselves in such activity.

However, human nature being what it is, we find that some things that are specifically individual obligations according to Jewish law, such as visiting the sick and care of the poor, were often transferred to the community council. Regulations were drawn up and provisions made for a fund for caring for the poor, widows, and orphans, and a committee for visiting the ill. In Spain, there were special "brotherhoods" or guilds, voluntary organizations for these and other matters, such as burial societies, educational guilds to maintain the schools, and to provide for the weddings of orphans or the poor. In some communities, money from the communal treasury was given to these charitable organizations for their expenses, while in others the brotherhoods themselves took on these expenses.

Paying for It All   As we see, a considerable amount of money was needed to maintain all these institutions and to pay the salaries of community officials. There were two sources of funding for this, taxation and donation. It is not at all clear, according to talmudic law, that the councils had the right to impose taxes (a legal loophole was found in the concept of *hefqer beit din hefqer*, in which a court could declare certain property "abandoned" and designate its use). Nevertheless, such taxes were imposed in nearly every Jewish community. Usually, these were property taxes but sometimes also head taxes, or assessments on all adult males.

Other taxes, particularly in Spain, included the sale of meat or wine and often other commercial activity. All these were in addition, of course, to the taxes imposed by the king and local governing officials. Charitable institutions and property, including private property whose income was donated for charitable institutions, were exempted by the kings of Spain from taxes.

Donations came from private persons, some wealthy and others not. A sense of personal obligation for such donations was part of Jewish life, and children were educated in this also. Several cases of the donation of property, houses, or fields, are also found. It was also customary to include in wills a bequest of money or property and sometimes both for charitable purposes or for use of the synagogue or school. Some Jews in Spain also made such bequests to the Christian community, with a stipulation that it be administered by the priest or bishop. It is possible that some Jews in other Christian lands did this as well, although records of this seem not to exist (again, the documentation is much richer for medieval Spain than for any other country).

COMMUNITIES AND PROBLEMS

In spite of the theoretical statements with which we began this chapter, belonging to the community could sometimes bring with it problems. Examples of this include conflicts of customs and observances. Many communities developed their own customs over a period of time with respect to such things as holidays, marriage practices, and even prayers. Difficulties could arise if someone moved to another community that had different customs. The most serious example of this concerned a group of Jews from Catalonia who moved to Provence and there continued to observe customs that were completely opposed to those of their new community. However, also in Muslim Egypt and North Africa there were problems that resulted from immigration from "Babylon" (Iraq) or Jerusalem.

Another problem, again better documented in Spain than elsewhere, concerned taxation, whether local community taxes or taxes imposed by the government. Some individuals, in order to avoid these taxes, claimed another home elsewhere where the payments were less. Others moved outside the town or city, much as in modern life people flee to the suburbs or smaller communities to avoid high taxes in the city.

On the whole, however, membership in a particular community was valued. In European lands, it provided a sense of security and protection, and everywhere there was usually a strong sense of identity and group cohesiveness.

NOTES

1. For the background to these concepts and some implications for modern Jewish life, see Norman Roth, "*Am Yisrael*: Jews or Judaism?" *Judaism* 37 (1988): 199–209.

2. Some important discussions of this are G. Ladner, "The Concepts of Ecclesia and Christianitas," *Sacerdozio e regno da Gregorio VII a Bonifacio VIII* (Rome, 1954; Miscellanea historiae pontificae 18), 49–77, and E. Lewis, "Organic Tendencies in Medieval Political Thought," *American Political Science Review* 32 (1938): 849–76. This relates closely to the old argument about the alleged "corporate personality" of the biblical Israelites. Of course, Christian unity was never more than theoretical, and the concept was utilized in large measure as propaganda to distinguish the "true faith" from its enemies, Islam and, although less a real threat, the Jews.

3. This is not theoretical but a reality. An interesting example of this was the embassies sent by Otto I of Germany in 953 to the caliph of Cordoba, which included Jews who were able to converse with Hasdai Ibn Shaprut, the Jewish minister of the Muslim ruler; see Roth, *Jews, Visigoths & Muslims in Medieval Spain: Cooperation & Conflict* (Leiden, 1994), 82–83. There are, of course, numerous examples of medieval Jews who spoke Hebrew when traveling to other lands.

4. See briefly for details the article "Expulsion from Other Lands" in Roth, ed., *Medieval Jewish Civilization: An Encyclopedia* (New York, 2003).

5. See Roth, *Conversos, Inquisition and the Expulsion of the Jews from Spain* (Madison, Wisc., 1995; revised paper ed., 2002), particularly chapter 2.

6. See the important discussion in Gaines Post, *Studies in Medieval Legal Thought* (Princeton, N.J., 1964), Chapter 10 (which, however, focuses entirely on royal power and legal theorists), and the interesting article of Guido Kisch, "Nationalism and Race in Mediaeval Law," *Seminar* (Catholic University School

of Canon Law) 1 (1943): 48–73. See also Pearl Kibre, *The Nations in Medieval Universities* (Cambridge, Mass., 1948). From a Jewish perspective, see Salo W. Baron, *Social and Religious History of the Jews* (Philadelphia, New York, 1952–1983), 11: 193–201. There is a definite need for a thorough study of this neglected subject.

7. Baron, *Social and Religious History*, 60.

8. For details on the medieval rabbinate, see the article "Rabbis" in Roth, *Medieval Jewish Civilization* and the bibliography there.

9. Commentary on *Avot* 4. 6, in Moses b. Maimon, *Mishnah im peirush ... Neziqin* (Jerusalem, 1963), 288–90, Hebrew text translated according to the Arabic by Joseph Kafi. I have made my own translation from the Arabic text.

10. Simon b. Semah Duran, *Sefer ha-tashbetz* (Lemberg, 1891; photo reprint Tel Aviv, s.a.), Part 1, nos.142–48.

11. See details on the careers of the rabbis named here, also on Maimonides and Nahmanides, in Roth, *Medieval Jewish Civilization*. There are articles on each of the rabbis, and see also the index there for others.

12. Duran, *Sefer-ha-tashbetz*, part 3, No. 78.

13. See Joseph Shatzmiller, "An Aspect of Social Life of Provençal Jews," *AJS* (Association for Jewish Studies) *Review* 2 (1977): 231. This has nothing to do with Provence, but it was discussed in relation to the objection in Manosque, in Provence, to a boy leading the prayers; see also 235–36, on community agreement on appointing cantors.

14. Judah Minz (ca. 1408–1508), *He la-khem zera le-tsedakah* (*She'elot u-teshuvot*) (Fürth, 1766), No. 7.

15. Samson bar Tsadoq, *Sefer tashbats* (Warsaw, 1875), No. 512; the author was a student of the renowned Meir b. Barukh of Rothenburg (thirteenth century) and an important rabbi in his own right.

RECOMMENDED READING

Baron, Salo W. *A Social and Religious History of the Jews*. New York, Philadelphia, 1971, vol. 5, ch. 23.

Cohen, Mark R. *Jewish Self-Government in Medieval Egypt: The Origins of the Office of Head of the Jews, ca. 1065–1126*. Princeton, N.J. 1980.

Goitein, S. D. *A Mediterranean Society: The Jewish Communities of the Arab World as Portrayed in the Documents of the Cairo Geniza*. Berkeley, Calif., Los Angeles, London, 1967–1993), vol. 2.

5

SYNAGOGUES, CUSTOMS, AND OBSERVANCES

While, as noted, the synagogue was certainly not the center of Jewish life in the Middle Ages (or, indeed, any period until perhaps in contemporary America), it was an important institution. The exact origin of the synagogue is still a matter of debate, but undoubtedly it began in the First (Babylonian) Exile as compensation for the loss of the Temple in Jerusalem. Certainly there were synagogues both in the Land of Israel and in the Diaspora during the period of the Second Temple.

According to Jewish law, a true synagogue, *beit ha-keneset* (house of the congregation) or *beit ha-tefilah* (house of prayer, used rarely), is to be used only for the purpose of prayer. It may be a special building or even a private house, but in either case a particular sanctity attaches to it and it may not then be used for any other purpose. Obviously, few communities, particularly small ones, could afford the luxury of such a building, and indeed it is far down on the list of required buildings that a community must have (both schools and a *miqveh*, or ritual bath for immersion by women, are ahead of synagogues).

Far more common was the *beit ha-midrash* (house of study), used primarily as the name indicates for the study of Talmud and in which services were also held. Since the sanctity of such a building is less than that of a true synagogue, one may also eat or sleep there, and public meetings were also held there. None of this is allowed in a synagogue; it should be noted that even today, buildings that are called synagogues are usually not technically such, since all these activities take place (sleeping if only during sermons, perhaps). Also in the medieval period, the term

מעל **הבית** נבע בתוכו שאומרים **היהודה**

Sister Haggadah (fourteenth century Spain). Interior of a synagogue. The reader, with a white shawl covering his head, stands at the elevated reading platform and is reading from a scroll of the Prophets. The members of the congregation include men, women, and children. The stone ark houses the scrolls of the Torah. Copyright held by The British Library.

beit ha-keneset was loosely used to refer, in fact, to what was technically a *beit ha-midrash* (that term came to apply more specifically to a *yeshivah*). Vernacular terms used for the synagogue, by Christians as well as Jews, include *scola, schule* (German), *sinoga* (Spanish) and the less common *synagoga*. In Arabic, *kanisiya* or sometimes *bi'a* were used. It should be noted that the Latin term *scola* and German *schule* both reflect the primary function of a house of study.

In practice in medieval countries, whether Muslim or Christian, almost every community had at least one synagogue and usually more, depending on the size of the community. Sometimes, particularly in the later medieval period, people moving from one community or country to another would take their local customs with them and create their own synagogue, usually named after the community from which they came. This, too, continued to the modern period. In major American cities until recently it was common to find synagogues named after a particular city or town in eastern or central Europe. Most such synagogues have now disappeared or merged into larger congregations.

Particularly in Provence and parts of Italy, it was common to find different synagogues for Ashkenazim and Sefardim, for immigrants from these countries and with differing customs.

Another factor that led to the synagogue being a *beit ha-midrash* rather than a *beit ha-keneset* was the talmudic requirement that a synagogue as such be the highest building in the community. In some Jewish communities in the early medieval period, indeed, this was the case, but objections by Christian authorities, including popes, resulted in decrees prohibiting synagogues from being as high as (much less higher than) the church. The largest and most elaborate medieval synagogues are of course not to be compared in size or luxury with the local cathedral.

The synagogue (including the *beit ha-midrash*, which as mentioned was the most common type) had as its main features an ark for the keeping of Torah scrolls and scrolls of books of the prophets read in services. In Europe and also Christian Spain, these were elaborate decorated wooden or even stone or brick built-in structures, usually with embroidered or gilded curtains covering them. In Muslim countries, and parts also of Christian Spain, scrolls were kept in decorated cases, often gilded or made of silver, rather than in an ark; however, in some synagogues in Muslim communities (for example, Fez and parts of Egypt), the cases were also kept in arks with carved wooden doors. These cases were placed in a standing position on the reading desk and the scrolls thus read still inside the case, unlike the practice in European synagogues where the scrolls were placed flat on the reading desk and unrolled as read. The Torah scrolls were usually tied with a cloth band, also often decorated. In Ashkenazic communities, particularly, it became a custom for mothers of newborn infants to donate the swaddling clothes of the baby to be made into such bands for the scrolls.

Further decoration for the Torah scrolls included metal (silver, gold, or brass) ornaments placed on top of the wooden rollers that held the scroll. These were richly decorated and sometimes with small bells attached to them. Instead of these, some scrolls were topped with a large metal crown, also elaborately decorated. The breastplate, hung by a chain over the mantle covering the scroll, and the silver or ivory pointers for use in reading from the scroll, both of which are standard in modern synagogues, seem to have been used rarely if at all in the medieval period.

A perpetual light, in the form of a hanging lamp, was kept burning in front of the ark in those synagogues that had one, or else suspended near the lectern, in memory of the eternal flame kept burning in the

Temple. Some German synagogues had lights, or candles, on a stand made of wood or stone, perhaps marble, in front of the ark. Larger synagogues in Europe, but few in Spain, also had large candelabra on either side of the ark, again as a symbol of the *menorah* (candelabrum) in the Temple. The same symbol often decorated the curtain covering the ark; other decorations included the tablets of the commandments, a lion rampant, or special religious objects used for particular holidays (the *lulav*, palm branch, and *etrog*, citron, for Sukkot, and/or the *shofar* or ram's horn for Rosh ha-Shannah and Yom Kippur. Representations of human figures, quite common in manuscript illuminations, were not to be found in the synagogue, but animals and geometric or floral designs were common. Nevertheless, some rabbis objected strenuously to such decorations, just as in Spain there were rabbis who objected to certain Muslim designs on prayer rugs that then were hung as curtains for the ark.

The other main features of the synagogue were the large reading desk on which the scrolls were read at Sabbath and holiday services, and a lectern from which prayers were led and sermons sometimes preached, especially in Muslim countries, often on every Sabbath, just as Muslim preachers gave sermons in the mosque on Fridays, although in Spain and Europe generally, sermons were rare other than special Sabbaths. In Muslim and Spanish synagogues, in imitation of the mosque, such lecterns were elevated and covered with a small roof, and the leader of prayers or the preacher would ascend by a tall row of steps to a height well above the congregation. Another difference was that the reading desk, or *bimah*, remained always in the center of the synagogue in Muslim and Spanish communities, whereas eventually in many European congregations it was moved closer to the ark. In some Spanish synagogues, the *bimah*, called the *almemor* in imitation of the Arabic term, was the elevated lectern mentioned above. This, again, was copied from the Muslim mosques, whereas in European synagogues there were strong influences from Gothic church architecture and design of furnishings.

Seating, if any, also varied from place to place. In synagogues that had benches or, in rare cases, individual seats, these positions were highly prized and paid for and often inherited from one generation to another. Many disputes are recorded over the ownership of such places and the proper place of honor that an individual felt he deserved. Some Italian synagogues of the fifteenth century and perhaps earlier had not only seats but large carved wooden desks for use of the worshipers. In some Spanish synagogues, on the other hand, there were no seats at all, perhaps to avoid the constant disputes that arose over rights of ownership or of place of honor.

In European synagogues, women had their own gallery, either elevated above the main hall or in a separate annex, known as the women's synagogue. Only in a few Spanish synagogues, such as the famous Toledo synagogue, formerly the church of El Transito and now the national Jewish museum, were there such separate galleries (that synagogue dates from the fourteenth century). As in Muslim congregations, women in Spanish synagogues usually sat, or stood, together with the men with no separation of any kind.

The rabbi, not being the ceremonial leader of services or "Jewish clergyman" of modern times, rarely if ever had any special seat. For one thing, there were often several rabbis who attended a particular synagogue, and the official rabbi of the community, if there was one, was not necessarily given any greater honor than other local rabbis. Some rabbis in northern Europe did not regularly attend synagogue services at all, but rather prayed privately at home, or if they were teachers, held services in their homes for their students. In some European synagogues, however, the custom already was developing of providing a seat of honor for the main rabbi, as well as for official community leaders.

Lighting was provided by windows (as previously mentioned, at least one German synagogue had glass windows) and by hanging oil lamps, or chandeliers with candles in some European synagogues. Synagogues in Muslim lands, and in southern Spain, had open windows, sometimes covered with lattices. It was considered a great honor to provide lights for the synagogue, and oil for them, with individuals competing for the privilege. Bequests were often made for ongoing donations of oil for lamps in the synagogue or *yeshivah*. In synagogues in Spain and Muslim countries, oil lamps were often made of glass, which was quite expensive and considered at least as prestigious as gilded or silver lamps (the same was true for decanters that held wine for Sabbath or holiday meals in private homes).

In Europe, including Italy, synagogues were frequently dark and gloomy, nevertheless, and often were designed in such a way as to conceal their nature from what could be a hostile Gentile mob. Those in Muslim countries and throughout Spain, where there was far less danger of such things, were often more elaborately designed buildings with considerable light entering through many windows (where possible, 12 windows in memory of the 12 tribes). They usually had typical Muslim-style pillars and arches running the length of the synagogue. Walls, often of marble, were carved with simple or more complex decorations, often including verses from the Bible in Hebrew and inscriptions of the names of donors, and so on, in Arabic carved into the walls. Coats of arms of the kingdoms were not uncommon in synagogues in Christian Spain.

Synagogue buildings themselves were sometimes donated, or paid for by wealthy individual benefactors. This was the case, for example, with the famous synagogue of Toledo and some others in Spain. Others were associated with legend, claiming that they were the sites of famous rabbis or even biblical figures such as Moses. In Egypt one such synagogue was said to have been built on the site where Moses planted a tree.

In Aleppo (Syria) was a synagogue said to have been built by Ezra, as was another on Mt. Ararat, the alleged site of Noah's ark. In later North Africa, particularly Morocco, several synagogues were associated with famous rabbis or mystics who came to be venerated exactly like Muslim saints, and indeed Muslims also venerated these synagogues.[1]

FAMOUS MEDIEVAL SYNAGOGUES

Aside from these legendary synagogues, there were several synagogues in the medieval period that were particularly famous. The synagogue of the Exilarch (*rosh galut*), or official head of the Jewish community in Babylon and theoretically the whole Diaspora, in Baghdad, was described by the renowned traveler Benjamin of Tudela in the twelfth century as being adorned with colored marble pillars and gold and silver, with gold inscriptions of Psalm verses. The small Rabbanite (traditional) Jewish community of Jerusalem, as opposed to the larger Qaraite (heretical sect) community, had a synagogue but it was not of particular importance. However, the fanatical Muslims who had continued the Byzantine prohibition on the building of new synagogues nevertheless permitted a small synagogue at the Cave of the Machpelah in Hebron, which was the alleged burial site of the patriarchs and matriarchs. Shortly after, another was built there. These synagogues had great symbolic value, although few Jewish travelers actually went there. When the Crusaders took control of the Holy Land, they banned Jews from using the synagogues.

That the so-called Ramban synagogue in Jerusalem, built by Nahmanides (*Ramban* refers to Rabbi Moses b. Nahman, although in fact he was never a rabbi) in 1267 is also a legend. There was, in fact, a synagogue there, as reported by another famous traveler in the fifteenth century, but he does not mention any association of it with Nahmanides. The synagogue was destroyed by the Jordanians in 1948 and today is represented by a commemorative arch (and the perpetuation of the legend of its founder).[2] There is also extant in Fez (Morocco) a synagogue alleged to have been that used by Maimonides when he and his family lived there.

In Fustat, the suburb of Cairo where Jews were permitted to live, was the famous synagogue of the Palestinians, that is, built by immigrant Jews from the Land of Israel. It was destroyed by the half-mad and fanatical ruler al-Hakim in 1012, when he ordered the destruction of all churches and synagogues, but was rebuilt in 1025. This is the synagogue that housed the famous Cairo Genizah.

In spite of the importance of the French Jewish communities, no famous medieval synagogues are known. This is not the case with Germany, however. The chief synagogues were those of the three most important communities, Speyer, Worms, and Mainz. These served as refuge during the attacks of crusading mobs in 1096, although in fact the Speyer synagogue was burned then and again in 1195.

Interior of the Altneuschul synagogue in Prague, Europe's oldest synagogue. Gothic, thirteenth century. Altneuschul Synagogue, Prague, Czech Republic. Erich Lessing/Art Resource, NY.

The most famous of all European synagogues (aside from the Altneuschule in Prague, only part of which was medieval and all of which was destroyed by fire and later rebuilt) was that of Worms. Again, the fame of this synagogue rests on legend, since it came to be known as Rashi's synagogue, and an annex known as Rashi's chapel may indeed date to the original synagogue of the eleventh century. However, that famous biblical and talmudic commentator is not known to have ever been in Worms. The synagogue, with its remarkable architectural details (much of the interior dates from later centuries), was destroyed by the Nazis but has been reconstructed on the basis of excellent photographic records.

None of the synagogues of the numerous Jewish communities in Muslim Spain has survived, nor do we even have manuscript illustrations to provide details. From Christian Spain, however, a few synagogues have survived, in whole or in part. The most famous of these are the aforementioned so-called El Transito synagogue of Toledo and the Santa Maria la Blanca synagogue of Toledo, and also the smaller synagogue of Cordoba. The second Toledo synagogue, which fortunately has not seen the heavy restoration carried out on the El Transito, is the earlier of the two and in many ways the more beautiful. From it, indeed, may be gained some idea of what synagogues in Muslim times may have looked like. It is open and airy, with two rows of graceful arched columns and with a minimum of decoration, which is very tasteful.

The other synagogue, now a museum, is a far more imposing structure of two stories, built probably in 1357 under the patronage of Samuel ha-Levy, the famous treasurer of Pedro I, whose own impressive house is nearby. The much smaller synagogue in Cordoba of course is not from the time of Maimonides, although it is near the alleged site of his family home, but from a later period. Its decorations are reminiscent of the El Transito, but of a more simple kind.[3]

The only other synagogue completely extant, although remodeled as a church, is in Segovia. It was made into a church in the early fifteenth century when the entire Jewish community converted. At the present, access to the building is restricted. There are remnants or ruins of other Spanish synagogues, some of which are quite small, while others, such as the main synagogue of Barcelona (of which one wall survives), must have been imposing structures. Some few remains of synagogues, or what may have been synagogues, survive in England, France, Germany, Austria, and Hungary, as well as the famous synagogue on the island of Djerba, off the coast of Tunisia.

BLESSINGS AND PRAYERS

Strictly speaking, a Jew is not required to pray in a synagogue, and indeed there are conditions under which according to talmudic law one is not *permitted* to pray in a synagogue; for example, workers who are hired by the hour may not interrupt their work but should say their prayers even in the top of a tree if that is their job. Travelers at sea, of course, could not recite prayers in a synagogue, and in the memorable words of Maimonides they should simply direct their hearts to their father in heaven and pray.

However, when possible prayers are supposed to be said, if not necessarily in a synagogue, at least with a quorum (*minyan*) of ten adult males (over the age of 13). So important was this obligation considered that many communities made regulations enforcing attendance at a synagogue. Nevertheless, as noted, even some rabbis neglected this duty and preferred to pray at home.

The obligation of prayer, loosely defined, includes several things. First and foremost is the obligation to recite the so-called creed, *Shema Yisrael*

("Hear O Israel," consisting of the recitation of Deuteronomy 6.4–9, 11.13–21, and Numbers 15.37–41). This must be recited twice a day, in the first third of the morning and at night, accompanied by certain blessings and verses before and after the recitation. Since it is one of the obligations dependent on a particular time of the day, women are exempt (although many still did, and do, recite it). In practice, it is often recited at home and then again in the synagogue with the entire congregation. The Sefardic practice is to recite it in unison, aloud, whereas the Ashkenazic practice is to recite it silently. The first passage (Deuteronomy 6.4–9) is also recited at night in bed before going to sleep. While prayers may in accordance with rabbinical law be recited in any language (and in fact there are opinions that they should be recited in a language that is understood rather than in Hebrew–and Aramaic–if that is not understood), the *Shema* should only be recited in Hebrew. The distinction is that the recital of prayers is a rabbinical commandment (authorities disputed whether there is a general biblical commandment to pray), whereas the recital of the *Shema* is a biblical commandment.

The rabbis in the talmudic era instituted certain blessings that must be recited every morning, and others for particular functions or events that occur (the latter includes such things as seeing lightning or a rainbow, as well as seeing a king, or a famous scholar–whether Jewish or Gentile). The goal is for the pious person to recite a minimum of 100 such blessings during the day. Every drink taken, every fruit or vegetable eaten separately from a meal, requires its own blessing. German rabbis instituted their own forms of blessings for certain things, some of which are quite charming, such as this upon seeing trees beginning to bud in the Spring: "Blessed are You, Lord, king of the universe, who has not diminished in his world anything, and created in it pleasant creations to be enjoyed."[4]

In early modern European communities, and perhaps also in the medieval period, one of the ways in which a father might test the knowledge of a young prospective bridegroom would be to place a bowl of different kinds of fruit before him to see which he selected first, since certain fruits are metaphorically compared to the Jewish people (such as the pomegranate, the Jew being said to be full of good deeds as the pomegranate is full of seeds). There continues to be great debate about certain fruits and vegetables, whether they fall technically into the category of a fruit (which should grow from a tree) or vegetable (which grows on or as a plant).

Although the debate as to whether there is a biblical obligation to pray at all continued, the talmudic authorities in the Land of Israel established eighteen (later another was added) benedictions that must be recited three times a day. This recitation is known as the *amidah*, or standing, because it is recited while standing out of respect to God. Collectively, they are also referred to as the silent devotion since they are to be said silently. It was further established that there should be three periods of prayer each day, commemorating the order of Temple sacrifices: *shaharit* (morning), *minhah* (afternoon) and *ma'ariv* (evening). Sabbath and holiday services include also an additional (*musaf*) recitation, in commemoration of that additional service in the Temple.

Thus, services are held in the synagogue, or, alternatively, in a gathering of ten or more males in a private house or, of course, in a *yeshivah*, three times a day. In order not to impose an undue hardship on workers, the afternoon service usually was immediately before the evening service, which may begin with sunset; although the evening recital of the *Shema* must await the appearance of the evening stars.

The recitation of the morning prayers, only, requires the wearing of the *tefilin* (phylacteries) and the *talit* (so-called prayer shawl); the latter has varying customs, with some reserving it only for married males while in other communities every adult male wears it. The *talit* only is worn also for Sabbath and holiday morning services, and for the entire day on Yom Kippur. The *tefilin* are considered a "sign" according to the Torah, and since the Sabbath and holidays are also a "sign," or remembrance of God's mercies, only the one sign is sufficient . Although women are exempt from wearing the *tefilin*, again because it is a commandment dependent on a specific time, some women in the medieval period in fact did put on *tefilin*. The "small *talit*," a four-cornered garment worn either under or over the clothing so that the required fringes may be attached to it and worn all day, was sometimes also worn by pious women in Germany. We do not hear of this custom in Spain.

While adult males, and often minor boys as well, usually attended all of these services during the week, women rarely did (nor were they obligated to do so). Women, however, accustomed themselves at least to hear the reading of the Torah on the Sabbath and holidays, and they also took their minor daughters with them to get them used to attendance at the synagogue. Young boys, although also encouraged to go with their fathers to the synagogue, often were noisy and disturbed their fathers at prayers. Adolescent males, in spite of being considered adults in Jewish law, often left during the reading of the Torah and congregated outside in the street (a problem not unknown in modern times as well).

As previously mentioned, even when traveling one was required to recite these prayers, alone if a Jewish community could not be found.

SABBATH AND HOLIDAY SERVICES

The day begins, in accordance with biblical understanding, with the evening before, so that the Sabbath begins on Friday at sunset, and also every holiday.

Prayers may be led by any adult male, which again means of the age of 13 or over. In practice, many rabbis decided that it was not respectful of the congregation to have someone so young conducting services and ruled that at least the appearance of a beard is required, and preference should be given to older men and scholars. The office of a cantor was virtually unknown in the early periods. The *hazan* mentioned in various sources was more typically a teacher and reader of the Torah in the synagogue, although already in the Muslim period in Spain there are indications that some included the leading of prayers as part of their duties. This became more common with the passing of time. The problem was that, of course, there were no printed books and individual manuscript (that is, codex, bound pages) copies of prayers were expensive.

Furthermore, in communities where there was no legal enclosure to permit carrying, it was forbidden to carry such books to the synagogue on the Sabbath. Thus, there was a need for a knowledgeable preceptor of prayers who either knew the prayers by heart or in any case had his own prayer book that was kept in the synagogue. Those who could not recite the "silent devotion" by heart could fulfill their obligation by listening carefully to its repetition aloud by the *hazan*. Unfortunately, and for reasons that are not clear, many a *hazan*, at least in medieval Spain, was not of the best character. They were often implicated in sexual and other scandals and were generally the subject of ridicule in Hebrew *belles lettres*.

Sabbath and holiday and fast day morning services included also the reading from the Torah. In addition, portions of the weekly reading were also part of the weekday morning service on Monday and Thursday, and also at the afternoon service of Sabbaths and fast days. This required at least one properly prepared and written Torah scroll, but in the event (frequent enough) that an improperly written word or even a letter were found, another scroll should be available from which to continue.

Many problems arose about this, and also the interesting question of what to do in the communities, apparently many, where there was no Torah scroll, whether it was permissible to read from a manuscript codex.[5] Individuals were honored by being called to the reading of the Torah. Originally, they would actually read a portion of the Torah, but as knowledge of the proper reading of the unpointed text of the scroll declined it became customary merely to recite a blessing and the *hazan* or other official reader would actually read the portion. Following the complete reading, another scroll of the prophets was brought out and the weekly portion of one of the prophets was read.

Sabbath morning services are considerably longer than weekday ones, with numerous additional prayers and recitation of verses of poetry and the complete reading of the weekly Torah portion and a selection from the prophets. Already in the period of the *geonim* there was a custom to come early to the synagogue and recite the entire book of Psalms before the actual service began. That custom continues to be observed, although rarely, by some Sefardic Jews (at one time, and perhaps still, in the main Yemenite synagogue in Jerusalem this was observed, with the worshipers seated on cushions on the floor). In the early medieval period both in the Land of Israel and more particularly in "Babylon" (part of the

Persian Empire, later Iraq), religious poems were composed and many of these came to be recited as part of the Sabbath and holiday services. This aroused great debate and considerable opposition by many notable authorities, not only because these were seen as an interruption in some of the prayers, but because the poor grammar and obscure vocabulary made many of them virtually incomprehensible. On the other hand, some famous poems of this kind (*piyutim*) composed by poets in medieval Spain, and a few in other countries, after the rules of grammar had been established became and remain a part of the services.

HOLIDAYS AND SERVICES

Jewish holidays are divided into two categories: biblical and rabbinical. The biblical holidays, those commanded in the Torah, are Passover, Sukkot, Shavu'ot (commemorating the receiving of the Torah), *Rosh ha-Shannah* ("Beginning of the year") and *Yom Kippur* ("Day of atonement"). Modern custom, particularly among non-Orthodox Jews, is to refer to the latter two as the "High Holy Days," but in fact they are not more holy, or significant, than the Sabbath. Rosh ha-Shannah, besides commemorating the beginning of the Jewish year, is a day for introspection and reflection on improving one's life, whereas Yom Kippur is a day of fasting and atonement, but in fact it is called in rabbinical literature the Sabbath of Sabbaths, precisely to avoid the idea that it is somehow a more important holiday.

In all communities, in Muslim countries as well as Christian Europe, it was the custom to wear special clothing used only for these holidays, and particularly for Yom Kippur when a special white robe was worn by the men (in some medieval communities this, or a similar, robe was worn by the head of the household at the Passover *seder* table). Later, it became the custom in Ashkenazic communities for men to be buried in this garment. In some medieval German communities, however, the garment for Yom Kippur was far from the simple cloth robe of later times but was rather an elaborate and costly garment. As a result, some congregations banned the use of such robes so as not to shame poorer people who could not afford them.

Elaborate holiday food was prepared for the eve and the midday meals of Rosh ha-Shannah and for the eve of Yom Kippur (from sundown until the following night was a day of complete fasting).

Certain symbolic foods, such as some fruits, were eaten as a commemoration for the beginning of the new year. Originally, and again today, in the Land of Israel Rosh ha-Shannah was celebrated only for one day. Due to the uncertainties of the calendar and determining the exact day for holidays, this and all other biblical holidays were celebrated in the Diaspora on two consecutive days. The exception is Yom Kippur, which being a fast was considered potentially dangerous to observe on two days.

Unlike the custom in nearly all other cultures, the Jewish New Year is not a time of riotous celebration as it is in many cultural traditions, but rather a time of soul-searching and reflection on one's deeds during the past year. The ten intermediate days between Rosh ha-Shannah and Yom Kippur are known as "Days of awe," or the ten days of repentance, during which special prayers are recited and attention given to repentance. One must also seek the forgiveness of others who may have been offended or hurt by one's actions; only after this may God's forgiveness be expected.

The services for these two holidays, particularly those of Yom Kippur, which last until nightfall, are much longer than others. Numerous additional prayers and liturgical poems are included in the service, again with significant differences between the Ashkenazic and the Sefardic rites. These elaborate rituals were written in a special prayer book, called *mahzor*, for each of the holidays (there were also such special books for the other biblical holidays). Since the content was so completely different from Sabbath prayers, it became almost essential for at least the head of the household to have a personal copy of the *mahzor*. These could be either simple written codices or elaborate books prepared by a professional scribe and, if the owner could afford it, richly illuminated with illustrations and colored lettering. Unlike the Sabbath, carrying is permitted on holidays, and thus even on Rosh ha-Shannah such books could be carried to the synagogue, even in communities where there was no legal enclosure, which allowed carrying on the Sabbath. However, Yom Kippur is observed as the Sabbath of Sabbaths, and thus carrying would not be permitted without such a fictitious enclosure.

Perhaps a word of explanation is in order. The enclosure (*eruv*) requires some recognizable boundary, often a wire or rope, which delimits a particular area, or the entire Jewish community (in Spain, often the entire city), as a "private" domain in opposition to the "public" domain. Thus, carrying is permitted within that boundary. It was necessary to have the consent of the Gentiles sharing this space, and in Spain such agreements were readily made, although they undoubtedly were more difficult in European communities.

In some communities the enclosures would only be made for courtyards shared in common with Christian neighbors, thus permitting, for example, carrying water from the common well. The renowned thirteenth-century German scholar Meir b. Barukh of Rothenburg ruled that a Jew living in a village surrounded by a wall, in which his was the only Jewish family, need not request permission from the entire town in order to carry on the Sabbath; but if there were more than one or two Jewish families they must ask permission not only of the overlord of the city but of all the Christian residents in order to make an *eruv*.[6]

In Mainz in the fourteenth century the rabbi, a famous scholar, was accustomed to make an *eruv* in his own courtyard on the eve of every

Sabbath and not rely on the one made for the entire city once a year, since it might become broken. It once happened that he forgot to make his *eruv,* and he sent for a city official to investigate the general *eruv,* which indeed was broken (note here the cooperation of city officials with the Jews). The rabbi sent students from the *yeshivah* to warn all the Jews not to carry on that Sabbath.[7]

The *shofar,* a ram's horn, is blown during the service if it is not the Sabbath (when playing an instrument of any kind is forbidden), in order to aid in arousing feelings of repentance. In some medieval communities, the same instrument was used to announce the approach of the Sabbath.

Passover is probably the holiday best known to non-Jews. It is in commemoration of the exodus from Egypt, a week during which the eating (or even possession) of unleavened bread and certain other food is forbidden. The holiday begins with the *seder* ("order," that is, of reading the Hagadah and of special symbolic foods) in the home at nightfall. In the Middle Ages, as in all times, this was an important family gathering and often many relatives would join together or else friends would be invited.

The home was thoroughly cleaned prior to the holiday and all forbidden food items either disposed of or ceremoniously "sold" (temporarily) to Gentiles. The *seder* involves the telling (*hagadah*) of the story of the exodus and additional stories from the Talmud, together with explanations of the symbolic foods used, and is read from a special book, called the Hagadah. In the medieval period this was, of course, a handwritten manuscript, elaborately bound and if the owner could afford it also richly decorated and illustrated in colors. Special additional prayers and liturgical poems were added to the holiday and daily synagogue services during the week. The first and last days are full holidays.

Aside from the symbolic foods used for the *seder,* no particular food customs were associated with Passover, except that the eating of any form of leavened food was, of course, forbidden and the *matzot* (unleavened bread) were eaten for the entire week in place of bread.

Sukkot is the other holiday that lasts for a week. It commemorates the period in the wilderness when the Israelites dwelled in "booths" or "tabernacles" (*sukkot*), temporary makeshift rooms with thatched roofing. Each family constructed such a *sukkah,* with open ceilings upon which are placed living branches of trees (in Muslim lands and southern Spain, palm branches). When weather permits, the requirement is that the family at least eat meals in the *sukkah,* and adult males often sleep in them as well. Study of the Talmud also takes place there. The *qidush,* or sanctification—blessing of wine——is recited on the evening of the first and last days. The *sukkah* was decorated with hand-made drawings and ornaments. Special holiday prayers also were recited in the synagogue.

Barcelona Haggadah (fourteenth century Spain). A
man at the top holding two *matzot*. Cherub-like figures in the four corners are blowing trumpets, representing the four winds or directions. The shields
in the center are of the city of Barcelona. Copyright
held by The British Library.

A particular obligation, a biblical commandment (Leviticus 23.40), is the
taking of the "four kinds," a palm branch, myrtle and willow twigs, and
the *etrog* (citron). The latter is a rare fruit grown only in certain parts of the
world and is therefore often quite expensive. In Germany, for example,
myrtles were not to be found and were brought in by merchants together
with the citrons from France (even there, only in parts of Provence would
they be found).[8] Often, they were so scarce that only one or two sets of
the required species would be used by all members of the community,
and kept in the synagogue. Where possible, these four species were carried by each adult male to the synagogue and used in the service. In some
European communities, after the holiday was over children would collect
the bundles and burn them in the street, a custom that was discouraged
by some rabbis because of lack of respect for objects that had been used
to fulfill a commandment.

The final day of Passover is a holiday and also the final day of Sukkot. In the Diaspora, as with Rosh ha-Shannah, this became two days, the most important being the last, *Simhat Torah,* or rejoicing over the completion of the cycle of reading the Torah and beginning it again.

Shavu'ot ("Weeks," so named because it comes seven weeks after Passover) is a one-day (again, in the Diaspora two-day) biblical holiday commemorating the revelation on Mt. Sinai. Special prayers are recited in the services, but no other particular observances are associated with it.

Rabbinical holidays include one mentioned in the Bible but not in the Torah, Purim, commemorating the events of the book of Esther. Other rabbinical holidays are Hanukkah, commemorating the rededication of the Temple after it was defiled by the Assyrian Hellenistic soldiers (not "Greeks"), and various minor celebrations or fasts. Many of the latter were already largely ignored even in the medieval period. It is important to note that the so-called intermediate days, *Hol ha-mo'ed,* of the major holidays of Passover and Sukkot are also "semi-holidays" decreed by rabbinic law; that is, certain types of work may not be done and special prayers are recited.

The appearance of the New Moon, and thus the beginning of the Jewish month, is also a semi-holiday, which in fact was more generally observed in the medieval period than at present. At least in Germany, these days were observed by women as full holidays in the sense that they performed none of the work (creative activity) forbidden on biblical holidays.

Holiday services were more joyous than Sabbath services, with the synagogue often decorated appropriately (flowers and greenery, and other decorations). Special garments were worn both by men and women, either for Sabbaths and holidays or if one could afford it, separate garments for each. The aforementioned holiday of *Simhat Torah* was a particular time of joyous, sometimes raucous, celebration with singing and dancing. Two distinguished members of the community would be given the special honor of reading the concluding portion of the Torah cycle and the beginning of the new cycle (starting with Genesis). In Germany and probably elsewhere, the men so honored afterwards invited everyone to their homes where a feast was celebrated, at no small expense. It was also not unusual to invite Christian friends to attend the services in the synagogue on *Simhat Torah.* This tradition remained, particularly among the Sefardic Jews. In eighteenth-century London, the famous diarist Samuel Pepys recorded his own visit to the Sefardic synagogue on that holiday.

The other such holiday, perhaps with even more celebration, was *Purim.* The *megilah,* or book of Esther written on a scroll, was read aloud and great noise was made, usually with some kind of mechanical noise-maker, at every mention of the name of the evil Haman. In Spain the question arose concerning women, many of who could not understand the Hebrew of the text, since every person is required to hear the reading of the book and understand it (women are included since this is not a commandment dependent on a specific time but can be done anytime during the holiday). Some rabbis ruled that the book may be read in whatever language is understood, and thus it was in fact read in Spanish in many communities. However, not all agreed with this practice.[9] This was probably the practice also in European and Muslim countries, but there is little information compared to the sources for Spain.

The two (rabbinical) commandments for the holiday are hearing the *megilah* and sending gifts (usually food) to friends and to the poor (food or money). Clearly the intent was for such gifts to be sent to fellow Jews; however, the custom arose everywhere to include Gentiles as recipients of such gifts, which therefore were sent to one's neighbors and to Gentile as well as Jewish poor people (indeed, this was already mentioned in the Talmud, *Gitin* 61a), as a general obligation to support Gentile as well as Jewish poor). Whether or not the special type of cookie baked for that holiday, known to Ashkenazim as *Hamantaschen* ("Haman's ears"), were known in the medieval period is doubtful. However, other kinds of sweet foods were prepared.

Hanukkah, the other rabbinical holiday, has only one observance, the lighting of the *menorah* or candelabrum for the eight nights of the celebration. In most medieval communities, as in many modern homes, the light was provided by oil rather than candles, which were expensive and smelly. The *menorah* is supposed to be placed where it may be seen from the street as well as by the family, to publicize the miracle. In practice, many Jews in medieval Europe kept it indoors, whereas in Muslim countries and in Spain generally the custom was to place it actually outdoors, at the entrance of the home.[10] It was, and is, customary to give gifts to the children during the week of this celebration. In the medieval period, such gifts were in fact small and inconsequential, for instance nuts or candies.

Minor rabbinical holidays include *Lag ba-omer,* the thirty-third day of the "counting of the *omer*" (Leviticus 23.15) in the period between Passover and Shavu'ot. This period was observed in the Middle Ages, and beyond, as one of mourning, or remembrance of the deaths of the students of Rabbi Aqiva (*Yevamot* 62b). Allegedly, that ceased on the thirty-third day, which is therefore celebrated as a kind of holiday, particularly by children and in the medieval period by women.[11] An interesting custom in Germany was the celebration on that day of a man's achieving his sixtieth year (considered a milestone in talmudic tradition), even though birthdays as such were not celebrated. It was the custom not to cut the hair during this period until *Lag ba-omer*.

On that day also it was the custom to send gifts to Christian neighbors, as also on the Christian New Year (*Natale* or *Calend*, the eighth day after the birth of Jesus, which in the Middle Ages was observed as the New Year) and on Pentecost.[12] Christians reciprocated in part by providing leavened bread to Jews at the end of Passover (during which they were forbidden to eat or even possess leavened products). One important Jewish legal source explains that the sending of gifts to Christians, particularly on Purim, was considered a moral obligation since the Christians often assisted Jewish neighbors on the Sabbath by doing things for them that they were not permitted, such as lighting fires and the like.[13] In some German communities, the *etrog* (citron) used for the holiday of Sukkot was given to Christian neighbors after the end of the holiday, and this aroused the opposition of some rabbis because it was an object that had been used for the fulfillment of a commandment and ought to be treated respectfully.

In Spain, Christians often sent or gave gifts of food and other things to Jews, and sometimes this raised questions as to the permissibility of eating certain kinds of food or game. On Passover it was quite common for Christian neighbors to visit a Jewish house while eating leavened or forbidden food, which again raised legal problems (a good thing for the historian, as otherwise we would not know of these practices).

Learning being a major part of Jewish life, a special customary holiday was a celebration upon completion of the learning of a tractate of the Talmud, and even more when an entire Order (such as *Nezikin*, "damages," or *Nashim*, "women") was completed. Such celebrations, which included a feast, were held either in the person's home or in the synagogue or *beit midrash*. Similar celebrations occurred when a new scroll of the Torah was written.

OTHER CUSTOMS

The Sabbath began in the home, as did the holidays, with the lighting of two lights (usually oil lamps, more rarely candles) by the wife. These symbolize the dual commandment to "Keep" and "Observe" the Sabbath, but originated in fact in the period of the *geonim* in order to refute the heretical Qaraite practice of sitting entirely in darkness during the Sabbath in the belief that the use, as well as kindling, of fire was forbidden. After the evening service, mercifully short, the meal was eaten. It began with the recitation of *qidush* (sanctification) over a cup of wine, usually of silver or even gold but sometimes of expensive glass. In European lands, but not apparently known in Muslim countries and Spain, it was customary to recite a special song welcoming the Sabbath angels into the house. Songs were also sung during the meal, and at the end of the meal the praise of the woman of the house (Proverbs 31.10–31) was recited or sung. The second, or noonday, meal also began with the recitation of the *qidush* and the blessing over two special Sabbath loaves of bread, as at the Friday evening meal. A third, smaller, meal, was also eaten before the end of the Sabbath.

On the Sabbath, after services, in European lands it was customary to visit the sick and to comfort mourners. In the afternoon, following the meal, people strolled along rivers or lakes and often fed the fish. In Germany and other places, they would also go to hear public announcements from officials of the city or the government, particularly news about wars or local conflicts. Other time was spent in reading; especially popular were various stories and parables as well as ethical books. Rabbis often attempted to discourage reading on the Sabbath general works about Gentile history, and Maimonides especially opposed the reading of such Arabic works.

The final evening service that concluded the Sabbath, and also biblical holidays, was followed by a special ceremony, *havdalah* (separation), which marked the end of the Sabbath and the beginning of the secular week. This was also recited over a cup of wine and also a lamp or candle (symbolizing the permissibility to kindle lights) and spices that were smelled in order to restore the body, which has been symbolically deprived of the "additional" soul said to enter the body on Sabbaths and holidays. Special songs were also then sung, one honoring the prophet Elijah and expressing messianic hopes, and even in Germany, as well as Spain and Muslim countries, various religious poems of famous Spanish poets, such as Ibn Gabirol and Moses Ibn Ezra(h).

FAST DAYS

Only one fast is biblical in origin, Yom Kippur. As with all days in the Jewish calendar, it begins with sunset and lasts until after the appearance of the first stars the following night. In addition, there are several rabbinically instituted fast days, the most important of which is Tishah B'Av (the ninth day of the Hebrew month of Av, usually August). This commemorates the traditional date of the destruction of both the first and second Temples (it is, of course, improbable that both were on the same day, but it became convenient to combine the events). On these major fast days, no food or liquid of any kind is consumed, bathing and shaving are prohibited, and leather shoes may not be worn. Tishah B'Av is observed with the reading of the biblical book Lamentations (*Eikhah*) in the synagogue and special prayers. However, the day service does not last the entire day, as does that of Yom Kippur. Some very pious Jews also arose at midnight to recite special prayers. Minor children were exempted from all these fasts, except in the opinion of some extremist rabbis.

There are also minor fast days, including that for firstborn sons on the day before Passover, which while rarely observed today were universal in the medieval period. In times of great danger to a Jewish community, or in periods of drought, local leaders could ordain a temporary fast supposedly to avert the disaster. In addition, some communities (particularly in Germany and Austria) observed fasts of atonement on Mondays and Thursdays, and many individuals in all places observed personal fasts for such things as nullifying the portent of danger or death in a dream.

CELEBRATIONS AND MOURNING

Marriages, including the betrothal (see Chapter 3), as well as circumcisions of newborn infants, were occasions of community celebration. Feasts were held, usually in the home of the celebrant but in some countries in the Jewish community hall. It was customary for the celebrant to give a gift to the synagogue. Whether or not presents were given on such occasions is unknown, since our sources are silent about that, but undoubtedly this was the case. The birth of a child was a cause for celebration not only for the family but for the entire community. A naming ceremony for the infant would also take place in the synagogue. In more superstitious communities, such as in Germany, the legend that Lilit (the mythical other wife of Adam), jealous of children she was not able to have, would attempt to steal the infant boy before he could be circumcised; thus, a special "Watch Night" (*Wachnacht*) would be observed the night preceding the circumcision (which is on the eighth day after the birth).[14]

The circumcision ceremony took place usually in the synagogue and was performed by a specially trained *mohel* ("circumciser"). A particularly pious and learned man, not necessarily a relative, would be chosen to act as *sandiq*, a sort of "godfather," whose duty was to hold the baby but also to serve as a kind of spiritual guide. According to one German rabbi, this position was more important than that of the *mohel*, and he ascribed various mystical associations to it.[15]

The modern Bar-Mitzvah (son of the commandment) ceremony celebrated when a boy reaches the age of adulthood (13) was not yet known, although it began in the medieval period in some communities with the custom of calling the boy to his first public reading from the Torah. Quite often the boy would be required to deliver an explication of a difficult talmudic passage, either in the synagogue following the service or at his home, but this seems not to have begun until the late medieval period.

Mourning was the opposite side of the coin, so to speak. Death in the traditional Jewish community was far from the remote and "sanitized" experience customary in modern life. The body of the deceased was washed and prepared for burial by immediate members of the family, assisted by a special brotherhood of men whose sole purpose was this function. The body must be buried almost immediately following the death. Funeral rites did not normally take place in the synagogue but in the home and were quite brief, with specified prayers and a funeral oration only in the case of the death of an important scholar. The entire community was obligated to attend the burial, which took place, of course, in the Jewish cemetery. The coffin had to be a simple wooden box, nor were flowers allowed either at the funeral or on the grave.

Rabbinical law requires a period of seven days of intensive mourning for close relatives, and during this period the mourners remained at home, not even attending services (prayers were conducted in the home

Tomb of Rabbi Meir of Rothenburg (1220–1293) in the Jewish cemetery of Worms, Germany. Rabbi Meir was imprisoned by German King Rudolf von Habsburg and died in prison in the tower of Ensisheim (thirteenth century). Jewish Cemetery, Worms, Germany. Erich Lessing/Art Resource, NY.

of the mourner), and they had to sit on the floor; nor was the mourner allowed to change clothes or to wear leather shoes or to cut the hair. It was considered a religious duty to visit and comfort mourners, particularly on Sabbaths and holidays as previously noted.

In modern times, male mourners must not shave, but this was not a distinction that usually would have been observed in the Middle Ages, when most Jewish males grew their beards (and often their hair) long. There were different rabbinical opinions about shaving, some forbidding it altogether and others permitting it with scissors (which existed in the Middle Ages) but not a knife. Manuscript illuminations do show some Jewish males who are clean-shaven, but usually they are with beards. Some important German rabbis nevertheless apparently did not grow beards.[16]

A second period of mourning lasted for thirty days, with fewer restrictions than the initial seven-day period. Finally, a general mourning of one year was observed (again, only for close relatives), during which no celebrations of any kind, other than the observance of holidays, were permitted.

Not everything that in later periods came to be considered obligatory, or prohibited, was necessarily so in the medieval period. For example, the practice of males covering the head at all times, indoors and out, became actual law among Ashkenazic Jews in the seventeenth century or later, and at the present among most Sefardic Jews in Israel, but this was not the case in the Middle Ages, nor indeed among Sefardim until recent times. Some Spanish rabbis insisted that a head covering be worn inside the synagogue, and in any case most Jews wore some kind of hood or cap in the streets, but this was not the opinion of all.

Women and children were accustomed to play various games, including cards (gambling became a big issue in medieval rabbinical decisions). Very popular in European Jewish communities was a game involving rolling nuts down a board, presumably to see which one arrived first. These and other games were played also on Sabbaths and holidays, and as noted in chapter 3, playing with balls was also allowed, although in later centuries this was strictly prohibited.

Most surprisingly, perhaps, the playing of musical instruments on the Sabbath, and even a kind of organ in some synagogues, was not unknown, both in Germany and central Europe and also at least among some Catalan Jews, where we hear of the playing of various instruments including guitars. This custom scandalized one of the rabbis of Provence when he discovered that newly arrived Jews from Catalonia, including *yeshivah* students, engaged in this.[17]

While being Jewish is not solely a matter of religion, what we would describe as religious practices and customs played a central role in the daily life of the Jew. These not only were fulfillment of biblical and rabbinical laws but also served to define the Jew and to foster strong family and community ties.

NOTES

1. On legends related to synagogues, see the article "Synagogues" in Norman Roth, ed., *Medieval Jewish Civilization: An Encyclopedia* (New York, 2003), 620–21 and in the bibliography there.

2. See further details, ibid., 622.

3. Details on these, and other medieval synagogues, ibid., 624–28 and the bibliography.

4. Samson bar Tsadoq, *Sefer Tashbats* (Warsaw, 1875), 27a. The author was an important thirteenth-century rabbi and student of the renowned Meir b. Barukh of Rothenburg.

5. See the article "Bible, Manuscripts" in Roth, *Medieval Jewish Civilization*, especially 87–88 and 95–96 ("Responsa").

6. Reported by his disciple Samson bar Tsadoq, *Sefer Tashbats*, Nos. 74, 75.

7. Jacob b. Moses Mölln (or Molin), *Sefer Mahari"l*, ed. Shlomo Spitzer (Jerusalem, 1989), 225–26. The author, a rabbi in Mainz (1365–1427), was a foremost legal authority in his time.

8. Ibid., 392. A problem for which I have found no answer, since no source known to me discusses it, is how they obtained palm branches, which had to be fresh and remain so during the whole week. The scarcity of these species is shown by the fact that in some smaller communities they were not found at all, and one such community requested from a Jew in a nearby city who owned his own set that he send it to them, to which he agreed since all the Jews of that community would benefit from it (ibid., 397, No. 13).

9. When the renowned Isaac b. Sheshet became rabbi of Zaragoza (ca.. 1375), he objected to that practice, which he said had been the custom there for 30 years, on the basis of rulings by Nahmanides and another important authority, and that also there were errors in the translation being used. He wrote to another famous scholar, Nissim b. Reuben of Gerona, about this, who agreed with his opinion (Isaac b. Sheshet, *She'elot u-teshuvot* (Vilna, 1878; with notes; photo reprint Jerusalem, s.a. [1967]), no. 388, and Nissim's reply there, no. 390. The statement of Nahmanides is in Moses b. Nahman, *Hidushey ha-Ramban, Shabbat, Eruvin, Megilah,* ed. Moses Herschler (Jerusalem, 1973), 17a, col. 20 (there are problems related to Nahmanides' reasoning there that are too complex to discuss here). After he received Nissim's opinion, Isaac wrote also to Hasdai Solomon, rabbi of Tudela, who replied at length (*She'elot,* no. 391).

10. An eleventh-century Muslim calendar of Jewish festivals from Spain mentions this practice; the calendar is edited by Juan Vernet, "Un antiguo tratado sobre el calendario judío en las 'Tabulas probatae'," *Sefarad* 14 (1954): 59–78 (see 69 [text], 76 [translation]).

11. In fact, modern scholars accept none of the theories associated with the period between Passover and Shavu'ot, or the semi-holiday of *Lag ba-omer* (which may, in fact, reflect the influence of Christian mid-Lenten celebrations); see Efrat Zarren-Zohar, "From Passover to Shavuot," in Paul F. Bradshaw and Lawrence A. Hoffman, eds., *Passover and Easter: The Symbolic Structure of Sacred Seasons* (Notre Dame, Ind., 1999), 71–93, particularly 82–87. It should be noted that the confusion as to the dates for observance of the holidays, which he mentions, relates only to the talmudic period. In the Middle Ages the dates of Shavu'ot and of Lag ba-Omer were set definitely. The peculiarity of the entire observance is that there was nothing heroic in the death of Aqiva's students, who supposedly died because they were jealous of each other.

12. Abraham Berliner, *Hayei ha-yehudim be-Ashkenaz* (Warsaw, 1900; photo reprint Jerusalem [?], 1969), 19.

13. Ibid., 20.

14. It is peculiar, and highly ironic, that some modern Jewish (and even non-Jewish) feminists have chosen this mythical evil creature as their special symbol.

15. Jacob Mölln *Sefer Mahari"l*, 476–77. Some synagogues had the so-called "chair of Elijah" on which the *sandiq* sat while holding the infant. Elijah was supposed to actually visit the ceremony and sit on that seat (ibid., 477, No. 4).

16. On the Jewish borrowing in Spain of the peculiar practice of Muslim men of shaving the armpits and pubic hair, see Norman Roth, *Jews, Visigoths & Muslims in Medieval Spain: Cooperation & Conflict* (Leiden, 1994), 168–69. For important German rabbis who are said to have grown their beards only during the mourning period between Passover and Shavu'ot, and shaved on the semi-holiday of Lag ba-omer, see Jacob Mölln, *Sefer Mahari"l*, 157, No. 8. However, the statement may mean trimming the beard rather than shaving completely.

17. See Roth, *Medieval Jewish Civilization*, 463–64 and 468.

RECOMMENDED READING

Berliner, Abraham. *Hayei ha-yehudim be-Ashkenaz*. Warsaw, 1900; photo reprint Jerusalem [?], 1969.

Goitein, S. D. *Mediterranean Society: The Jewish Communities of the Arab World as Portrayed in the Documents of the Cairo Geniza*. Berkeley, Los Angeles, London, 1967–93, vol. 2.

Roth, Norman, ed., *Medieval Jewish Civilization: An Encyclopedia*. New York, 2003. Articles on "Synagogues," and in index: "holidays," "Sabbath."

6

OCCUPATIONS AND PROFESSIONS

The earliest records we have concerning Jews in the Middle Ages show that most were engaged in agriculture, with a small number in commerce and international trade. Not surprisingly, these had been the traditional occupations of Jews both in the Land of Israel and in the Diaspora in earlier times. Only gradually over centuries did this situation change, with an increasing number leaving agriculture and moving to towns and cities where they began new occupations, usually in crafts and trade. Nevertheless, Jews never abandoned agriculture throughout the medieval period.

With, as usual, the exception of Spain and southern Italy in the Christian lands, and all Muslim countries, professions were closed to Jews, other than the traditional ones associated exclusively with the Jewish community (rabbis, teachers, scribes, and others mentioned in the previous chapter). True, in the early medieval period there were Jewish "physicians," poorly trained and with little knowledge, in France, Germany, and England. However, they were frequently suspected of poisoning their Christian patients, including some kings, and also were subject to constant complaints by church authorities, because Christians were not supposed to utilize the services of Jews. From at least the thirteenth century on, therefore, Jewish "physicians" in these lands were mostly local individuals, men and women, who used folk medicine and even magic for their cures, confined exclusively to Jewish clientele. The true profession of medicine as practiced by Jews in Muslim lands, and also Christian Spain and Italy, will be discussed later.

AGRICULTURE: CROPS AND WINE

Agriculture, including the growing of grapes and production of wine, had been an important part of Jewish life throughout history, first in the Land of Israel and then in Babylon and elsewhere in the Diaspora. Certain things must be produced for themselves by Jews, or at least supervised by them, in accordance with Jewish law; for example, wheat for the making of *matzot* (unleavened bread) for Passover, and wine. Strict Jews also insisted that dairy products be produced from milk that had been taken from cows by a Jew, or at least the milking supervised by a Jew (to avoid the possibility of pig's milk being substituted). This concern extended also to milk products, such as butter and cheese.

The majority of early Jewish settlers in all lands, not just Christian Europe, were involved in agriculture either as growers or sellers (or both). Whereas rabbis in the talmudic era in Babylon had discouraged Jews from agriculture due to the uncertain conditions and poor prices, Maimonides wrote that one should not sell fields in order to engage in business, but rather the reverse: he should sell possessions (even a house) in order to purchase agricultural property.[1] Obviously by his time (twelfth century) agriculture had become a reliable and profitable source of income.

Contrary to much scholarly speculation, there is little evidence that Jews abandoned agriculture in Europe, either because of attacks in Germany during the First Crusade or for any other reason. One of the constantly repeated claims of the old theory about the First Crusade as a "turning point in Jewish history" is that Jews supposedly abandoned rural settlement and agriculture in favor of moving to the more "secure" cities (even though it was precisely in German cities that the Jews were attacked).

There is no evidence to support that, and much that contradicts it. We hear a great deal in medieval Jewish sources of the period, both German and French, about Jews in agriculture; most interesting, perhaps, is the testimony of Rabenu Tam, the son-in-law of Rashi, that Jews and Christians worked together in the harvesting of grapes. He objected to the practice of having Christians join Jews in stomping the grapes to extract the juice for wine but permitted them to help in filling the vats. In addition, it as precisely in the twelfth century that there was great general expansion of towns, and it is likely that some Jews were in fact part of that general movement.[2] Other examples include such things as partnerships with Christians in the ownership of fields or cows. Jews and Christians frequently helped each other at harvest time. In the thirteenth century, a renowned German rabbi discussed the legal situation of Jews and Christians in partnerships in fields and owning cows.[3]

Throughout the Muslim world, including Spain, Jews benefited from the advanced agricultural knowledge of their Muslim neighbors, learning from them how to grow rice, palm trees (for dates), apricots, peaches, guavas, and many other kinds of fruits and vegetables, such as artichokes, cauliflower, and cucumbers, virtually unknown in Christian Europe. While Jews in the biblical period had been expert at irrigation, this had been largely forgotten. They now learned also from Muslims the system of three-crop rotation (especially in Muslim Spain). It has been claimed that Jews introduced olives into Spain; in any event, they played a significant role in the growth of olives and production of olive oil there. In medieval Persia (Iran), Jews also apparently had a monopoly on the ownership of olive presses and were skilled gardeners whose services were sought by Muslims.

Contrary to popular belief, wine was *not* prohibited to Muslims in general, and thus it may be assumed that Jews also learned certain important aspects of quality wine production from Muslims (only later in the medieval period did more strict religious laws prohibit Muslims from drinking wine). Of course, Jews had always produced their own wine, both in the Land of Israel and throughout the Diaspora (in the talmudic era, wine from the Land of Israel was renowned throughout the Roman Empire). Surprisingly, the wine of Egypt, where we would not expect it, was also famous.

In Spain, and certainly also in Italy and France, both red and white wine was produced, and Jews valued white wine more than red, customarily using it for sanctification ceremonies on Sabbaths and holidays. Contemporary manuscript illuminations, for example, show white wine in glass decanters on tables during the Passover meal, and written sources confirm the preference.

In France, wine was also important. Famous rabbis such as Rashi (Solomon b. Isaac of Troyes, 1040–1105) and his family supported themselves by growing grapes. More would be produced, of course, than could be consumed by any one family, and excess grapes and even wine would be sold to Gentiles.[4] Jews were actively involved in the growing of grapes and production of wine also for Christians, in France. Following the expulsion of the Jews from the royal domain in France by Philip II in 1182, several acres of vineyards that had belonged to Jews were sold by the king's order.[5] It is not clear whether Jews in the region (the Ile-de-France around Paris) resumed their wine production after they were recalled in 1198. (Jews, particularly in France, were constantly expelled and then recalled when they were needed for economic reasons, chiefly taxes.)

Jews in Germany, where less wine was produced, and of lesser quality, were involved in the import and sale of wine from as far away as Hungary, although this was considered inferior to French wine.

Jews in medieval Poland,[6] where there was already a very substantial population by the early thirteenth century, were also primarily involved in agriculture, as in most other countries. Unfortunately, we have little information about many of the countries in central Europe.

In fact, the majority of Jews in the Middle Ages were owners of land, something almost unknown for the average Christian peasant, who was a vassal to his overlord and forbidden from owning property.

COMMERCE

The second most important occupation of Jews, after agriculture, was commerce. This also had been an area of activity of extreme importance, particularly to Jews in Babylonia during the talmudic period. Also in the Byzantine Empire, Jews played a major role in the dyeing and sale of silk. In the tenth century, however, there was a law that raw silk was not to be sold to Jews or other merchants for resale outside the capital. While guild restrictions may have prevented Jews from being involved in the manufacture of silk in the early period, at least by the twelfth century many Jews were involved in it, both in Constantinople and Syria. Under Frederick II (1194–1250), Jews had a monopoly on silk manufacture and dyeing in Sicily.[7]

Spain was the main center for production of silk during the Muslim period, followed by Sicily. According to Muslim sources, Jews had a monopoly on the production of crimson dye in Muslim Spain. Other dyestuffs were imported, particularly brazilwood, and Jewish merchants such as the famous Ibn Jau brothers amassed vast fortunes. Jews in both countries continued to be active in the silk trade and the import and export of other cloth throughout the medieval period. In Zaragoza in 1401, Jews complained that they were not being allowed to sell cloth in stores in their own quarter, but only in the Christian quarter. The city council agreed with their complaint, noting that the manufacture of cloth was the principal occupation of many Jews, especially widows, who worked in their own homes, and that their cloth was known to be of much better quality than that made by Christians. In 1481 this privilege was extended to allow all kinds of Jewish craftsmen and artisans to maintain stores either in the Jewish or Christian quarter.

Jews in Barcelona and Majorca in particular were engaged in maritime commerce on a large scale. By the end of the fourteenth century, the majority of the Jews in the latter island community were in such trade.

Jewish merchants with international trade connections were particularly valued by Christian countries. As we have seen, the privileges of settlement granted to Jews by rulers in Germany, and later also in France, especially favored such Jewish merchants, who were often granted exemptions from taxes and freedom of travel and trade.

This was not, of course, because Christians were in any way incapable of such activities, but because Jews had particular advantages not available to Christian traders. Chief among these was a knowledge of languages. Precisely because Jews lived in many different countries and frequently moved from one country to another, they tended to know several languages. If all else failed, they could always fall back on Hebrew when communicating with fellow Jews in other lands. In addition, Jewish merchants had the advantage of a ready-made intersnational network of contacts that allowed them to travel virtually anywhere in the world and be assured of a welcome reception from other Jews, who would assist them in obtaining merchandise for trade at fair prices.

A particularly interesting example, because it has received so much scholarly attention, is the class of merchant travelers known in Arabic sources (tenth century) as *Radhanites*. This is a generic term, referring to merchants from a particular district in southern **The Radhanites— International Merchants** Iraq, which indeed was a major center of Jewish population. In fact, it would appear that most if not all of the Radhanite merchants were Jews. These merchants were particularly adept at languages, fluent in Persian, Arabic, Greek, the Romance languages, and even Slavic. They traveled throughout the known world, to North Africa and Spain, then to France (or more probably Christian Italy), Egypt, India, and China. Sometimes they went also to other lands, as far away as Arabia. They were responsible for an increasingly important exchange of exotic spices, silk, and other goods from the Muslim world for furs, timber, and various things (including slaves) from Christian lands much sought after in the Muslim world.[8]

Since the slave trade has been mentioned, some explanation is in order. The entire Muslim world in the Middle Ages (and beyond, for that matter) was dependent on slaves. Slaves were acquired as merchandise **Jews and Slaves in the Medieval World** from other countries, including blacks from Sudan and Libya and the highly prized, and high-priced, fair skinned and often blond northern Europeans, generically called Slavs (from which, through Arabic, the word *slave* derives). In the early medieval period, and in fact through the thirteenth century in some cases, these European slaves were from countries not yet Christianized, partly or at all. Christian raiders thought nothing of capturing them and selling them into slavery to Muslims. Some Jewish merchants, such as the Radhanites and others in southern Spain, were involved in this trade. Many Jews in Muslim lands, and later even in Christian Spain, also owned slaves (in Christian Spain, these could also be Muslim slaves).

Entirely too much has been made of Jewish involvement in the slave trade, however, particularly in general medieval histories (where often this, along with "usury," is the only thing mentioned about Jews at all). In fact, a very small minority of Jews was ever involved in the purchase or reselling of slaves to the Muslims. Primarily this was, as mentioned, one of the things in which the Radhanite merchants engaged, and we know of another example at one particular brief period of time in a part of Muslim

Spain. In fact, only one Muslim source mentions Jews involved in this at all; it is not confirmed by other sources. It can certainly be argued that any Jewish involvement in such trade is contrary to the sensibilities of biblical and rabbinical ethics (an argument made by medieval rabbis), but it was scarcely a major part of Jewish economic life.

We know that Jews in Visigothic Spain and also in the Christian Byzantine Empire had slaves, from laws that sought to prevent them from holding Christian slaves or from converting their slaves to Judaism. There is no evidence as to what percentage of Jews owned slaves or how many slaves were owned.

Most slaves in the Muslim world served in the household or worked in various businesses or government offices. Women slaves tended to the kitchen and waited on table and did other chores. Male slaves were also not uncommon in the house. Slaves sometimes accompanied Jewish and Muslim businessmen on trips abroad to acquire merchandise. Among Muslims, some slaves rose to high positions of power, some even becoming rulers.

There is, nevertheless, no denying that there was significant discrimination and prejudice against slaves among Muslims, particularly blacks (some of the Muslim poetry and other literature is extremely racist). While blacks are mentioned in some Hebrew poems, there is no indication of this racist attitude. It is uncertain whether Jews had any black slaves at all, since this is never mentioned in the sources. However, at least one manuscript illumination from Spain appears to show a black female slave at a Passover meal. Slaves were traditionally allowed to eat such meals at the table with the family, and they often accompanied their masters to the synagogue on holidays.

According to Jewish law, a slave could only be held for a certain period of time, not longer than a year in any case, after which he or she must be given the choice either of converting to Judaism or being freed (of course, conversion also brings freedom but the slave becomes part of the Jewish community). We know from rabbinic sources that this rule was not always observed, however. Jewish law was very strict as to how slaves should be treated. Any slave who was abused was immediately freed, and in general slaves had to be treated kindly.

Travel and Trade   The vast number of documents made available from the Cairo Genizah reveal the extent of international trade and travel. Jewish merchants from Spain or Sicily regularly traveled overland in caravans through North Africa to Egypt and from there by ship to Asia Minor and again overland through Iraq and Iran as far as Samarkand in lower Russia (some even to China) or to northern India. Others journeyed by sea around the Arabian peninsula to reach the coast of India. Journeys such as this by merchants were not a once-in-a-lifetime event, or even once a year, but often repeated several times during a year. There were, nevertheless, constant dangers from bandits, pirates, and storms at sea.

Traveling with Children

In 1149, a Jewish spice merchant, Abraham b. Perayah Ibn Yijū [or Yajū; on the name, see S. D. Goitein, *Medieval Society* I, 435, n. 82] wrote to his brother Mevasser in al-Mahdiyya in North Africa [see maps in end papers of Goitein] to inform him of his return from India and that he had arrived in Aden safely with his "money, life and children" and had sufficient money to support himself and his brothers and sister. He was angry that his brother had gone to Cairo but not to Aden to meet him. "And I have already sent by the ship [or caravan] of the *shaykh* Majmun [a Jew] to you at Cairo … some 50 *uqiya* [exactly 50 ounces] of spices worth 40 *dinars.*" He complains that in spite of this, his brother had not been at Cairo to receive the shipment, which was then sent on to him at Sicily by a "faithful Jew." He again begs his brother to come at once to Aden, where he can take from him his son and daughter (while Abraham himself returned to India?) and the money, "better [this] than that the people of Djerba should take it." He also asks his brother to select the best of the sons of their brother Joseph or sister Berakhah to marry Abraham's daughter.[9]

Just as merchants from Spain (or more rarely from Italy) faced dangers from pirates on the sea or robbers attacking caravans, so merchants in Europe faced constant dangers on the roads. In one case of which we know, and which must have been repeated many times, merchants brought **Robbery and the Danger of Travel** wool from Cologne and were robbed by Christians who then sold the wool to two other Jews. One of those, acting on the instructions of his partner, took the wool to Mainz and sold it to a Jew there, who gave him partial payment and promised to pay the remainder by a certain date. Meanwhile, the original Jewish merchants who owned the wool heard of this and went to Mainz to recover their wool. The Jewish purchaser there bribed the officials and the courts of the city in an effort to keep the wool, and when he thus succeeded he sought to deduct the expenses of the bribe from the remainder of the price he was to pay for the wool. We hear frequently in these sources of Jewish merchants traveling between Cologne and Mainz.[10]

Abraham b. Isaac of Narbonne (d. ca. 1178) wrote that there are many places in France where Jews cannot safely go from place to place in general unless they dress in Gentile clothing, which he said is not a severe violation of Jewish law if it is necessary for safety, but even worse is the fact that some dress as monks, carrying crosses and other religious symbols to ensure their safety from attack by robbers, the existence of which is "well known," or if one kingdom should make war against another and rob and plunder travelers on the road. Over a century later, in Germany, another rabbi warned against dressing like a monk or priest so as not to be recognized as a Jew and attacked.[11]

Jewish   It has been stated that there were at least three important
Innovations   contributions by medieval Jews to economic development
in Commerce   in general:[12]

1. Introduction of interest on capital; charging interest on loans. This allowed for the development of further capital. However, in fact interest was charged also by Muslims and, at a later period, also by Christian merchants and bankers even though this was contrary to church law.
2. Protection of the possessor of an object illegally gotten (e.g., by theft) without his knowledge and yet sold, or pledged for a loan, in good faith. The application of this Jewish law in medieval German law concerning Jews has a long and fascinating history.
3. Bills of exchange, or letters of credit. As one noted scholar put it, "more or less the same significance for monetary exchange as the railroad has for transportation and the telegraph for dissemination of news."[13]

However, it was not only bills of exchange and letters of credit that were innovations but also checks, exactly like modern checks except that they were written in Hebrew or Arabic.[14]

The danger of carrying large sums of money, gold and silver coins, and the probability of loss due to rates of exchange, is obvious. Jewish merchants could avoid this by simply carrying letters of credit, which they presented to local Jewish merchants, guaranteeing payment in internationally recognized currency. We see this at work extensively on the part of Jewish merchants traveling to fairs in Europe to buy and sell goods. In Muslim lands there were bankers (actually, currency changers and investors) through whom such transactions could be made. Although we have very little evidence in the sources, presumably Jewish merchants from countries such as Germany and France traveling to Muslim countries would also avail themselves of these services.

Commerce is thus a very broad term, including the truly significant import and export of goods or commodities on a large scale, but also this kind of exchange at European fairs, and even local shopkeepers who sold items to other Jews or to Gentiles. Unfortunately, our sources are nearly silent about such shops in Europe, but in Muslim (and later Christian) Spain they often occupied the lower floor of a home and were either rented to a merchant or else the merchant himself lived in the house.

Partnerships were frequently established, in accord with detailed laws (both Muslim and Jewish, and later also Christian). Full partnerships involved usually an equal share in expenses, with one partner actually undertaking the voyages to distant lands to acquire merchandise for sale and then sharing the profits. Limited, or investment, partnerships involved one or more people investing a percentage of money and then sharing in the profits in accord with the investment.

In Christian Spain in the later medieval period, it was common to enter into all kinds of business partnerships, temporary or permanent, with Christians as well as Jews.

So important was the Jewish contribution in sales of merchandise and produce in the local communities that Christians found it necessary to change the market days and days of selling at fairs from Saturday to another day in order to accommodate the Jews. Already in the ninth century Agobard of Lyons wrote that royal orders were given to change the day of fairs from Saturday to any day Jews preferred, including Sunday. In Spain, too, such laws were enacted, noting that Jews constituted a major part of the market.

OTHER OCCUPATIONS

Testimony from Muslim sources of the ninth century and later indicate that Jews had a virtual monopoly on certain occupations: tanners, copper workers, butchers, and cobblers. In Egypt and Syria in the tenth century, it is reported that most bankers (see further discussion on the term), dyers of cloth, and tanners were Jews, while, surprisingly perhaps, most physicians were Christians. However, these sources may reflect a typical Muslim attempt to denigrate the status of Jews, since many of the occupations mentioned were considered demeaning (particularly tanners and dyers, as is still true in Morocco today). In fact, the considerable documentation from the Cairo Genizah and other sources indicates that many Jews were engaged in local businesses or in international trade. Jews paid a large percentage of taxes in the Muslim world, in addition to supporting the talmudic academies of the *geonim* and the expenses of the Exilarch, or official head of the Jewish community, in Baghdad.

The famous twelfth-century traveler Benjamin of Tudela reports that Jews in Antioch and Tyre were manufacturers of glass, and in Tyre, also ship owners, as well as continuing the aforementioned monopoly on silk in the Byzantine empire and in Jerusalem.

In Muslim countries, including Syria and the Land of Israel, and especially Egypt, Jews were employed in all **Artisans and** sorts of skilled crafts, including glass making, leather work, **Craftsmen** metal working (copper, silver and gold), and later in the thirteenth century paper making. In Spain, both Muslim and Christian, Jews were active in all of these trades and many others, throughout the medieval periods. While they were excluded from Christian guilds (which in fact were religious in nature), they formed their own guilds and usually experienced no discrimination in their trade. There were also highly skilled craftsmen, particularly jewelers and makers of astronomical instruments, several of whom were in the service of rulers and their families. An interesting example was the Jewish shoemaker in the service of Prince Juan of Aragon-Catalonia at the end of the fourteenth century. In the thirteenth century, Jewish teachers were also employed by members of the royal family to instruct their children. There were a few Jews in highly skilled occupations such as musicians and artists, as also in Italy.

As noted in the chapter on marriage and the family, adolescent children were often apprenticed to craftsmen or merchants. This was particularly true in Muslim countries, where such apprenticeships could also serve to strengthen ties between businessmen or artisans. Strong bonds often developed between apprentices and their masters, from whom they learned a trade or the ways of commerce that served them in their own later livelihood. In Spain, some Jewish families apprenticed their children to Christians, and vice versa, often for years. The apprenticeship contracts specify that the children must be permitted all their respective religious observances, and in the case of Jewish children must be provided kosher food by the Christian family.

In Christian Europe, Jews continued to be active also in all kinds of trades and crafts. In Paris in the early medieval period, there were many Jews involved in at least the sale (if not perhaps the production) of cloth. According to the exaggerated statement of one contemporary Christian source, "half of Paris" was owned by Jews. Nevertheless, Jewish cloth merchants were indeed prominent in the city and elsewhere.

In Germany and France, there were fewer Jews involved in a much more restricted number of crafts, and they were explicitly excluded from participation in the Christian guilds. They were therefore restricted to agriculture or the previously mentioned trades, although some craftsmen such as carpenters, glaziers, and tailors are found.

BANKERS AND MONEYLENDERS

It is actually something of a misnomer to refer to bankers, Jewish or otherwise, in the Middle Ages, for they were mostly merchants who engaged in short-term lending or transfer of funds, and sometimes served as "deposit bankers;" that is, funds would be placed on deposit with them to guarantee the creditworthiness of a merchant or for transfer as payment for merchandise. Essentially, they were involved in money-changing and determining the value of various international currencies offered for exchange.

The most famous Jewish bankers were Yusuf b. Pinhas and his son Netiyrah and their colleague Aaron b. Amram in the tenth century in Persia (Iran). They were immensely wealthy merchants who in addition to collecting taxes were also deposit bankers for the vizier and loaned him huge sums of money. There were also several other Jewish bankers in the Muslim empire during the same period. In Egypt during the eleventh century and after there were also some Jewish bankers, once again primarily money-changers.

Only in late medieval Italy were there, to some extent, true bankers in the way we would understand this term, and several of these were Jews.

While they did open accounts and hold money on deposit, their main function was lending money, including loans made to city and regional governments (in spite of opposition by the church).[15]

Money-lending by Jews (so-called usury) has received undue attention in general medieval histories. In fact, few if any Jews ever made a living entirely by lending money. Those who had extra capital on hand would be approached by Christians, individuals such as neighbors, or on a larger scale by rulers and even church officials, for loans on interest. While lending money on interest was theoretically prohibited by church law, Christians nevertheless ignored the law and also made such loans (famous are the Lombard bankers, or merchant associations). In some instances, Jews and Christians would join together to make particularly large loans, as in 1221 when a Jewish moneylender joined with several Italian Christians to lend a huge sum of money to Countess Joan of Flanders for the ransom of her captive husband. Incidentally, not only in France but even more in Spain, Jewish women were also involved in lending money to Christians.[16]

While the attitude of Jewish authorities toward lending money to Gentiles was very cautious in the beginning, by the late thirteenth century it had become so widespread that one famous rabbi, Mordecai b. Hillel of Germany, said that there is no profit to be compared to it.

So important were Jewish loans for the functioning of business, agriculture, and even the government that most countries soon imposed tight regulations and record-keeping for such loans. Both France and England had official records kept of every loan made by Jews. In Spain this was not done, but local notaries often recorded such transactions. The existence of several such documents from medieval England provide some of the most important information we have about Jews there.

Problems arose, of course. Jews were accused of charging exorbitant interest (in spite of the fact that this was usually controlled by law, as in Spain and other countries), and there were riots and killing of Jews, individually and in whole groups, in England, France, and Germany (the unique example in Spain, in the summer of 1391, only in part was due to complaints about loans). Ultimately, this was also the cause for the frequent expulsions of Jews from France and Germany and the permanent expulsion from England. On the other hand, businessmen and nobles protested that they needed the Jews for economic survival and sometimes successfully intervened to prevent their imprisonment or expulsion. Jews were also recalled to France and Germany because their financial contributions were missed.

There were frequent instances of cancellation by rulers of debts owed to Jews by Christians, which of course made the risk of such loans even greater. It is often assumed that the Crusades resulted in such a cancellation of all debts of the crusaders to Jews. Indeed, Innocent III had ordered this and the Fourth Lateran ecumenical council of the Church (1215) finally decreed this, but in fact both Philip the Fair of France (1214) and

Blanche, the powerful countess of Champagne, resisted and ordered the repayment of all loans to Jews prior to departing on the Crusade. In Aragon-Catalonia also, Pedro III twice ordered (1278) the officials to see that all debts to Jews were paid by those "taking the cross" to go on Crusade (in this case, the campaign against Sicily). In 1280, he noted that many deliberately tried to avoid their debts to Jews by joining the Crusade, and he therefore ordered a delay of one year before anyone was allowed to do this, during which time all debts to Jews must be paid.[17]

The church somewhat hypocritically protested against Jewish usury, while at the same time gladly borrowing money from them (popes, bishops, monasteries, and local clergy). Church officials, including popes, also loaned money themselves, and at interest rates that no Jew would have dared to consider. While the maximum rate of interest of 33 percent for loans by Jews may seem outrageously high by today's standards, it must be remembered that the risk involved of actually recovering the loans made to Christians was considerable.

At least in medieval Spain, we have many examples of Jews themselves borrowing money from Christians and Muslims as well as lending to them. There is some evidence of this also in other countries.

JEWS AS MINTERS OF COINS

One of the unusual occupations of medieval Jews (also beyond the Middle Ages) was that of minters of coins.[18] As early as the seventh century we find Suhayr *al-yahudi* (the Jew) in Damascus operating as mintmaster, purveyor of metals, and financial administrator (ca. 695). He replaced the Byzantine coins circulating in the Land of Israel (then part of Syria) with Muslim coins, which later Jewish legend considered an indication of the coming of the messiah, so much were the intolerant Byzantines hated.

In Barcelona in the ninth century lived Judah "the Jew" who is described as a minter of coins, probably only for the city. In the eleventh century, also in Barcelona, there were two Jewish minters of coins, David b. Jacob and Berzellay (Barzillay) the goldsmith, whose father had also apparently held that position. He was the father of the famous Jewish scholar Judah b. Barzillay. A certain Joseph b. Aziz (d. 1100) was a minter of coins in Leon. Very important was Abu Ghalib b. Abu Thair ibn Shibr, a Jewish official of the mint at Baghdad (died in 1204/1205) and whose father was a banker and head of the Jewish community there. In the fourteenth century in Spain there were several Jewish minters appointed by various kings. In Germany (Hesse) in 1180 David ha-Kohen minted coins, and Solomon, the Jewish mintmaster of the duke of Austria, was killed by a Crusader mob in 1195. Bishop Otto of Wurzburg, overlord of the city (1202–1223), also had a Jewish minter of coins.

Perhaps most interesting are the coins minted by Jews in Poland in the twelfth century, some of which have Hebrew inscriptions and some also with the names of the minters.

SPECIALIZED PROFESSIONS

Medicine and pharmacy were both important professions, particularly in the Muslim world and in Spain, and this topic is dealt with in detail in the following chapter.

Mention should be made of the importance also of Jewish translation. In the Muslim world, Arabic translations of medical and scientific works from Greek, Persian, Egyptian, and even Indian languages made available most of the knowledge of the ancient world. Thus, Galen and Hippocrates, for example, were known there long before they were in Christian Europe. Jews also played an important role in making these translations. Later, especially in Spain (including Provence) and in Sicily, Jews made even more significant contributions in the translation of scientific, medical, and philosophical treatises into Hebrew and Spanish. In Aragon-Catalonia, several Jews served as official Arabic translators for the kings.

NOTES

1. Moses b. Maimon, *Mishneh Torah, Mada: "De'ot"* 5. 12.

2. See the older studies of Henri Pirenne, and the responses to them, but especially Carl Stephenson, *Borough and Town* (Cambridge, 1933) and the more recent bibliography in *Cambridge Economic History* (1952) 3: 531–56. "Rabenu Tam" as reported in *Tosafot* on *Avodah zara*, 55b; see also Rabenu Tam's *Sefer ha-yashar* (responsa; Berlin, 1898), 26., no. 15; and the German authority Mordecai b. Hillel on *Baba Batra*, no. 481. Numerous other sources for continued Jewish agricultural activity after the Crusade could be adduced.

3. Meir b. Barukh of Rothenburg, *She'elot u-teshuvot*, ed. Moses Bloch (Budapest, 1895), No. 452.

4. Incidentally, the claim by William Chester Jordan, in an otherwise generally excellent book, that churchmen (clergy) forced Jews out of commercial activity that they considered inappropriate (such as selling wine to Christians) is not supported by the secondary studies he cites, few of which are reliable in any case; *The French Monarchy and the Jews* (Philadelphia, 1989), 27.

5. On Jews and slaves, see generally Norman Roth, *Jews, Visigoths & Muslims in Medieval Spain: Cooperation & Conflict* (Leiden, 1994), index (and especially 152–62), and the index in Roth, *Medieval Jewish Civilization* ("slave trade," "slaves of Jews").

6. See the article "Poland" in Roth, ibid.

7. Robert S. Lopez, "Byzantine law in the seventh century," *Byzantion* 16 (1944): 445–61; cf. the laws of the "Book of the Prefect" in Robert S. Lopez and Irving W. Raymond, eds., *Medieval Trade in the Mediterranean World* (New York,

London, 1968), 22; Benjamin of Tudela, *Itinerary*, ed. and tr. M. Adler (London, 1907), 11 ff.; Joshua Starr, *Jews of the Byzantine Empire* (Athens, 1939), 28 ff. and Documents LXXXV, CXV, and CLXXXII.

8. See the article "Radhanites" in Roth, *Medieval Jewish Civilization*, with the most current bibliography.

9. Text edited by Joseph Braslavsky in *Zion* 7 (1942): 135–39; article in Hebrew.

10. Meir b. Baruch of Rothenburg, *She'elot u-teshuvot* (Prague, 1608), No. 828, see also, for example, Nos. 773, 904.

11. Abraham b. Isaac, *Sefer ha-eshkol*, ed. Hanoch Albeck (Jerusalem, 1928), II, 132–33. Judah b. Samuel "*he-Hasid*," *Sefer hasidim* (Berlin, 1893), Nos. 201, 203.

12. Wilhelm Roscher, the leading German economic historian of the nineteenth century. His theories concerning Jewish economic contributions are important, with qualifications. See the important article of Guido Kisch, "The Jews' Function in the Mediaeval Evolution of Economic Life," *Historia Judaica* 6 (1944): 1–12; however, see Salo Baron, "The Jewish Factor in Medieval Civilization," American Academy for Jewish Research, *Proceedings* 12 (1942): 39–41 (article, pp. 1–42), who argued that Kisch really did not support Roscher's position. See also on the general subject Toni Oelsner, "Wilhelm Roscher's Theory of the Economic and Social Position of the Jews in the Middle Ages," *YIVO Annual* 2 (1958): 183–212 and "The Place of Jews in Economic History as viewed by German Scholars," *Year Book of the Leo Baeck Institute* 7 (1962): 183–212.

13. Roscher, "The Status of the Jews in the Middle Ages Considered from the Standpoint of Commercial Policy," tr. Solomon Grayzel in *Historia Judaica* 6 (1944): 19–20.

14. S. D. Goitein, *A Mediterranean Society: The Jewish Communities of the Arab World as Portrayed in the Documents of the Cairo Geniza* (Berkeley, Calif., Los Angeles, London, 1967–1993), 1: 230 complained about "exaggerated statements" concerning the use of checks and bills of exchange (he does not mention who made these "exaggerations"), but Walter Fischel, *Jews in the Economic and Political Life of Medieval Islam* (London, 1937; reprint N.Y., 1969), 17, demonstrated the reality of these things beyond question (Goitein nowhere cites Fischel's important book), and Goitein himself describes medieval checks, 241: "very similar to a modern check."

15. For further details, see the article "Banking" in Roth, *Medieval Jewish Civilization*.

16. For medieval France, only, see William C. Jordan, *Women and Credit in Pre-Industrial and Developing Societies* (Philadelphia, 1993), part I, 13–49.

17. Innocent's letter to Philip in Solomon Grayzel, ed. and trans., *The Church and the Jews in the Thirteenth Century*, (Philadelphia, 1933); vol. 1, 139–41; Honorius III's letter concerning Blanche, ibid., 151–52; the orders of Pedro III in Jean Regne, ed., *History of the Jews in Aragon, Regesta and Documents 1213–1327*, ed. Yom Tov Assis (Jerusalem, 1978), Nos. 698, 701, 825).

18. See sources and bibliography in the article "Minters of Coins" in Roth, *Medieval Jewish Civilization*.

RECOMMENDED READING

Fischel, Walter. *Jews in the Economic and Political Life of Medieval Islam.* 1937 London; reprint New York, 1969.

Goitein, S. D. *A Mediterranean Society: The Jewish Communities of the Arab World as Portrayed in the Documents of the Cairo Geniza.* Berkeley, Calif., Los Angeles, London, 1967–1993, vol. 1.

Roth, Norman. *Maimonides: Essays and Texts.* Madison, Wisc., 1985.

Roth, Norman, ed. *Medieval Jewish Civilization: An Encyclopedia.* New York, 2003. Articles on "Agriculture, "Banking," "Commerce," "Medicine," "Minters of Coins," "Moneylending," "Translation."

7

MEDICINE

Jews were interested in medicine since biblical times. The Talmud is particularly rich in information about disease and healing, and it is obvious that there were already professional physicians both in the Land of Israel and in Babylon at that time. Other ancient civilizations developed special expertise both in pharmacology (the study and use of drugs) and in medical practice, for example, the Egyptians, Greeks, and Indians. Jewish practitioners may have benefited directly from this knowledge, but it was especially the Muslim conquest of Persia, Babylon, and Asia Minor in the early seventh century C.E. that brought significant advances in the knowledge of medicine. Translations of Greek works, particularly of Galen and Hippocrates, by Syrian Christians were soon translated from Syriac into the cognate Arabic, as were other medical and pharmaceutical writings directly from the Indian and Egyptian languages, as well as some from Persian.

THE MUSLIM WORLD

Jews living under Muslim domination were not at all persecuted, nor did they suffer particular discrimination, other than special taxes. They quickly adopted Arabic as their spoken and written language, and soon many were proficient and even expert in mathematics, astronomy, and medicine.

Many famous doctors whose writings were read also by Muslims are known from at least the eighth century. The earliest known Jewish physician and author, Asaf *ha-rofe* (the physician), may have lived as early as the sixth century and probably studied at the famous medical school at Jundishapur near Baghdad.[1] Other famous Jewish physicians included Masarjawayh, ca. 701–720, whose work was still well-known to Muslim and Christian scholars centuries later, and Sahl al-Tabari in the ninth century, who was also a famous astronomer and made the first translation of the *Almagest* of Ptolemy.

While Jewish physicians were certainly a minority of the total number in the medieval Muslim world, their importance is not quantitative but qualitative.[2] It is remarkable enough that Muslim writers from the ninth through the sixteenth centuries praised these physicians and wrote accounts of their lives and works. It should be remarked also that without exception these Jewish physicians received their training from outstanding Muslim physicians and at such medical schools as the one previously mentioned

The Jewish physician most famous among Christian students of medicine in the medieval period was Isaac Israeli, also in the ninth century, who was born in Egypt and lived and wrote in Qayrawan (in modern Tunisia). His treatise on fevers, but particularly his work on urine analysis, remained standard throughout the medieval period and beyond.

In Muslim Spain lived Hasdai Ibn Shaprut, a Jewish official in the service of the caliph Abd al-Rahman III (912–961) in Cordoba. He was also an accomplished physician, praised also by Muslim writers, who later was able to cure Sancho, the grandson of the queen of Navarre, of his obesity; Sancho later became king of Navarre. However, Ibn Shaprut is most famous for his translation of what became the most important pharmaceutical work of the Middle Ages and for centuries after, the treatise of the Greek physician Dioscorides. This manuscript was sent from the Byzantine emperor as a gift to the caliph of Muslim Spain, but as it was written in Greek no one was able to translate it. Hasdai, who himself certainly did not know Greek, worked together with a monk who had brought the manuscript and thus was able to produce an Arabic translation. Equally important was his discovery of the means of synthesizing the Greek "wonder drug," which became the virtual penicillin of the Middle Ages.[3]

Following this period there certainly were other Jewish physicians in Muslim Spain, but it is not until nearly two centuries later that we again find those who achieved fame, who wrote medical works in Arabic. Two of these were also important Hebrew grammarians, contributing substantially to the development of knowledge in that area, the renowned Jonah (Abu'l-Walid) Ibn Janah of Zaragoza and Ishaq (Isaac) Ibn Qastar of Denia.

Other Jewish physicians from Muslim Spain treated the Almoravid ruler Ali b. Yusuf Ibn Tashufin in Morocco in his final illness in 1143.[4]

Both Abraham Ibn Ezra (d. 1167), famous biblical commentator, scientist, and poet, and Judah ha-Levy (ca. 1075–1141), equally famous poet and author of the *Kuzari*, whose daughter married Ibn Ezra's son Isaac, practiced medicine on occasion, in order to support themselves. As noted in Chapter 1, medicine was part of the standard curriculum in the education of Muslim and Jewish boys (in Muslim lands), and thus it was possible for at least the best students to practice medicine temporarily when they needed an income.

The most famous Jewish physician of all time, Maimonides (1138–1204), who was born and educated in Cordoba, is an example of this. He perhaps had not intended to become a physician, but after moving with his family to Egypt his brother David died on a sea voyage. David was a merchant, who supported the family, and following his death Maimonides (Moses b. Maimon) had to support himself, which he did by becoming a physician.

Maimonides

At first he treated Jewish patients in Fustat, and then also Muslims in nearby Cairo, and his fame reached the court of the sultan so that he was appointed official physician to the court. His duties kept him there half of the day, after which he rode to the Jewish suburb and attended to Jewish patients and also to his duties as head of the Jewish community (although not a rabbi, he was the most renowned authority on Jewish law). At night he fell exhausted onto his bed, where he dictated his extensive writings and also answers to legal questions, which came from all over the world.

His medical treatises, in Arabic, soon became famous also among Muslim physicians; ultimately some of these, through Latin translations, were equally famous among Christian physicians. His son Abraham, also an accomplished Jewish scholar, succeeded him as an outstanding doctor, particularly renowned (again, among Muslims) for his surgical skills. Maimonides is credited with certain important discoveries concerning such things as digestion and the capillary circulation of blood.

While much of his medical writing (most of it translated now into English, although not always accurately) is technical, he was also possessed of much common sense, and his sound advice on health and healthy living was centuries ahead of its time. Some examples, concerning diet, have already been mentioned. Others include his concern with the psychological, as well as physical, well-being of the patient. Indeed, one contemporary Muslim praised him by saying that while Galen's medical works are for the body alone, those of Maimonides are for both body and mind, adding: "Had the medicine of the Age come to call upon him, through knowledge he would have cured it of ignorance's ills."

He prescribed actual aerobic exercise, vigorous rapid motion "in which the respiration alters and one begins to heave sighs," the importance of which has been rediscovered only in recent times. Similarly modern are his statements that only whole wheat bread, made of unrefined flour, should be eaten and that fatty meat be avoided. He also recommended wine in moderation as being very beneficial. He was aware of environmental issues also, commenting on pollution in crowded cities due to narrow streets and high buildings, saying that one should preferably live in open cities or in houses with broad open courtyards where the air can be purified and the sun penetrate.

Maimonides on Health and Doctors

If man were to conduct himself as he manages the animal he rides, he would be safeguarded from many ailments. That is, you find no one who throws fodder to his animal haphazardly, but rather he measures it out according to [the animal's] tolerance. Yet he himself eats indiscriminately, without measure. Moreover, he takes into consideration the activity of his animal and exercises it, so that it does not always stand still and be ruined. Yet he does not do this for himself, or pay attention to the exercise of his own body, which is the cornerstone of the conservation of health and the repulsion of most ailments.[5]

The physician should not treat the disease but the patient who is suffering from it.[6]

Concern and care should always be given to the movements of the psyche; these should be kept in balance in the state of health as well as in disease, and no other regimen should be given precedence in any wise. The physician should make every effort that all the sick, and all the healthy, should be most cheerful of soul at all times, and that they should be relieved of the passions of the psyche that cause anxiety.[7]

Do not consider a thing proof because you find it written in books; for just as a liar will deceive with his tongue, he will not be deterred from doing the same thing with his pen. They are utter fools who accept a thing as convincing proof because it is in writing. The truth of a thing does not become greater by its frequent repetition, nor is it lessened by lack of repetition. Let the truth and right by which you are apparently the loser be preferable to you to the falsehood and wrong by which you are apparently the gainer.[8]

It should be mentioned that Maimonides was not, in fact, the author of the well-known "Prayer for Physicians," which still continues to be hung on the walls by some doctors. Far more important than that is the kind of advice quoted above.

There were other renowned Jewish physicians in Egypt, at least one of whom was also the author of medical treatises (no longer extant), including a commentary on Hippocrates.

Joseph Ibn Shimon of Ceuta, Maimonides's most famous student, for whom he wrote the "Guide of the Perplexed," his renowned philosophical treatise, in about 1185, became the court physician in Baghdad, where he served not only the local ruler but also the son of Saladin (this is perhaps the source of a long-standing but incorrect legend that Maimonides himself was a physician to Saladin).

EUROPE

Italy was the first Christian country to have important Jewish physicians. Shabbetai Donnolo (died after 982) may have studied in one of the medical schools in southern Italy, where he lived. He was an important author, particularly for his commentary on the mystical work *Sefer Yesirah*, and his authorship of a pharmaceutical work of which only fragments remain.

However, it is not until the thirteenth century that other important Jewish physicians appeared in Italy, including Benjamin and Abraham *Anav* (humble), with some others in the fourteenth century. The most renowned Italian Jewish physician of the Middle Ages was Elijah di Sabbato (Elijah Be'er) of Viterbo and then Rome (1405) , where he was granted the honor of Roman citizenship. He also became the physician to Pope Martin V, neither the first nor the last pope to have a Jewish doctor.

Medieval France, Germany and Austria had no Jewish physicians as such, certainly because of the total opposition to secular studies of any kind in those Jewish communities. There were at best one or two in England. Only in the very early period do we hear reports of possible Jewish physicians, in the false charges that some poisoned various rulers (it is doubtful, in fact, that such physicians really existed). Medicine in those countries, as indeed to a large extent also among the Christians, was primarily superstition and folk medicine. These practitioners, often women, were always suspect of magic and the black arts and used various kinds of remedies and concoctions of herbs and potions.

Among the Jews expelled from England in 1290 who settled in France, many earned a living selling folk remedies to non-Jews, which brought orders from the French king, Philip IV, prohibiting this and punishing those who continued the practice.[9]

For lack of Jewish physicians, Jews in these and other countries turned to Christians, either lay practitioners or slightly more professional "doctors." Rabbis, although opposed to such reliance, had no choice but to allow it. Judah b. Asher b. Yehiel, son of a great rabbi who came with his family from Germany to Toledo in the early fourteenth century (Judah later succeeded his father as head rabbi of that important community), wrote that in his youth he had poor eyesight and was nearly made blind by the treatment he received from such a Christian woman practitioner in Germany, but he was saved by the treatment of a Jewish woman. Even in Christian Spain, where there was no lack of well-trained and highly skilled Jewish physicians, some Jews chose to see Christian doctors.

In Spain (which included Castile-Leon, Aragon-Catalonia, Majorca, Valencia, Galicia, and part of Portugal, Cantabria, the **Christian** Asturias, Navarre, and for part of the medieval period nearly **Spain**[10] the whole of Provence, and later also Sicily), there were more Jewish physicians in any period than in all the rest of the world combined. So many and so famous were they that there is no point in even trying to

list the names. Instead, we shall consider as examples the careers of some
of the most outstanding.

Just as some renowned scholars and poets earned their living at least temporarily by practicing medicine in Muslim Spain, so also in Aragon-Catalonia
some famous scholars were also physicians, including Nahmanides, Nissim
Gerundi, and Simon b. Semah Duran.

Kings regularly had personal physicians who were Jews. Nearly every
king of Castile had at least one Jewish physician and most had more than
one. Some of these were also officials in other capacities or leaders in the
Jewish community. Jewish physicians who served Alfonso X were also
renowned scientists and translators of the first astronomical and other
scientific work into Romance. His son Sancho IV had two Jewish physicians from the Ibn Waqar family in his service, both of whom received
large salaries. That dynasty, lasting to the end of the fifteenth century and
beyond, included many outstanding physicians.

In the fourteenth century both Pedro I of Castile and his enemy,
Muhammad V of Granada, had Jewish physicians. Ibrahim Ibn Zarzar,
the doctor of the Muslim king, in 1358 was summoned to Fez to treat the
sultan. When the king of Granada was forced into exile the following
year, Ibrahim went to the court of Pedro and stayed there until 1364 when
the king sent him as head of an embassy to Muhammad, who had been
restored to power in Granada. Ibrahim's son Moses, one of the physicians
of Enrique IV, wrote a Spanish poem on the birth of the king's son, the
future Juan II.

The famous philosopher Joseph Ibn Shem Tov was the physician of
Enrique IV in the fifteenth century, and another of his Jewish physicians
(there were, in fact, several), Rabbi Jacob Aben Nunez, continued to serve
Enrique's sister and successor, Isabel. *Maestre* ("doctor") Samaya, one of
Enrique's Jewish physicians, was paid an enormous salary, fifteen times
that received by the aforementioned physicians of Sancho IV (of course,
the value of the money had deteriorated meanwhile). He was appointed
also as chief justice of all the Jewish communities in Castile in 1465 or earlier. Both Fernando and Isabel had their own personal Jewish physicians,
as did Pedro Gonzalez de Mendoza, cardinal of Spain and one of the most
important officials of the time. This physician, Rabbi Abraham, was one of
the many who converted in 1492.

Similarly, virtually every king of Aragon-Catalonia had Jewish physicians. Jaime I, whose daughter Constanza was married to Juan Manuel
of Castile (1282–1348), nephew of Alfonso X and a famous author, wrote
to her upon hearing the news of the birth of a new baby that she should
not raise this one as she had her other children solely on the advice and
with education received from her Jewish physicians. Juan Manuel trusted
his Jewish physicians in all things, including seeking their advice and
assistance on matters that had nothing to do with medicine. Particularly
famous physicians in Catalonia included Abraham Caslari, physician of

Jaime II, who was also a scholar. He saved the life of the young Pedro, Jaime's son, who became ruler as Pedro III.

Juce Orabuena, chief rabbi of Navarre (ca. 1385–1394), was the physician of the king of Navarre (then an independent kingdom). The most renowned physician in Navarre, however, at about the same time, was the philosopher Shem Tov Ibn Shaprut.

There were several Jewish surgeons whose specialty was the care of the eyes. One of these, Crescas Abnar, physician to Juan II of Aragon-Catalonia in 1469, operated on the king's double cataracts and restored his sight. When the king became terminally ill from fever ten years later, many Christian physicians were consulted, but the royal council insisted on consulting also two Jewish specialists. Pedro IV had numerous Jewish physicians, including members of the famous Caravida and Cabrit families and an important scientist, Cresques Elies.

Another capacity in which Jewish physicians served with distinction, and at times held a monopoly, was as official doctors of cities and towns. Such doctors were salaried by the city council. Nearly all of the city doctors of Burgos in the thirteenth and fourteenth centuries were Jews. Guadalajara, Toledo, Seville, Murcia, and numerous other cities and smaller towns had such official Jewish physicians and surgeons on their payrolls from the thirteenth through the end of the fifteenth centuries. The same situation existed in many towns in the kingdom of Aragon-Catalonia, and no doubt there were more than our records indicate.

The life of a doctor, Jewish or not, was not always easy or free from danger. Jewish physicians in royal service, particularly, needed to be especially skilled. The lives of the most important patients in the kingdom were in their hands and had they failed in their cures, much more if the patient had died, the doctor could be in great danger. Local Jewish physicians, or those on city council payrolls, had to treat patients of all kinds, including the indigent, and like modern doctors were constantly exposed to various diseases, but unlike modern doctors also to the recurring plagues. Some Jewish physicians lost their lives in the great Black Death, or plague, of 1348–1349. Jonatas Marcos, an important Jewish physician in Majorca, was granted special privileges by the king because of services during the plague "at risk of his life." He is apparently the physician "Marchii" who was captured by the Genoese while returning from Cerdana (Sicily), where he had been sent by the king to cure his chamberlain there; the king secured his release. He may also be the doctor who wrote a Hebrew treatise on the plague, a manuscript that remains to be published.

MEDICAL EDUCATION AND LICENSING

The exceptional skills of Jewish physicians in Spain, many of whom were surgeons or specialists in eye care and other areas, was due to the education they received and, sometimes as a substitute for formal education, apprenticeship to a renowned doctor. In Muslim Spain, where as far as we know there were no formal medical schools, apprenticeship was the only form of education. In Christian Spain, however, particularly, or exclusively, in the kingdom of Aragon-Catalonia (which as mentioned earlier included Provence), there were specialized schools of medicine at some universities. Only in Salerno was there another such school. According to legend, it was founded by four masters, one of whom was a Jew. This, and the alleged presence of Jewish doctors on the faculty, appears not to be correct, however. By the early thirteenth century, in any case, the importance of this school had declined and was replaced by the schools at the universities of Bologna, Paris, and Montpellier.

Only the last named university permitted Jewish students, and only to study medicine. The extent of Jewish involvement in this school, which actually dates to the eleventh century, is still a matter of debate. Five years of study were required of those who already had a master's degree in an area other than medicine and six for those who did not. An internship of at least six months was also required before one could be fully licensed. By 1340, Jews were no longer allowed to attend the school (by that date, Montpellier had ceased to be part of the Spanish kingdom). Nevertheless, by the end of the century Jews were again attending the school, and in fact surgery was taught primarily by Jews.[11] It is interesting to note that at the University of Paris surgery was not taught and indeed had been forbidden by the Fourth Lateran Council of 1215. Christian physicians had to swear not to perform surgery.

There were also specifically Jewish schools of medicine, at Lunel, Arles, and Narbonne and possibly elsewhere, of which very little is known.

In Catalonia itself, the most important school was at the university of Lerida (Lleida), which began in 1300; by royal decree no one in the kingdom could study medicine anywhere else (this obviously was not observed, however). Certainly in the late fourteenth and throughout the fifteenth centuries, Jewish, Christian, and Muslim physicians were trained at this university. Presumably also physicians from Castile, where we do not hear of any medical schools, also studied at Lerida or Montpellier.

Every physician had to be licensed, and the regulation of this was left up to local communities. Either a board of examining physicians or in some cases a particularly outstanding local physician examined the candidates, which examination often included general knowledge of science and other matters as well as medicine. In Aragon-Catalonia, Jewish physicians were allowed to be examined and licensed by Jewish boards or individuals. Those who practiced medicine or surgery without license (and there were some, including at least one woman) were heavily fined. In Castile, also, physicians had to be licensed, and the texts of some licenses of Jewish physicians have survived. Peculiarly in Murcia in the late fifteenth century, there was a law requiring Jewish physicians and surgeons to be licensed (already required by laws of the kingdom) but exempting Jewish eye doctors from such examination.

While there were some Jewish women "doctors" in Egypt, in fact they had no formal medical training. In medieval **Women** Germany there were women who practiced folk medicine **Physicians** but who lacked any kind of medical training. There was no necessity, according to Jewish law, for women physicians to examine women, and famous male physicians such as Maimonides and Nahmanides treated women. Only in Christian Spain do we find Jewish women physicians who received a medical education equal to that of men, and who were examined and fully licensed to practice as doctors and even as surgeons.

The names of several such women are known, and mention has already been made of some. We do, however, hear of rare cases of Jewish women folk healers in Aragon.

In 1326 in Marseilles a woman taught medicine privately, and in Sicily (then part of Aragon-Catalonia) in 1376 a Jewish woman was licensed to practice throughout the kingdom. Several physicians and surgeons were licensed there in the fourteenth and fifteenth centuries, including Jamila, the widow of Yucaf, who was also licensed as a surgeon . Among the Jewish women doctors were two eye specialists in Seville in the fifteenth century: dona Leal and Juana Levi, who was also an official "judge," or supervisor, of physicians in 1455.

Jewish pharmacists (or apothecaries) practiced in Muslim lands and in Christian Spain and Italy. Numerous Arabic **Pharmacists** treatises were devoted to the description of drugs, both natural and synthetic. As previously noted, the great treatise of Dioscorides, translated in Cordoba by Hasdai Ibn Shaprut, a Jewish official of the caliph, was particularly important in this regard, leading to the discovery of the first "miracle drug" in medicine.

The danger in the Middle Ages (and for centuries after in Christian Europe) was that individuals could go to a pharmacist and obtain medicines to cure themselves without the intervention of a doctor. Much depended, therefore, on the knowledge and skill of the pharmacist. In some cases in the fourteenth century in Spain, we know of Jewish pharmacists who achieved a great reputation because of their skill. There were many Jewish apothecaries or pharmacists in Spain, and at least in Castile and Murcia and probably elsewhere they also had to be licensed. In Toledo there was a complaint that "many Jews" had come to the city from elsewhere and were practicing medicine or pharmacy without the required examination.

The preaching campaign in the early fifteenth century of the fanatical Vicente Ferrer resulted in the conversion of several Jewish pharmacists (along with thousands of other Jews), and prejudice led to some local laws that prohibited employing Jews in this capacity. In Murcia in the fifteenth century, Yucaf Ibn Ya'ish, member of a famous Jewish family, was a physician, surgeon, and pharmacist. However, in 1488 the city council of Murcia prohibited Jews from being pharmacists. There is an interesting description of a pharmacy, including the mention of various drugs, in a sermon of Joseph Ibn Shem Tov (1452).[12]

Hospitals   There were also many hospitals in Spain, including some Jewish hospitals. There reportedly were some in Europe, particularly in Germany, but given the virtual nonexistence of real medicine there, these were probably not much more than hospices. In Spain, as in the Muslim world, true hospitals existed where surgery and other medical procedures were carried out. While public hospitals were supported by taxes, Jewish hospitals of course depended on donations.

So famous were Jewish surgeons that one of the greatest of all medieval Christian physicians, Bernard de Gordon, who lectured at the university of Montpellier, wrote that "Jewish soap" is prescribed for washing wounds after lancing, and a "bland" form of Jewish soap is to be used generally by surgeons.[13] Washing of the hands, not practiced until the early twentieth century among American doctors, was routine among Jewish physicians. Especially interesting is the same author's observation that hemorrhoids is known as a "Jewish affliction" for three reasons: Jews are constantly in fear and anxiety (according to another edition, because they are constantly idle; and the second reason, omitted in the earlier text, is that of anxiety); the third cause being because of divine wrath and eternal punishment![14]

BOOKS AND JEWISH PHYSICIANS

As we have seen, from the earliest period of records of Jewish physicians in the Muslim world they were authors of books; indeed, were it not for records of these books, most of which have since disappeared, we probably would know nothing about many of those physicians. Some of the books, such as those of Masarjawayh and Isaac Israeli, were eventually translated into Latin (that of Isaac Israeli also into Spanish) and became important medical textbooks in the later medieval period in Christian Europe. Others, such as the numerous works of Efraim Ibn al-Zafran, physician to the sultan of Egypt in the eleventh century, and his student Salama b. Mubaraka Ibn Rahman, also a physician and philosopher, have been lost. The medical works of Asaf and of Sabbetai Donnolo have had a better fate, both with modern editions. The book of Asaf was apparently studied by Nostradamus.

There were several physicians who were authors, of medical and other works, in medieval Spain. Moses b. Samuel ha-Selai of Toledo and Seville in the fourteenth century was a poet and also translated the aforementioned medical work of Bernard de Gordon into Hebrew. In 1360, he converted, taking the name Juan de Avinon, and wrote the very important work *Sevillana medecina* (in Latin) on the plagues of 1391 and 1419.

There were, as might be expected, many Hebrew works on medicine, most of which remain unpublished, some of which are extremely important. Others were in Spanish, such as the still unpublished "Secreta medica" of Meir Alguadix, about 1400, an important rabbi and physician of Enrique III (nor is this the only medical work he wrote). This was translated into Hebrew in 1546 (also unpublished). Samuel Esperial (or Esperel) of Cordoba wrote a Spanish work on surgery for one David of Jaen, extant in various manuscripts, as did Solomon Marik (unpublished).

In Aragon-Catalonia, the aforementioned Abraham Caslari (flourished ca. 1320–1362), physician of Jaime II and also a teacher of medicine, was the author of several medical works in Hebrew (in manuscript), including an important work on fevers.[15] There was also a considerable amount of translation by Jews of medical works, particularly from Arabic, in Provence and throughout Aragon-Catalonia. A listing of these would run into many pages. The kings were well aware of the extensive personal libraries of medical books owned by Jewish physicians, from which they sometimes borrowed or advised Christian physicians to consult.

The most famous library of a Jewish physician, extensively discussed by scholars since the nineteenth century, was that of Judah (Leon) Mosconi, also known as Leo Grech among the Christians. Born in Okrida, Turkey in 1328, after much travel he settled in Majorca where he became physician to the king of Majorca and also was on the city payroll of Inca, where he lived. In 1365 he moved to Tlemcen in North Africa and died in 1377. Many of the books in his vast library, which remained behind with his wife in Majorca, were sold to other Jewish physicians. However, Pedro IV wrote to the governor of Majorca that there were many books in the library that he had not seen and therefore he ordered that all the books be sent to him.

CHURCH OPPOSITION AND OTHER DANGERS

All was not sweetness and light and cooperation between Christians and Jews, however. From the earliest period of the Middle Ages, Jewish physicians faced intense hostility from elements of the church. There were rumors of poisoning of patients, including royal ones. The alleged Jewish doctors of Carloman (Frankish ruler, 870–874) and Hugh Capet (French king, 987–996) were said to have poisoned them, and such charges were made against others who attended kings in later periods. Even in tolerant Spain there were some such accusations, none of which was ever proven. The most serious accusation was against the aforementioned rabbi and physician Meir Alguadix, that he had poisoned Enrique III. Moses Rimoch in Sicily was falsely accused of poisoning some Christian patients and was martyred in Salerno around 1400. He was only 24 at the time.

In certain periods in Provence special permission was required for Jewish doctors or surgeons to treat Christians. This was not the case in Spain, of course, where as mentioned Jewish physicians were often on city payrolls and in many cases were the only physicians. Not only kings and members of the royal families but also cardinals, archbishops, and important nobles had their personal Jewish physicians.

Canon (church) law prohibited Christians from being treated by Jews, and there were frequent repetitions of this by local church councils in Europe. The penalty was excommunication for the Christian patient (legally, the church could do nothing against Jewish doctors or practitioners). The Council of Vienne (1267) even prohibited Jews from visiting sick Christians, which we know was frequently done in Germany, especially by Jewish women, who also visited Christian prisoners. The ecumenical Council of Basel in 1434 prohibited Jews being appointed as public physicians, on city or town payrolls as was done in Spain before and after that decree, which was simply ignored.

In spite of all these pious attempts to prohibit the use of Jewish physicians, many popes had their own private Jewish doctors. One of these, Isaac b. Mordecai, the physician of Boniface VIII (1296–1303), interceded with the pope when there was danger to the Jews of Rome. This has led, apparently, to the widely believed but unproven claim that Jewish doctors of the popes in general used their influence on behalf of Jews. Other popes of the fourteenth century also had Jewish physicians. As previously noted, the famous Elijah di Sabbato (Elijah Be'er) was the physician of Martin V (1417–1431) and his successor Eugene IV (1431–1447). Both popes treated him generously and granted him a pension. Pius II (1458–1464) was served by Moses Rieti, author of a small Hebrew work in imitation of Dante (devoid of literary merit, nevertheless), and of more important medical commentaries. Sixtus IV (1471–1484) wrote in strong terms condemning the freedom of Jews generally in Castile and particularly the Jewish physicians and pharmacists who were consulted by Christians; yet hypocritically the pope had his own personal Jewish physician.

Official opposition and false accusations did nothing to prevent the use of Jewish physicians. On the contrary, especially in Spain, there were frequent examples of glowing testimonials by individual Christians and entire cities as to the services of their Jewish doctors. It happened that if a Jewish physician who was particularly respected decided to leave a community, for example Zaragoza, virtually the entire Christian population signed petitions and sent letters to the king urging that everything be done to retain his services. Obviously the respect for Jewish physicians and surgeons helped foster the general friendship and cordial relations that existed between Christians and Jews.

NOTES

1. See especially Aviv Melzer, *Asaph the Physician—the Man and His Book* (unpublished dissertation, Madison, University of Wisconsin, 1971; available on microfilm, Ann Arbor Microfilms, 1972), with an excellent edition of the Hebrew text. Less useful is Suessman Muntner, *Mavo le-sefer Asaf ha-rofe* (in Hebrew; Jerusalem, 1957). See most recently Elinor Lieber, "Asaf's 'Book of Medicines': a Hebrew Encyclopedia of Greek and Jewish Medicine," *Dumbarton Oaks Papers* 38 (1984): 233–49.

2. Joseph Shatzmiller, *Jews, Medicine, and Medieval Society* (Berkeley, 1994), 12, apparently saw no inconsistency in reporting that one Muslim authority records less than ten percent Jewish names in his biographies of physicians from 750 to 1230, and yet a modern scholar has found no less than 44 such physicians in the eleventh century alone; nor were other important sources for physicians in the Muslim world consulted.

3. Full details on his career are in Norman Roth, *Jews, Visigoths & Muslims in Medieval Spain: Cooperation & Conflict* (Leiden, 1994), 79–86; see also generally the index there, "Physicians."

4. See Norman Roth, "Jewish and Muslim Physicians of Ali Ibn Tashufin," *Korot. The Israel Journal of the History of Medicine and Science* 10 (1993–1994): 83–91.

5. *Moses Maimonides' Two Treatises on the Regimen of Health,* tr. A. Bar-Sela, H. E. Hoff, and Elias Faris (Philadelphia, 1964), 17.

6. Moses b. Maimon (Maimonides), *Treatise on Asthma,* trans. S. Munter (Philadelphia, 1963), 89.

7. *Two Treatises on the Regimen of Health,* 27.

8. Norman Roth, *Maimonides: Essays and Texts* (Madison, Wisc., 1985), 29, 31–32 (see there for sources).

9. William Chester Jordan, *The French Monarchy and the Jews* (Philadelphia, 1989), 184.

10. I have spent years studying the documents and sources relating to Jewish physicians in medieval Spain, which are too complex to detail here. In a forthcoming book, all of this will be discussed.

11. Vern L. Bullough, "The Development of the Medical University at Montpellier to the End of the Fourteenth Century," *Bulletin of the History of Medicine* 30 (1956): 508–23; I am not entirely convinced of this conclusion (522), however. It is certain that Jews were being examined and licensed there in surgery. There are many other articles and books that deal with the school at Montpellier.

12. Translation in Marc Saperstein, *Jewish Preaching, 1200–1800* (New Haven, Conn., 1989), 170–71.

13. *Lilio de medecina,* first published in Seville in 1495; critical edition by John Cull and Brian Dutton (Madison, 1991), 37, and 252 (not "soap of Judea," as misunderstood by the editors, *xabon judaico* and *xabon blando judaico;* in fact, Jews in Spain were in general involved in the manufacture of soap).

14. Ibid., 261–62.

15. This only has been the subject of modern investigation, J. O. Leibowitz, "Abraham Caslari's Hebrew Ms. 'Pestilential Fevers'," *Korot* 4 (1968): 69–72 (in English), 517–20 (in Hebrew).

RECOMMENDED READING

Friedenwald, Harry. *The Jews and Medicine.* Baltimore, 1944; reprinted New York, 1967, 2 vols. Includes several serious errors, however.

Rosner, Fred. *Medicine in the Mishneh Torah of Maimonides.* New York, 1984.

Roth, Norman. *Maimonides: Essays and Texts.* Madison, Wisc., 1986.

———, ed. *Medieval Jewish Civilization: An Encyclopedia.* New York, 2003. Article on "Medicine."

Shatzmiller, Joseph. *Jews, Medicine, and Medieval Society.* Berkeley, Calif., 1994. Disappointing and incomplete in many respects.

8

LITERATURE
AND THE ARTS

An important part of the daily life and culture of any people is what may be broadly defined as the arts, including everything from simple decoration and folk art to the most skilled painting, sculpture, music, theater, and dance. Included also is literature, whether oral folk tales and poetry or formal compositions. These are the things that not only make life enjoyable, or at least bearable, but also express the creativity and cultural values of the people.

Throughout its history, from the biblical era to the present, Jews have been productive in all of these areas. The Temple in Jerusalem, as we know from the surviving artifacts (unfortunately the very existence of which are not widely known even among Jews), was richly adorned with carved ornamentation and other decoration, and so were many private homes, some of which even included mosaics depicting pagan deities (merely decoration, however). Early (fourth to seventh century) synagogues that have been discovered also are decorated with mosaics and carved stone decoration. The richest of these, the famed Dura-Europas synagogue in Babylon, has every inch of every wall covered with paintings, as well as decorations on the ceiling, doorways, and the niche for the Torah scrolls. While none was ever so elaborate, such decoration was continued in medieval synagogues.

Literature begins, of course, with the Bible, but also includes such extrabiblical writings as the Dead Sea Scrolls (which contain also some secular poetry) and early Greek secular and religious writings, in addition to the Apocrypha and Pseudepigrapha. Music and dance also, even though little detail is actually available, began with the biblical period.

ART IN JEWISH LAW

For the Jews, certain aspects of this cultural creativity were (and, for traditional Jews, are) defined by biblical and rabbinical law. The most famous of such laws is the biblical prohibition: "Do not make for yourself a statue (carved image) and any image which is in the heavens above and [or] in the earth below and in the water below the earth" (Exodus 20.4, correctly translated). Contrary to popular myth, this (the second of the Ten Commandments) does not prohibit the making of any kind of art, including sculpture, whether of the human body or anything else. What it was intended to prohibit, as the concluding verse clearly states, is not to bow down to or worship such images. So strict, indeed, was the prohibition against idolatry that images used for such worship found in the Land of Israel were to be completely destroyed. Of course, large numbers of the early Israelites themselves practiced idolatry for centuries.

Talmudic law focused on the interpretation of the above biblical commandment, noting that this includes images of the sun, moon, and stars as well as astrological and zodiac signs. From this, it is clear that the rabbis actually did interpret the commandment as a prohibition against the making of such images for whatever purpose. Nevertheless, this continued to be debated in the Middle Ages. Authorities like Maimonides and Nahmanides, who disagreed on many points of law, concurred that the making of human images, at least, in any form and for any purpose was forbidden. Nevertheless, the great German authority Meir b. Barukh of Rothenburg (ca. 1220–1293) stated that the Talmud did permit the drawing of animals and birds in prayer books and the like, although he objected to this because such drawings might distract the worshiper, who should concentrate his heart on "his Father in heaven."[1]

In spite of such rulings, Jews nevertheless portrayed the human figure, and certainly animals, the planets, and the zodiac, in manuscript illuminations and in popular (private) drawings, as well as in synagogue art (not, however, human figures).

ART IN PRACTICE IN MEDIEVAL JEWISH LIFE

There were at least two kinds of art in the Jewish world of the Middle Ages, which we may term professional, and naive, or popular. The chief purpose of the first kind was the illumination, or illustration and decoration, of important manuscripts, primarily but by no means exclusively religious in nature. These included Bible codices (Torah scrolls were never to be illustrated or decorated, but in spite of this prohibition some did have gold letters and other adornments), the Passover Hagadah, holiday and occasionally daily prayer books, or codes of law such as the

Mishneh Torah of Maimonides. Talmud manuscripts, as far as we know, curiously were never illuminated. However, only a very small number of these have survived from the Middle Ages. In addition, some important secular works were illustrated and sometimes also richly decorated, such as books of parables or tales (particularly the famous *Meshal ha-qadmoni*, "Parable of the ancient one," a series of tales by Isaac Ibn Sahulah of Spain, 1281, which was popular in Italy and even Germany, and indeed it is from these lands that we have our illustrated versions) or medical works, such as the famous "Canon" of the Muslim philosopher and physician Ibn Sina ("Avicenna").[2]

These manuscripts were commissioned by wealthy patrons, or by communities for use in the synagogue perhaps, and scribes carefully wrote the Hebrew lettering in a manner not unlike that used for Torah scrolls, except that sometimes vowel points (*niqudot*) would be included. Then

Pessach. Page from the Darmstadt Haggadah. Israel ben Meir of Heidelberg (fifteenth century). Hessische Landesbibliothek, Darmstadt, Germany. Snark/Art Resource, NY.

highly skilled artists, sometimes more than one (in the case of very important manuscripts, a whole workshop of professionals, perhaps including non-Jewish artists), would decorate letters or important passages in colors and gold leaf and with elaborate backgrounds and borders, imitating in this way the illumination of the large initial letter of Christian manuscripts. Since Hebrew has no capital letters, an entire opening word, or even sentence, of a passage would be thus decorated.

Often, the scribe who wrote the manuscript was also the illustrator. One such highly skilled scribe-illuminator, Joel b. Simon from Germany, went to northern Italy in the fifteenth century, where he was the head of a workshop of scribes and illuminators. Some famous scholars in Spain were also scribes and illuminators of important biblical and other manuscripts.

Other artists, or sometimes the same one, would draw beautiful illustrations that either depicted events mentioned in the text or associated with the story. For example, the famous Sarajevo Hagadah, so called because the manuscript, written and illuminated in medieval Spain, eventually made its way to Sarajevo, has a series of illustrated "cycles" of the creation, the life of Moses, and the exodus. Similar, if less elaborate, cycles of illustrations adorn other Hagadot. Other illustrations found include, fortunately for the historian, full-color depictions of contemporary rabbis teaching or, in one case, an astronomer demonstrating an astrolabe, or an apothecary in his shop. These have little or nothing to do with the works in which they appear and were nothing more than an opportunity for the artist to show off his skill. The *matzah* (unleavened bread) and other special foods for the Passover *seder* were frequently depicted, and the *matzah* in particular was sometimes drawn against an elaborately colored and decorated background, in at least one case with cherubic figures in the four corners of the borders, representing the winds, or directions, blowing trumpets. Coats of arms of the kingdoms of Spain, and in the later medieval period also Portugal in manuscripts from that land, often adorned the pages.

Illustrations in Medieval Manuscripts Of particular interest are the numerous biblical manuscripts from Spain that depict, often in full page illumination and with heavy gold leaf, the various utensils (candelabrum, shewbread table, altars, etc.) of the Temple. Some of these illustrations are extremely realistic, while others are quite stylized and merely suggestive of their subject, the main intent being decoration.

Another important aspect of illustration, whether of Bible manuscripts or Hagadot, is the inclusion of scenes or elements of contemporary life, and not always of Jewish life. Thus, we have hunting scenes (although, at least in Spain, Jews did hunt) and portrayals of knights and kings, armies in battle, and other such things, all of which serve as additional sources of information for life in the Middle Ages. From the illustrations, we learn not only what Jewish homes were like, and how the family lived, but what cities and buildings in general looked like. It should be mentioned, however, that we are rarely certain whether all of these illustrations are by Jewish artists or, more likely, whether at least some were by Christians. It also appears that in some cases artisans in a Christian workshop may have done the background decoration and left space for the Hebrew words and their illumination, which were then done by Jews.

It has been incorrectly suggested that the so-called Bird's Head Hagadah from Germany, in which human figures are drawn with the heads of birds, is due to the alleged prohibition on portraying human figures. However, one of the earliest illustrated prayer books, also from Germany (1272), shows figures with human faces and also with birds' heads, so that clearly this is merely decoration. We also find this, and figures with animal heads, in some Spanish manuscripts as well, indicating that more probably it was simply a humorous element.

Few of the manuscripts from France, Germany, or other European countries, aside from Italy, have the sophistication or elaborate nature of illumination that characterize all of the Spanish and Portuguese manuscripts. While not lacking in artistic talent, the Jewish artists in those lands expressed themselves with a more simple style and choice of color. The illustrations are, indeed, primarily of importance for showing styles of dress of both men and women. One German manuscript stands out, however, the famous Darmstadt Hagadah. A full-page illumination, clearly with Christian Gothic influence, remarkably shows women studying together with and even teaching men. We know that this was not some imaginative fancy, for there were such women scholars, as previously noted.

Important illuminated biblical manuscripts from Germany also exist, such as the Ambrosian Bible (1236–1238), which has two full-page illuminations at the end, one depicting mythological figures of the afterlife, such as the wild ox and Leviathan (a mythical giant fish, named in the Bible), with a scene of the righteous in the world to come eating and drinking at a table. More interesting is the Schocken Bible (ca. 1300) with its full-page illumination at the beginning of Genesis in red and blue background and border with no less than 46 roundels, or circular medallions, each containing miniatures depicting scenes from Genesis, including human figures.[3] There are, or more correctly were, several other illuminated manuscripts produced in Germany, including some secular works. Unfortunately, these were not published and few have survived the destruction by the Nazis of Jewish manuscripts and books not only in private collections but in all the major libraries that fell under their control.

Denmark, fortunately, escaped this fate, and the magnificent collection of the royal library in Copenhagen contains priceless treasures, including a magnificent illuminated manuscript of the *Mishneh Torah* of Maimonides. A published edition of this would be a great contribution. These manuscripts, of course, originated from other countries, including Spain and

Provence (from the fourteenth century, no longer a part of Spain with the exception of some areas).[4]

Most of the Italian manuscripts that have survived are from the late medieval period and the Renaissance and are elaborately illustrated and decorated in a rococo style very similar to the late Portuguese manuscripts. This is not surprising, given the influx of Spanish and Portuguese Jews in the fifteenth century, some of whom arrived in Italy even prior to the expulsions from those lands (similar rococo decoration is found in some fifteenth-century manuscripts from Provence). The life these manuscripts portray is inevitably of wealthy Jews, in expensive costume and rich homes. This, of course, was the class able to afford such extravagant and expensive manuscript illumination.[5]

Recent years have seen the publication of some of the important manuscripts from the vast collection in the Vatican and of other Italian masterpieces such as the Rothschild prayer book. One manuscript of particular interest shows a Jewish dancing master instructing his female pupils.

Micrography and Naive Art A special form of illustration employed in various kinds of manuscripts is micrography, the use of writing itself to form decorative elements.[6] Usually minuscule, the Hebrew letters of a biblical verse or other quotation are written in such a way that they form the outline of designs, which range from simple geometric or floral patterns to more complex figures of birds, animals, or human figures. A particularly elaborate German manuscript has a full-page micrographic drawing that includes a figure of a knight, a man hunting a deer with an axe, and another blowing a horn, as well as two peacocks. The figures themselves in this manuscript are drawn in a "naive" style, that is, certainly not the work of a trained artist.

Examples of such naive art are found in other manuscripts, including German Passover Hagadot that depict men baking *matzah*. From the post-medieval period have survived private manuscripts with extremely unskilled and hasty sketches depicting various ceremonial activities, and no doubt there were such manuscripts also in the medieval period that have not survived.

In Muslim Egypt, as no doubt in other lands, a children's primer, for learning the Hebrew alphabet, was a sort of coloring book, in which the child could fill in the colors of letters. Others are decorated with figures of snakes and the so-called Star of David.[7]

The Magen David—"Star of David" Since we have mentioned it, it might be of interest to discuss briefly this six-sided star, which unfortunately perhaps has come to be considered the symbol representing all things Jewish and almost the equivalent of the Christian cross, although it never had such a sacred connotation in Jewish history. In fact, it is not even Jewish in origin, but is an ancient symbol found already on Greek jars of the fourth century B.C.E. It was used also in other cultures, including Muslim. Most significant was its use in medieval Christian cathedrals, particularly in stained glass windows but also sometimes carved in stone, for example over the entrance. This certainly was not a Jewish symbol (ironically, the cathedral of Burgos has the symbol in a very large central window that would have been clearly visible in the nearby Jewish quarter; in the late fourteenth century, one of the important rabbis in Burgos converted and became bishop of the city).

Spanish Jews may have been responsible for the use of the star as a particularly Jewish symbol, as has been suggested, although this can hardly be established on the basis of its use in thirteenth-century Christian manuscripts. Nonetheless, the symbol is found in Jewish manuscripts of about the same time but is not restricted to Spain. It is also found in the decoration of the two surviving synagogues of Toledo. Increasingly in the early modern period it came to be used as an ornament in synagogue decoration and in illustrations, but with no particular religious significance. It was taken over by the Zionist movement as its symbol, both in western and eastern Europe. The Nazis, of course, imposed the wearing of the star by all Jews (it was rarely so used as part of the medieval "Jewish badge" legislation).[8]

OBJECTS OF DAILY AND SYNAGOGUE USE

Although some legal authorities, at least, had ruled that even sculpture, particularly of animals, was permitted, we have no knowledge of any in the medieval period. Even the bas-relief wooden carvings of lions that adorned some synagogues in the early modern period seem not to have been done in medieval synagogues. However, objects for daily use, such as lamps and dishes and probably more fragile things that have not survived, were often decorated. Elaborate brass or even gold-plated hanging oil candelabra, usually with several openings for the lights, are seen in many manuscript illustrations. In some countries these were in the shape of a star (not necessarily the star of David discussed previously), with a metal bowl attached underneath to hold any dripping oil.

Unfortunately, our manuscript illuminations do not allow any conclusions about the type of decoration used on such objects, since they are typically shown (including plates, pitchers and tableware) either gilt or in different colors.

More certain is the use of elaborate decoration for various ritual objects, both in the home and in the synagogue. Mention has already been made of embroidered Torah scroll covers, in Ashkenazic communities, or the gold or wooden cases in Muslim countries and in Spain. Also the "crowns" of silver or gold and the *rimonim* (pomegranate ornaments), of the same metals, which were placed on top of the rollers holding the scrolls. Some examples from medieval Spain have survived and indicate that the traditional design for these has remained unchanged to the present.

Cups used for the sanctification (*qidush*) of the Sabbath and holidays, filled with wine over which a blessing was recited at the evening meal, or for Passover, were also made of rich metals, or of pewter or even wood in poorer homes. These were often decorated with embossed designs and possibly some were even painted, at least so they appear in some German manuscripts. In Spain from the fourteenth century, and perhaps also in Italy, such cups and wine decanters were frequently made of glass, almost more valuable than gold or silver. Glass etching, of course, had not yet been invented, so that these objects were without decoration, although decanters had very graceful shapes.

The *havdalah* (separation) ceremony at the end of Sabbaths and holidays also required the recital of a blessing over a cup of wine, in addition to a special braided candle or perhaps oil lamps in some cases and spices (see Chapter 5 for a discussion of this). Both the candle holder, also often of precious metal, and the box that held the spices were decorated with various designs. Some medieval examples of these spice boxes have survived, the earliest of which is from thirteenth-century Spain, made of bronze in the form of a square tower with three levels and horseshoe-shaped windows (showing Muslim influence). Another from late fifteenth-century Italy is in gilded copper and is an imitation of a Christian reliquary.[9]

Special plates for use at the Passover *seder*, to hold the symbolic food items mentioned in the Hagadah, were also usually of precious metal. However, there is possibly one example from Spain (fifteenth century) that is of typical ceramic gold lusterware (the gold incorporated in the process of manufacture rather than painted on), with Hebrew lettering designating the various items on the plate. The authenticity of this plate, nevertheless, is in doubt.[10]

The *menorah*, or candelabrum for the holiday of Hanukkah, almost always with oil for the lights rather than candles, was of course another object for decoration. Since it is forbidden to copy the candelabrum used in the Temple, according to biblical descriptions, other forms were utilized. Particularly important is an example from Lyon, France (fourteenth century), triangular in shape with "rose windows" (such as found in churches) cut out in the metal backing. One from Spain, on the other hand, is in the form of a tray and made of ceramic.

Personal artistic expression included the embroidery or needlepoint designs made by women on tablecloths and linen covers for the Sabbath or holiday loves of bread, and in some European homes there were also wall paintings, even on the outside of the house in some cases. Unfortunately, no examples of any of this kind of art have survived and we know about such things only from brief mentions in written sources.

Jewelry for women and rings for both men and women were, of course, commonplace. Some information about the former can be gleaned from manuscript illustrations; however, although there were many skilled Jewish jewelers and craftsmen, particularly in Spain, there is no way of determining whether this jewelry was necessarily purchased from them or from Christian or Muslim craftsmen. The few rings that have survived from medieval Spain, on the other hand, have Hebrew lettering and other marks that indicate their Jewish origin. Some were mere decoration, whereas those worn by men served as signet rings with which to stamp and verify important letters or documents.

In several Jewish communities (Spain, Germany and other lands), important individuals as well as community councils also had seals, engraved with designs such as the moon and stars, the fleur-de-lis, a coat of arms and other symbols, along with Hebrew lettering indicating the name of the owner. Many such seals have survived and been described.[11]

JEWISH LITERATURE IN THE MIDDLE AGES

In addition to the fundamental obligations for every adult male to study at least the weekly Torah reading (and for those with sufficient learning, to study also the Aramaic translation, although later that was virtually replaced by the study of the commentary of Rashi), and for all but the most ignorant also the obligation—indeed, a rabbinical law—to study every day either the Mishnah or a section of the Talmud, there were also other forms of literature. Popular, of course, were various moral or ethical books, primarily those written by Spanish rabbis such as Jonah *Gerundi,* but also later in other countries, particularly the German *Sefer hasidim,* a peculiar mingling of laws, tales, and sometimes excessive moral instruction. Sermons, or homiletical interpretations of the Bible, while rarely preached in synagogues, were often written, and some individual sermons or collections became popular.[12]

However, we are interested here in another form of literature (in fact, what is generally understood by that term), secular stories or tales, including also proverbial or parable collections, and poetry. Furthermore, this literature is not restricted to Hebrew but includes that written in other languages.

The most important, and diverse, Hebrew literature was produced in Spain, as might be expected because the development of Hebrew grammar and lexicography began in Muslim Spain and continued throughout the Middle Ages, and because of the strong influence of Muslim culture, including literature and poetry.

Hebrew Literature in Spain

This influence was direct, the form known in Arabic as *maqama* and Hebrew as *maqamah,* which may have to do with sitting or, on the contrary, standing and referred to the oral recitation of tales in a group. This form of literature arose among the Muslims in the tenth century but became famous with the work of al-Hariri (1045–1122), which was translated into Hebrew by Judah al-Harizi of Toledo in the thirteenth century. He then composed his own *maqamah,* surpassing the model, which will be discussed later.

The first known work of this genre in Hebrew was written in the twelfth century by Solomon Ibn Saqbel, about whom little is known, including his place of residence, but obviously in al-Andalus. He initiated elements of the form, which were generally copied in all subsequent examples, including a parody of the "call" in a vision to biblical prophets. The hero of the story is thus "called" into action at the opening of the story, although the source of the call is not identified and is certainly not divine; we may assume it is the author himself. The other key element of such tales is found here also, the conflict or counterbalance between the protagonist (the hero) and an antagonist, usually a mythical character given an obscure biblical name. This work, *Noam Asher ben Yehudah* (Asher b. Yehudah speaks), like nearly all subsequent examples, is devoted to love and other pleasures and is interspersed with short poems that summarize the action or emotions of the hero up to that point. An absolute requirement of this form of literature, which distinguishes it from all other Hebrew literature, is that it is written in rhymed prose. This, too, is an imitation of the Arabic form.

The next example we have, which unlike the first has been completely preserved, is the most famous of all due to the fact that it has been translated into Catalan, English, and Castilian. This is *Sefer Sha'ashuim*, or *Book of Delights*, and was written not in Muslim Spain but in Christian Barcelona by Joseph Ibn Zabara, a physician, in the twelfth century.[13] It is not clear that he knew Ibn Saqbel's work at all, but his medical training means that he knew Arabic and was probably directly influenced by the Arabic model. It is a well-written collection of tales, which in fact holds together as a novella centered around the main characters of the protagonist and antagonist. While it is secular in nature, it also contains moral lessons and proverbs and in general lacks the humor and sophisticated eroticism of Ibn Saqbel's example, and later ones of this genre. While the work probably did not influence the famous *Libro de Buen Amor* of Juan Ruiz, as some have thought, one of the stories was certainly known and used by another famous medieval Spanish author, Juan Manuel, in his novel *Conde de Lucanor*. The English translation of the book is not entirely accurate, and written in an archaic style, but the Catalan and Castilian translations are quite good.

A very important work was written by Judah Ibn Shabetai, who lived in Toledo and also Zaragoza (both cities had been Muslim capitals and continued to have significant Muslim populations), also in the early twelfth century. This is *Minhat Yehudah* (the gift, or offering, of Judah), and is the first of the "wiles of women" motif, which was to become popular not only in Hebrew but also in other literature in later years. Far more humorous and in general better written than Ibn Zabara's work, and almost certainly influenced by Ibn Saqbel, it is more mildly erotic but makes fun of the deceitfulness of women in a humorous way. It is also the first work, perhaps the first in all medieval literature, in which the author openly enters the story himself and narrates events in the first person. It had a great influence on subsequent Hebrew literature, including Immanuel of Rome (discussed later).

However, there were those in Provence (at the time also part of Spain, but lacking the sophisticated secular culture) who took the book seriously as a criticism of women, shocking to Jewish sensibilities, and immediately wrote replies in defense of women.[14] While mere curiosities today, some are not entirely lacking in literary merit. In any event, the debate aroused a curiosity about this new form of literature also in Provence, and even important rabbis were soon seeking copies of some of the literary works from Spain.

As mentioned above, Judah al-Harizi wrote his own novella in this style, called *Tahkemoni* (a biblical word of uncertain meaning, perhaps also influenced by it being the name of the hero in Ibn Shabetai's book). It is the largest of any of the Hebrew examples, and is a strange combination of fiction and factual accounts of his own extensive travels, interspersed with poetry, and such things as chapters on the history of Hebrew poetry and important rabbis. There is also a considerable amount of moralizing in the work. While many of the stories are of literary merit, the work is also an important source for historians. It has been translated in English and Spanish (Castilian), the latter with a valuable introduction and notes.[15]

Hebrew adaptations, not literal translations, of the famous Barlaam and Joasaf story (ultimately of Indian origin, but best known in Byzantine literature), from the Arabic version, were also made in the thirteenth century. The most important of these, *Ben ha-melekh ve-ha-nazir* (The Prince and the Ascetic), is by Abraham Ibn Hasdai of Barcelona. While it is, again, a moralizing work, with many examples drawn from rabbinic (and Arabic) sources and even the Gospels, it also contains some original literary gems, such as the tale of the lust of a married woman for her slave. The popularity of this work is attested by the numerous editions throughout the years. There have been some bad German translations, and a modern one in Catalan.[16]

Jacob b. Elazar of Toledo, who was also a grammarian, translated the famous Arabic work *Kalila wa-Dimna* (also of Indian origin; translated into Persian and then Arabic, it influenced other Hebrew works). It is, again, also an adaptation rather than a literal translation. More of interest is his own original work, *Sefer meshalim* (Book of Proverbs, or stories), completely on erotic themes and written in excellent literary style. It is, in fact, the finest example of such literature and also far surpasses any of the Arabic examples. Nevertheless, it had a bad fate and was only rediscovered, and not entirely complete, in recent years.

By far the most popular example of such work is that of Isaac Ibn Sahulah (Gudalajara, 1281), *Meshal ha-qadmoni* (Parable of the Ancient One), which as previously noted was richly illustrated in all manuscripts and printed editions (the author himself at least indicated where such illustrations should be placed and perhaps drew his own examples). Numerous later works of this genre were produced by authors in the fourteenth and fifteenth centuries, when the literary center shifted from Castile to Catalonia. While some are not without merit, none of them approximate the quality of the earlier writings.

Hebrew Literature in Other Lands   While the importance for Jewish life of such things as legends or brief parables found in various collections of *midrashim* and the like cannot be denied, these do not constitute literature in the sense used here, entire fictitious narrative.[17] Even such collections of ethical tales as the work of Nissim b. Jacob Ibn Shahin of North Africa, originally in Arabic and translated into Hebrew as *Hibur yafeh me-ha-yeshuah* (Lovely [or important] composition of salvation), while very popular does not actually fall into the category of literature. There are also Hebrew versions of the stories of Alexander the Great, but again these belong to the area of legends.

However, the ever-popular fables or tales of Aesop (620–560 B.C.E.), which strongly influenced medieval literature in general, also found examples in Hebrew. At least two versions, again adaptations, have survived, derived from the Provençal vernacular versions, from the fourteenth and fifteenth centuries. An even more important example is a collection of "fox fables," or tales in which animals given human characteristics are the central figures, *Mishlei shu'alim* by the French writer and rabbi Berakhyah b. Natronai in the thirteenth century. While this is also a heavily moralistic collection, it is not lacking in literary style. It is possible that the author also drew upon versions of Aesop's fables (including probably an Arabic one), and very probably the adaptation, *Dits d'Ysop* by the twelfth-century author Marie de France.[18]

Another work, from Italy (1279), with some pretension to being called literature, is a Hebrew adaptation of the King Arthur stories, which actually had other Hebrew versions as well. Exaggerated claims have been made for the importance of these stories, without foundation,[19] rather than literature as such. The most important Hebrew work from medieval Italy, obviously influenced by the Spanish *maqamah* style, is by Immanuel b. Solomon of Rome (1265–1330), *Mahberet Immanuel* (Composition of Immanuel).[20] This work, in fact completely lacking in literary value, has been the subject of wild exaggeration, with claims made that the author is the "Hebrew Dante," no less.

True, he was personally acquainted with Dante, whom he hardly influenced, and on the contrary borrowed some aspects of Dante's *Inferno*, but any comparison is ridiculous. The book is completely a moralistic treatise, condemning to Inferno various writers and philosophers, both Greek and Jewish, of whom the author disapproved. On the other hand, and here the comparison is more legitimate, Immanuel achieved true excellence in his Italian sonnets, a form in which, as a Jew, he pioneered.

Problematic is the now well-known Hebrew version of the famous Sindibad tales, *Mishlei Sendebar,* carefully edited with a reliable English translation.[21] However, the claims of its editor that this Hebrew version is the original text of the stories is, of course, incorrect. In fact, those tales are of Indian origin, as I have elsewhere demonstrated, and became famous in general medieval literature as the "Seven Sages of Rome." The Hebrew version is probably an adaptation of a lost Arabic translation, with additions drawn from biblical and other sources.[22] It would be tempting to suggest Spain as the locale for this work, but the style of Hebrew is extremely simple and the work lacks the sophistication and wit typical of Hebrew literature of Spain. Thus, neither the place or date of its composition is known.

LITERATURE IN OTHER LANGUAGES

With the exception of the previously mentioned work of Nissim b. Jacob of North Africa, originally written in Arabic, we know of no Arabic (that is, written either in Arabic or Hebrew script) literature from Jews in the Middle Ages. This is actually surprising since for centuries almost all works written by Jews in Muslim lands, including Spain, was in "Judeo-Arabic" (Arabic in Hebrew script), and given the fact that popular Arabic literature was read and cited by Jewish writers in Spain, it is even more surprising that no such works were written by Jews.

Nor do we have any significant amount of literature written by Jews in the vernacular, except for Spain. Even there such work does not appear before the early fourteenth century (astronomical and other scientific treatises, of course, are not included here as literature). Jahuda Bonsenyor (d. 1331), the son of Astruch, official translator of Arabic for Jaime I of Aragon-Catalonia, and himself translator for two successive kings, Alfonso III and Jaime II, and physician to the royal family, wrote in Catalan the *Llibre de paraules e dits de savis e filosofos* ("Book of parables and sayings of the sages and philosophers") around 1305. He dedicated the work to Jaime II. It is drawn from a variety of sources, including Hebrew, and qualifies as literature only in the sense that some of the parables have literary motifs. The work has been edited and there is also a Castilian translation (1402) by Jacob Çadique of Ucles.[23]

The most famous Spanish-language work by a Jewish author is *Proverbios morales* (Moral proverbs) of Shem Tov de Càrrion (fl. 1350–1360). The author planned to dedicate the work to Alfonso XI of Castile, but when the king died the dedication was changed to his successor, Pedro I. The style, although often difficult, in fact is pure Castilian and of considerable literary merit. It became quite popular and was read and praised by Spanish nobles as late as the sixteenth century. There have been numerous editions and attempted translations (not entirely successful).[24] The same author wrote in Hebrew a debate between the pen and the scissors, as well as a liturgical poem.

POETRY

The Bible, of course, already contains a considerable amount of poetry, in addition to such obvious things as the Psalms. However, with some few exceptions in the Diaspora (chiefly in languages other than Hebrew), there was no secular poetry until the mid-tenth century, at the earliest. Muslims excelled in such verse in Arabic, and there also had been a long tradition of Persian poetry. Jews, particularly in Muslim Spain, were sensitive to the challenge of Arabic superiority over Hebrew because of this poetry and the Muslim claims as to the perfection of Arabic. Therefore, they responded on at least two different levels, the investigation (and in fact discovery) of Hebrew grammar, and the composition of secular poetry in Hebrew. This would not have been possible without a thorough knowledge of grammar, of course. Furthermore, this poetry originally was modeled on Arabic verse in that it borrowed both the meter and the motifs of that poetry.

The names of over 100 Hebrew poets of medieval Spain are known to us today, but only the poetry of a few of these has survived, although there are in some cases thousands of poems from an individual poet. This is the case with the first major poet, Samuel Ibn Naghrillah (993–1056), who was the prime minister and commander-in-chief of the Muslim city-kingdom of Granada, leading his troops in battle every year against other Berber troops who were enemies of Granada.[25] He was at the same time an important Jewish scholar and skilled in astronomy. He (or rather, his son, at his instruction) compiled three separate volumes of his poetry, named after biblical books: *Ben Tehilim* (Son of Psalms), *Ben Mishlei* (Son of Proverbs) and *Ben Qohelet* (Son of Ecclesiastes). Each book resembles in style and content the books after which they are named. Although there is some religious verse in the first, the majority of the poems are of a secular nature, about his battles, friendship, and songs of wine and love. The published editions of this poetry are large, with the total number of poems in the thousands.

Already in his poetry new meters, differing from the traditional Arabic ones, as well as new motifs were introduced. The quality of his style far surpassed that of any of the Arabic models. The following generation continued in this manner, with Solomon Ibn Gabirol (ca. 1021–1056/7), the famous philosopher, being the outstanding example.[26] While still young, at the age of 16, he was writing poems of significant quality. This was not in itself unusual, as we have many examples of poets who wrote at such an early age. One of his most significant poems, in some 400 verses (not all of which have survived), on Hebrew grammar was written at the age of 19. He is most known for his great mystical masterpiece, *Keter malkhut* (Crown of the kingdom), a long and beautiful poem that encompasses cosmological notions, philosophical and religious ideas, and deep mystical longing for union with God.[27] He was the author of numerous other religious poems, some of which were intended to be recited as part of Sabbath and holiday services and others for private devotional inspiration.[28] His secular poetry, very complex and highly sophisticated, often deals with his quest for wisdom and the conflict between the desire for pleasure and the attainment of intellectual perfection. Of a lighter nature are his many love and wine poems.

A contemporary of Ibn Gabirol was the slightly older Moses Ibn Ezrah of Granada (dates uncertain). He was the master poet of his generation, and indeed of all medieval Hebrew poets. He also composed religious poetry, intended for synagogue use, which earned him fame particularly as *the* poet of penitential, or confessional, poetry. While many of these poems continued to be recited in synagogues throughout the world to the modern period, unfortunately his real masterpieces, the secular poetry, were forgotten until their rediscovery in the nineteenth century.[29] This collection includes a separate book, *Anaq* or *Tarshish* (both words meaning *necklace*, referring to verses strung together), which is a series of usually short epigrams organized in "gates," or chapters, according to theme. He wrote on every theme common in Hebrew poetry, but particularly outstanding are his poems on nature and on love.

He was also the author of the only complete book on Hebrew poetics that has survived, although other writers devoted short treatises or a few remarks to the subject.[30] This book, written in Judeo-Arabic (Arabic in Hebrew letters), is a more or less detailed history of the development of Hebrew grammar as well as poetry. Individual poets are discussed and some poems, both Arabic and Hebrew, analyzed. Most important, however, is the complete analysis of the various rhetorical and thematic topics necessary for the composition of good poetry.

Judah ha-Levy (d. 1141), best known today for his philosophical (actually, anti-philosophical and polemical) work *Kuzari*, was also an important poet. Born and educated in Tudela, then a Muslim city, he was expert in Arabic and thoroughly acquainted with Arabic and Hebrew poetry. Like Ibn Gabirol and others, he had already written poetry as a teenager. He set out for Granada, to meet Ibn Ezrah but was temporarily prevented from completing his journey because of the wars between Christians and Muslims in Castile. He spent a few years in Toledo, where he was able to earn a living as a doctor. Ultimately, he got to Granada and became the protégé of the great poet.

He also wrote religious poetry. With some notable exceptions, his secular poetry is not of the same quality as that of his predecessors. He is best known, as a poet, for his "Zionide" poems, or poems praising the Land of Israel. Due to the Almoravid persecution in Spain, as well as his own intense longing, he decided to abandon his native country to live in the Holy Land. His fame as a poet had already spread to Egypt, however, and when he arrived there he was persuaded to remain for a year, during which period he continued to write the kind of secular poetry (especially love poems) that he had vowed to abandon after his commitment to his spiritual quest. Finally, however, he set out by ship for his destination, but the ship was lost in a storm and the poet never fulfilled his dream. His poems about the Land of Israel remained famous through the centuries, and the most important one in particular was translated into many languages.[31]

Abraham Ibn Ezra (ca. 1092–1167), the famous biblical commentator, scientist, and author of numerous works, was also born in Tudela.[32] He also was a poet of considerable skill, writing both religious and secular verse. His son Isaac, also a poet, married the daughter of Judah ha-Levy and accompanied him on his journey to Egypt but went on to Baghdad, where he apparently converted to Islam, although he later repented and returned to his former faith. If it is uncertain that we have all or even most of the poems of Ibn Gabirol or Moses Ibn Ezrah, it is absolutely certain that very little of Ibn Ezra's secular poetry has survived. This may be due to the fact that when he left Spain due to the uncertain conditions under the Almoravids, as did ha-Levy, he left all of his books behind, and this may have included his poetry. As a result, only a small amount of the secular poems have survived. His religious poetry, just as certainly the introductory poems to various biblical commentaries and other works, probably were written during his extensive travels in North Africa, Italy, France, and allegedly even England. A notable aspect of his secular verse, and an indication of what we may be missing, is humor and parody. While not lacking in other poetry, particularly that of Ibn Gabirol, the sharp wit of some of Ibn Ezra's verses is remarkable.

There were numerous other poets in the Muslim era in Spain, as well as those who continued the tradition following the Christian reconquest of most of southern Spain, culminating in the late thirteenth century. Poets such as the aforementioned Judah al-Harizi of Toledo and others merit comparison with the earlier poets. However, the tradition deteriorated into mere literary imitation, since much of the way of life in Muslim society that had inspired the poets had changed. The extensive poetry of Todros Abulafia (b. 1247), for example, while of a high quality, is not convincing in its themes of love and even in praise of wine. In his poems, these appear to be conventional literary motifs rather than reflective of real personal experience or conviction.

In the following centuries, the focus of poetic creativity switched from southern to northern Spain, chiefly to Aragon. Zaragoza, Huesca, and even smaller communities produced important Hebrew poets throughout the fourteenth and fifteenth centuries. If this poetry is also at times somewhat conventional, it nevertheless shows that the interest in proper use of Hebrew and in creativity in verse was not confined to the more sophisticated southern region.

An interesting byproduct of the generally cordial relations between Christians and Jews in medieval Spain is that some Christians learned Hebrew, whether from Jewish teachers or at one of the monastic schools. Some of these Christians, again in Aragon, actually exchanged Hebrew poetry with Solomon de Piera (d. after 1417), an important poet. One of these whom he mentions was the renowned don Juan Fernandez de Ixar, overlord of that town (Hijar) and whose collection of Spanish poetry (his and others) has survived and been published. Unfortunately, it appears that his Hebrew poetry has not survived.

Arabic and Hebrew poetry in Muslim Spain also has a unique genre known as *muwashshah* (plural, *muwashshahat*), or strophic poetry in which the final rhymed couplet (*kharja*) is in Romance, in the case of an Arabic poem, or Arabic or mixed Arabic and Romance in the case of a Hebrew poem.[33] These poems began to appear in the tenth century, and while considered vulgar and objectionable by Muslim theorists and by Jewish authorities like Maimonides, they were popular both among Muslims and Jews.

Muwashshah Poetry— a Special Style

In fact, the Hebrew examples far outnumber the Arabic ones, and the genre has become the subject of an amazing amount of scholarly debate due to the fact that these poems represent the earliest known written forms of Romance (i.e., Spanish). Nevertheless, there has been more heat than light generated in these discussions, and one of the problems is that there has not yet been a thorough study of all the extant Hebrew versions. Nearly all of the well-known Hebrew poets composed examples of this kind of poetry. Its popularity continued beyond the Muslim period in Spain, with examples being found in the poetry of Todros Abulafia and others (not, however, in the poetry from Aragon).

The commonly accepted theory is that the final couplet of such poems is a quotation from a popular song, the rhyme (and meter) of which determine that of the rest of the poem. Such a theory may (or may not) fit the Arabic models, but certainly not the Hebrew ones, in which, as stated, the final couplet may be either in Arabic or in Romance or very often a combination of the two. Clearly these cannot be quotations from popular songs.

Some earlier writers claimed, erroneously, that there was a courtier class, or aristocratic group of Hebrew poets in al-Andalus. Nothing could be further from the truth. With the exception of Ibn Naghrillah, none of the Hebrew poets fits such a description. Many (Ibn Gabirol, ha-Levy, Ibn Ezra and others) were actually quite poor and from undistinguished family backgrounds. Nor was the audience for these poems aristocratic. On the contrary, the poetry became immediately popular throughout the Jewish population, and not only in al-Andalus and other Muslim areas of Spain,

Popularity of Hebrew Poetry

but later in Christian Spain as well, including Aragon and Catalonia. There were also some Hebrew poets in Provence (then a part of Spain). The popularity of such outstanding poets as Ibn Gabirol and ha-Levy extended in their lifetimes to North Africa, Egypt, and even distant Yemen, where their poems were copied and circulated soon after they were written.

That people read this poetry, not only heard it recited orally (although that may also have taken place), is attested by its quotation in ordinary correspondence and in scholarly books. There is no doubt that this aided significantly in educating the Jewish public in proper Hebrew grammar and style. Important, too, is the fact that some of the poems, particularly love poems, were addressed to the poet's beloved, and thus obviously they were able to read and understand the often very complex Hebrew verse.

Hebrew Poetry in Other Lands Once the Spanish Jewish poets had created the genre, it was imitated, with more or less success, also in other Muslim countries. Already in the eleventh century one of the greatest of Jewish scholars, Hai (Hayey) *Gaon*, head of the talmudic academy in Baghdad and an important legal scholar, wrote secular Hebrew poetry of very good quality, including a poem in praise of Ibn Naghrillah.

Some secular Hebrew verse from Egypt has survived, and important also is the Hebrew poetry of members of the Qaraite sect (Jewish heretics who believed only in following the literal interpretation of the Bible and who denied the authority of all rabbinical tradition).[34] This poetry clearly shows the influence of Spanish Hebrew poetry. The poetry of Moses Ibn Ezrah served as the model for that of another important scholar, Joseph b. Tanhum *ha-Yerushalmi* (the Jerusalemite, born ca. 1262) who also lived in Egypt.

Judah ha-Levy's Zionist poetry was widely read, in particular his most famous one, "Zion, do you not seek," which was imitated in many religious and secular poems in other lands. The popularity of Ibn Gabirol's poetry, especially, in Yemen suggests the possibility that some Hebrew poetry may also have been written there in the medieval period.

Some few examples of Hebrew secular poetry from Italy, especially Sicily, are known, and there were even at least two poets in England whose work has survived. Hebrew poetry in Germany and France, and some other lands, continued to be strictly religious, however; particularly dirges on various calamities and persecutions.

Poetry in Other Languages As mentioned, there is very little Jewish literature in general in Arabic from the medieval period, and none in Persian that has survived (there were, however, Judeo-Persian—Persian written in Hebrew letters—poetic paraphrases of the Bible in the fourteenth century). However, there were some Jewish poets who wrote Arabic verse in al-Andalus, including poets who were considered to be the equal of or even superior to Muslim poets. Most of these are known only by name, but a few examples of the poetry of some have been preserved.

There was also at least one woman, among the several Muslim women poets, Qasmuna, the daughter of Ismail Ibn Baghdalah. She certainly was not, as mistakenly claimed by one writer and now popularly believed, the daughter of the aforementioned Samuel Ibn Naghrillah (whose only daughter died long before Qasmuna lived).[35] She is, however, the only example of a medieval Jewish woman poet whose poetry has survived. There is one Hebrew poem attributed to the daughter of Judah ha-Levy, but this is probably legend. We have to wait for the Renaissance period before again encountering Jewish women who wrote Hebrew poetry (see, however, the discussion further on about a woman who wrote in German).

Some important Jewish scholars in Muslim Spain wrote Arabic verse (indeed, we know that Ibn Naghrillah was one of these), such as Isaac Ibn Baron, a Hebrew grammarian (ca. 1100) and Abraham Ibn al-Fakhkhar (d. ca. 1240), an important rabbi and ambassador of Alfonso VII to North Africa. Saadyah Ibn Danan, rabbi of Granada (d. after 1505, in North Africa), is the last of the Jewish poets who wrote Arabic verse. He also wrote a brief treatise on poetics and was the author of a chronicle and of some responsa (answers to questions on Jewish law), all in Hebrew.

Ibrahim Ibn Sahl of Seville (d. ca. 1251/52) is the only one whose Arabic verse has survived in complete, or nearly complete, form. It was claimed that late in his life he converted to Islam, but it is difficult to know whether this is true.

Interesting are several poems apparently of the fifteenth century written in Judeo-Maltese (the Maltese dialect of Arabic, written in Hebrew script). These include some love poetry and satirical verses on wine. Since Malta was then under the control of Sicily, and thus part of Spain, the existence of such poetry is less surprising.[36]

There is also some secular poetry in Aramaic, including some by Ibn Naghrillah and at least one by Ibn Gabirol. Religious poems, or those intended for recitation in the synagogue, were also sometimes written in Aramaic, but as this became increasingly a language poorly understood, or not at all, this was abandoned.

An interesting person about whom little is actually known is the Jewish *minnesinger*, or troubadour, Suesskind von Trimberg (Bohemia) in the thirteenth century. He was a kind of wandering minstrel, well rewarded at courts for his recitation of his (German) poetry. He is portrayed dressed in an ermine trimmed cloak and luxurious clothing, but nevertheless with the typical Jewish hat. Only six of his poems have survived, on generally moral themes but not specifically Jewish. There may have been other Jewish poets who wrote German verse that has not survived. A woman, Litte of Regensburg, wrote a lengthy poem about David (still in manuscript).[37] She may perhaps be the same as "Liwa" of Regensburg (fifteenth century) who translated the biblical book of Samuel in German. Although Yiddish began to make its appearance in the medieval period, there is no poetry or literature from that time.

There are some examples of Romance poetry written by Jews. Moses Natan's Hebrew poem on chess was translated (ca. 1350) into Castilian, possibly by the poet himself. Moses Ibn Zarzar, physician of Enrique III, wrote a Spanish poem celebrating the birth in 1405 of the infant Juan, who would rule as Juan II. The style is adequate if not particularly outstanding. Solomon de Piera, an important Hebrew poet of the fifteenth century, mentions exchanging some poetry in Catalan with another poet, although none of this has survived. There is, however, some Catalan verse from Astruch Rimokh in correspondence with de Piera; Astruch later converted to Christianity.[38] The most important, and complete,

The Jews: Joshua, David, and Judas Maccabee. Burgkmair, Hans the Elder (c. 1473–c. 1553). Foto Marburg/Art Resource, NY.

work in Castilian is the *Coplas de Yoçef* (fifteenth century); actually, a rare example of Judeo-Spanish, since it is written in Hebrew characters. While significant from a linguistic point of view, the long poem is actually only a tedious retelling of the biblical story of Joseph.[39]

In addition to poems originally written in the vernacular, there were also some translations; for example, translations or adaptations (usually) of Arabic verse by Hebrew poets such as ha-Levy. Several *piyutim,* or liturgical poems, were translated in French, German, and Italian as well as Castilian and Catalan. Most, or all, of these are prose translations except for two Italian and six French translations, which are in rhyme.[40]

MUSIC IN JEWISH LIFE

Music has been a central part of Jewish life from biblical times to the present. Temple musicians and singers are mentioned in the Bible, as well as various musical instruments. Following the destruction of the Second Temple and the exile under the Romans, the rabbis prohibited the use of musical instruments as used in the Temple and the playing of any music except for celebrations such as weddings, because Jews are supposed to be in mourning over the loss of the Temple. Nevertheless, the singing of certain parts of the Sabbath and holiday prayers was permitted, and gradually this evolved into more and more elaborate forms and even the hiring of a special cantor (*hazan*) whose voice had to be pleasant and who often created new melodies in addition to the traditional ones; just as in some modern synagogues where the melodies of popular songs have been used, so in some medieval synagogues, as we hear from complaints to rabbinical authorities about the practice.[41]

In addition to the restrictions on the use of instruments, there is a talmudic prohibition against listening to the voice of a woman singing (for fear of erotic arousal), which was reinforced by a famous responsum from Maimonides, who also ruled that one may not listen to popular Arabic songs and particularly not to the kind of vulgar poetry (*muwashshahat*) mentioned earlier.[42]

Musical instruments were also sometimes played on the Sabbath, as mentioned in other chapters here, in spite of the prohibition on this, and were used at weddings and other community celebrations. We have no idea where the Jewish musicians, particularly in Germany, received their instruction or whether, more likely, they were self-taught. From at least one rabbinical source we see that some musicians, at least, did receive training from Gentiles. In addition to instruments, there were also special singers for such celebrations. In Germany, singers ate fresh eggs and various kinds of spices to sweeten their voices.

There are several sources referring to Jews playing instruments in Spain. Jews welcomed monarchs, such as Alfonso VII (1126–1157), when they visited a city, as we hear again with Fernando and Isabel in the fifteenth century, with the playing of instruments and drums. The psaltery was played by Jews at the rejoicing of Alfonso VII's victory over the Muslims in 1137, and again at the coronation of Alfonso XI in 1332. What exactly this instrument was is uncertain, but likely some kind of hand-held harp or stringed instrument. There were also professional Jewish musicians, at least one in the paid service of a king (Pedro III of Aragon-Catalonia), and we hear of several individual musicians hired by Pedro IV to accompany him and play for him. In fact, there were several Jewish musicians in the service of various kings. Fernando I of Aragon-Catalonia in 1415 sent his Jewish musician, Abraham Violant, to France for further study.

Juan Ruiz of Castile (fourteenth century), in his famous *Libro de Buen Amor* (Book of good love), wrote of Muslim and Jewish (male) singers for whom he had composed songs.[43]

Spanish Jews composed songs also in Spanish, and some few have survived, although not the original music. It is possible, but uncertain, that some of the later Sefardic songs and melodies may have been handed down from medieval tradition.

In Italy, even prior to the Renaissance, there was great interest in music. Nevertheless, there is little information about Jews and music until the late fifteenth century. The Jewish dancing master Guglielmo *ebreo*, who served at the courts of the renowned Sforza and d'Este families in Lombardy, composed a treatise on dancing that includes musical notation.

NOTES

1. For details, in brief, on these laws, see the article "Art, Jewish," in Norman Roth, ed., *Medieval Jewish Civilization: An Encyclopedia* (New York, 2003), 37–38, 47.

2. Examples of some secular manuscript illustration are discussed, ibid., 48–50.

3. Discussion of these and other German manuscripts, ibid., 42–43.

4. See Ulf Haxen, *Kings and Citizens* (New York, 1983), 2 vols. (paper), an illustrated catalogue of a Jewish Museum exhibit on the Jews of Denmark, including manuscripts of the royal collection.

5. See Vivian B. Mann, ed., *Gardens and Ghettos* (Berkeley, Calif., 1989), a catalogue of an exhibit at the Jewish Museum (N.Y.) on Italian Jewish life. Further details on particular manuscripts are in Roth, *Medieval Jewish Civilization*.

6. See especially Stanley Ferber, "Micrography: A Jewish Art Form," *Journal of Jewish Art* 3–4 (1977): 12–24. Examples mentioned in the following paragraph here are discussed in further detail in Roth, *Medieval Jewish Civilization*.

7. S. D. Goitein, *Sidrey ḥinukh biy-mey ha-geoniym* (Jerusalem, 1962), 42–43.

8. See Roth, *Medieval Jewish Civilization*, 49–50 for additional bibliographical references.

9. See Roth, ibid., 51 and bibliography there.

10. Ibid.

11. See details in the article "Seals" in Roth, ibid., with bibliography.

12. Information on all these topics may be found in Roth, ibid.; see also the index there.

13. *The Book of Delight* (sic), tr. Moses Hadas (New York, 1932); *Llibre d'Ensenyaments Delictables*, trans. (from the Hebrew) Ignasi Gonzalez-Llubera (Barcelona, 1931); *Libro de los Entremientos*, trans. Maria Forteza-Rey (Madrid, 1983).

14. There are no translations in any language either of Ibn Shabetai's work or of the rebuttals, but they are discussed in Norman Roth, "The 'Wiles of Women' Motif in the Medieval Hebrew Literature of Spain," *Hebrew Annual Review* 2 (1978): 145–65.

15. *The Tahkemoni*, trans. Victor E. Reichert (Jerusalem, 1965, 1973), 2 vols., including also the author's other poetry; *Las Asambleas de los Sabios (Tahkemoni)*, trans. Carlos del Valle Rodríguez (Murcia, 1988). This is also discussed briefly in Roth, "Wiles of Women."

16. *El principe i el Monjo*, trans. T. Calders (Sabadell, 1987).

17. See Joseph Dan's insightful article "Literature, Hebrew, Europe and the Mediterranean" (excluding Spain and Italy), in Roth, *Medieval Jewish Civilization*, particularly p. 405.

18. See the editor's insertions in the above-cited article, pp. 406, 407–8. In addition to Hebrew editions, there is also an English translation, *Fables of a Jewish Aesop*, trans. Moses Hadas (New York, 1967).

19. *King Artus, a Hebrew Arthurian Romance of 1279*, ed. and trans. Curt Leviant (New York, 1969).

20. English translation as *Tophet and Eden*, trans. Hermann Gollancz (London, 1921); most recent edition of the Hebrew text, as *Mahberot* (sic), ed. Dov Jarden (Jerusalem, 1957; reprinted 1984). The first edition was published in Brescia (Italy) in 1491.

21. *Tales of Sendebar*, ed. and trans. Morris Epstein (Philadelphia, 1967). See on it Roth "Wiles of Women."

22. See briefly my discussion of this in "Wiles of Women."

23. The Catalan text, *Llibre de paraules e dits de savis e filosofos*, ed. Gabriel Llabres y Quintana (Palma de Mallorca, 1889); the Castilian translation, *Libro de dichos de sabios e filosophos*, in *Cancionero de Juan Fernandez de Ixar*, ed. J.M. Azaceta (Madrid, 1956) 2: 628–60, and an important new Castilian translation, Libro de palabras y dichos de sabios y filósofos, by Jose Ramon Magdalena Nom de Deu (Barcelona, 1990).

24. For example, *Proverbios morales*, ed. Sanford Shepard (Madrid, 1985), and ed. Theodore A. Perry (Madison, Wisc., 1986). *The Moral Proverbs of Santob de Carrión*, trans. T. A. Perry (Princeton, N.J., 1992).

25. See the article on him in Roth, *Medieval Jewish Civilization*, with bibliography. Details of his career, and translations of excerpts of some of his poetry, may be found in Roth, *Jews, Visigoths & Muslims in Medieval Spain: Cooperation & Conflict* (Leiden, 1994), p. 89 ff. Some recent writings on him, by Ross Brann, Hava Lazarus-Yafeh, and various articles by David J. Wasserstein are without value.

26. See the article "Ibn Gabirol, Solomon" in Roth, ibid.

27. There are numerous editions, as well as translations in many languages. In English, *The Kingly Crown*, trans. and annotated by Bernard Lewis (London, 1961) is the best, despite the erroneous title and some mistakes in translation.

28. A few of these have been translated into English, generally accurately, as Ibn Gabirol, *Selected Religious Poems*, ed. I. Davidson and trans. I. Zangwill

(Philadelphia, 1923; reprinted New York, 1973 and Philadelphia, 1973 [paper ed.]). This also contains Zangwill's moving and spiritual translation of *Keter malkhut.*

29. Only a very small selection of his poetry, religious and secular, has been translated into English: Moses Ibn Ezra(h), *Selected Poems,* tr. Solomon Solis-Cohen (Philadelphia, 1945); the translations are not always accurate, but there is a good general introduction by Haim Brody, the editor of his collected poems in Hebrew. Some other poems have been translated and discussed by Roth; see the bibliography at the end of the article "Poetry, Hebrew" in Roth, *Medieval Jewish Civilization,* and further details in the article "Ibn Ezra(h), Moses" there.

30. *Sefer ha-iyunim ve-ha-diyunim* (*Kitab al-muhadara wa'l-mudhakra*), ed. and trans. (Hebrew, modern) by Abraham S. Halkin (Jerusalem, 1975). The translation is not always correct; there is a generally better Spanish translation, with the text edited in Arabic letters, *Kitab al-muhadara wa'l-mudhakra,* ed. and trans. Montserrat Abumalham Mas (Madrid, 1986) in two volumes. All of the other statements on poetics by medieval Jewish writers, published over the years in often rare books, have been gathered and edited with Spanish translations by Carlos del Valle Rodríguez in his splendid edition and translation of Dunash Ibn Labrat, the first known Hebrew poet, *El Divan Poetica* (Madrid, 1988).

31. Some, but not all, are also in the short collection of Judah ha-Levy, *Selected Poems,* trans. Nina Salaman (Philadelphia, 1928), with translations of uneven quality. There are better translations of some of his poems in Spanish anthologies. See further details in the article "Judah ha-Levy" in Roth, *Medieval Jewish Civilization,* with bibliography.

32. See the article on him in Roth, ibid. Virtually none of his poetry, secular or religious, has been translated.

33. Important anthologies include: Joseph Sola-Sole, ed., *Corpus de poesia mozarabe* (Barcelona, 1973); Alan Jones, ed., *Romance Kharjas in Andalusian Arabic Muwassah Poetry* (London, 1988); and F. Corriente and A. Sáenz Badillos, eds., *Poesía estrófica* (Madrid, 1991). As mentioned, there is a vast amount of secondary literature on the subject. On the Hebrew examples, some work has been done by Israeli scholars. Fundamental is Samuel M. Stern, *Hispano-Arabic Strophic Poetry* (Oxford, 1974), which deals with some of the Hebrew and Arabic poems, although it is incomplete and of course outdated.

34. See the article "Qaraites" in Roth, *Medieval Jewish Civilization,* with bibliography.

35. See details, briefly, in the article "Poetry in Other Languages" in Roth, *Medieval Jewish Civilization,* p. 518.

36. Godfrey Wettinger, "Late Medieval Juadeo-Arabic Poetry in Vatican Ms. 411: Links with Maltese and Sicilian Arabic," *Journal of Maltese Studies* 13 (1979): 1–16.

37. Leopold Zunz, *Zur Geschichte und Literatur* (Berlin, 1895; photo reprint Hildesheim, 1976), 173.

38. See details in Roth, *Medieval Jewish Civilization,* p. 521.

39. Originally published in 1935, transcribed in Latin characters, it was edited in the original Hebrew script by Moshé Lazar, *Poema de Yosef, Joseph and His Brethren: Three Ladino Versions* (Culver City, Calif., 1990); the work is not, technically speaking, "Ladino," however. Lazar previously translated the work into English in his *The Sephardic* [sic] *Tradition* (New York, 1972), pp. 77–119.

40. See Roth, *Medieval Jewish Civilization,* p. 521 and bibliography.

41. For this and what follows, see further details in the article "Music" in Roth, ibid, and the bibliography.

42. The responsum on music is well known and has been frequently published and discussed (see the bibliography in the article "Music" in Roth, *Medieval Jewish Civilization*, p. 471). I first discovered the text dealing with *muwashshahah* poetry, in the original Judeo-Arabic text, and published a translation of it in my *Maimonides: Essays and Texts* (Madison, Wisc., 1985), pp. 52–56 (see pp. 54–55). That scholars hitherto have overlooked this is an indication of the danger of relying on Hebrew translations instead of the original texts.

43. Usually mistranslated as "girls" instead of men; see details in Roth, *Medieval Jewish Civilization*, p. 467.

RECOMMENDED READING

Guttmann, Joseph. *Hebrew Manuscript Painting*. New York, 1978. Illustrated.

Metzger, *Jewish Life in the Middle Ages*. Seacaucus, N.J., 1982.

Narkiss, Bezalel. *Hebrew Illuminated Manuscripts*. Jerusalem, 1969. In English, color illustrations.

Roth, Norman, ed. *Medieval Jewish Civilization: An Encyclopedia*. New York, 2003.

Roth, Norman. "The 'Wiles of Women' Motif in the Medieval Hebrew Literature of Spain," *Hebrew Annual Review* 2 (1978): 145–65.

9

THE DANGERS OF BEING JEWISH

The life of a Jew in any age has not always been easy or pleasant. From ancient times to the present there have been, and continue to be, people who hate Jews. In the ancient world, enemies of the Jews included the Egyptians (long after the exodus), some Greeks and the Hellenized Syrians, and many Romans. It would not, of course, be correct to characterize all or even a majority of these peoples as anti-Jewish. The reasons for such hatred are many. Probably the best answer is found in the biblical book of Esther, the words of Haman to the king: "There is one people scattered and dispersed among all the people ... and their laws are different from all people" (Esther 3.8). In other words, the Jews were different, in customs and in beliefs. It is interesting to note that the brief Hebrew account of the attempt (which ultimately failed) by Robert II "the Pious" of France in 1007 to compel the Jews of his kingdom to convert also paraphrases this statement, allegedly when the king was told "there is one people scattered in all the cities and they do not listen to us and their laws and Torah [or observances] are different than [those of] all the people."[1] If we are to believe the somewhat stylized Hebrew account, several Jews were killed in this affair.

We must distinguish this ancient, and persistent, distrust and dislike of Jews from "anti-Semitism," which is a modern racial theory that emerged in the late nineteenth century. According to this, the Jews (for the term refers *only* to Jews) are a racially inferior people whose very presence has corrupted the "pure" Christian "race." Modern scientists, of course, dismiss any such nonsense. Even this theory, however, did have its medieval antecedent, in the perverse doctrine of "purity of blood" in fifteenth-century Spain, used by some bigoted "old Christians" to attack the "new Christians," or converted Jews. In spite of the fully substantiated devout Christian nature of these converts, some despised them and were jealous of their growing power and influence and saw this as the only way in which to destroy them. The result was the infamous Inquisition, which persecuted and killed thousands of these converts and their descendants and lasted for centuries throughout the Spanish world.[2] Note carefully, though, and this is an important distinction that many have failed to make, that this was applied *only* to Jewish converts to Christianity (*conversos*) and never to Jews as such.

Many other Jewish writers have claimed that anti-Semitism has antecedents not in this isolated example of Spain but in all of the medieval Christian hostile attitudes towards Jews.[3] I prefer to distinguish between anti-Semitism, the racist theory, whether of fifteenth-century Spain or the modern period, and what others have termed "anti-Jewish sentiment." The latter, present throughout history in greater or lesser degree, may be the result of certain myths or stereotypes about the Jews (as in the Hellenistic and Roman periods, and frequently thereafter) or religious differences, or economic and social jealousy.

Further, within the Christian manifestation of this, we must distinguish between "anti-*Judaism*" and anti-*Jewish*; that is, between essentially theological disagreements with official Jewish teachings, naturally repugnant to Christianity, and hatred of or attacks against Jews.[4] These are distinctions rarely made by current Jewish writers. Semantically, the problem lies in the area where such feelings crossed over into actions against Jews, including murder. While not technically anti-Semitic, in that they were not racially motivated, there is little doubt that they were inspired both by prevailing anti-Jewish sentiment and official Christian anti-Judaism. To the Jews when they were being robbed, beaten, forcibly baptized, raped, and murdered, such distinctions would have mattered very little.

The first part of this chapter discusses the general attacks on Jews, such as the Crusades, and myths concerning these, and expulsions of the Jews. The second part considers the personal safety of Jews and various more-or-less continual dangers they faced as individuals.

MYTHS AND MISCONCEPTIONS ABOUT CHRISTIAN ATTITUDES

Countless books and articles have been written over the years in an effort to explain both medieval anti-Jewish sentiment and modern anti-Semitism, largely without success.[5] To blame either of these phenomena on Christianity, or the Church, is a grave mistake, although this has been the attitude of many Jewish writers. In the first place, as noted, hostility towards Jews predated Christianity by centuries. Secondly, while it is true that some medieval Christian writers and theologians, as well as popes, expressed extremely negative attitudes, the official position of the church remained constant:

Jews must be preserved as "witnesses to the truth of Christianity" (first expressed by St. Augustine), and they must not be forcibly baptized and must be protected until the final coming of Christ when they will all convert.

From Pope Gregory I (590–604) through the end of the Middle Ages and beyond, every pope issued the famous *Constitutio pro judaeis* bull protecting the status of the Jews.[6] The medieval popes, of course, maintained an official position of anti-*Judaism,* but even while some of them also wrote virulently anti-*Jewish* statements they also recognized their responsibility to protect the Jews as far as it was in their power to do so. When the notorious badge legislation of the Fourth Lateran (Church) Council was enacted in 1215, requiring all Jews to wear some distinguishing sign to make them easily recognizable, Innocent III nevertheless wrote to all the archbishops and bishops of France that Jews must not be forced to wear something that would endanger their lives.[7]

Another aspect of this error is to refer to "the Church," as if this were a monolithic entity. It is not, of course; rather it is a theological (and legal) *concept.* When discussing the medieval Christian attitude toward and treatment of Jews, it is therefore necessary to distinguish several separate elements: the popes, canon law, theologians, archbishops and bishops, monastic and mendicant orders, and local clergy.[8]

Yet another thing that needs to be considered, and rarely has been, is the difference between medieval and modern access to polemical writings, theological works, and even legal codes or papal letters. The modern scholar has available an enormous and more or less efficiently organized **Availability of Books and Illiteracy** library containing virtually the whole of the written works of the world. Modern technology adds to this the Internet (for example, the entire collection of medieval Latin Christian theological and religious sources is available online).

However, in the Middle Ages all works were, of course, in manuscript and relatively few copies were made. Christian libraries, mostly monastic, were small and poorly organized, although some individual Jews in medieval Spain had larger personal libraries than even the most important of these Christian collections. Written works of any kind simply were not disseminated, or at least not to any significant extent. Another factor was widespread illiteracy. In the early medieval period, even some kings were illiterate, and illiteracy continued on a massive scale throughout the Middle Ages. Thus, few Christians, and even fewer Jews (who in any case could not read Latin), ever saw the books that are so easily accessible today. Thus, many of the harsh polemical attacks were unknown, or very little known, to anyone except their authors. Only in fifteenth-century

Spain, for example, do we encounter evidence of some Jewish awareness of such Christian polemic. There are isolated earlier examples from
Germany.

Jews as "Killers of Christ" An important example of why this is necessary to consider has to do with the often asserted claim that Jews in the Middle Ages were accused of "deicide," the killing of Christ. Indeed, it is safe to say that there is hardly a Jewish scholar (to say nothing of the public) who does not take this as a given. Yet it is false, or at least based on misinformation. A careful examination of all the Christian sources (biblical commentaries, theological writings, polemical literature) from St. Jerome throughout the medieval period reveals that those who made this accusation can be counted on the fingers of one hand, and this includes the many instances where it was applied not to contemporary Jews but to those living at the time of Jesus.

Many medieval Christian writers either made no statement of blame at all or blamed, correctly, the Romans, or allegorically, all of humanity. Of those few who did accuse the Jews, the most vitriolic statements were written in Greek, a language unknown in the medieval period outside of the Byzantine empire. Thus, what impact did these and other obscure writings have on the general population? Obviously, absolutely none whatever. True, the passion plays so popular in late medieval Germany (and in rare cases elsewhere) often did depict Jews as participating in the crucifixion, and the hysteria of the mobs sometimes led to attacks on Jews as a result. This was to become more of a problem in the post-medieval periods than in the Middle Ages, however. There were sometimes attacks on Jews during the Christian Holy Week, as a result of which laws were frequently enacted requiring Jews to remain indoors during this period; nor do we usually know what local preachers may have said in their sermons, when such were preached at all (a rarity). ·

PHYSICAL ATTACKS ON JEWS

Jews enjoyed peace and harmony with their Christian neighbors in France and Germany, and elsewhere, until the beginning of the eleventh century. Around 1007–1012, a few incidents of attacks on Jews, efforts at forced conversion, and the like began to occur. Why the sudden change? While no single answer is sufficient, it seems apparent that the most important factor was the rumor that reached Christian Europe at that time that the half-mad caliph of Egypt, al-Hakam II, had destroyed the Church of the Holy Sepulcher in Jerusalem. In fact, this was not true, although he had given orders to destroy churches and synagogues throughout his territories. It was this rumor that served as the cause for the infamous First Crusade.

Even a casual reading of medieval Christian polemical literature, as well as some legal sources, shows that there was a connection made between Muslims and Jews as "enemies of the faith." The distinction usually was that the former were real enemies, or perceived as such, against whom Christians must fight, while the Jews were a "theological" enemy. However, when rumors of the destruction of Christianity's most holy site reached Europe, this aroused harsh anti-Jewish attitudes as well. Indeed, this is found also almost unanimously in the Hebrew chronicles of the attacks on the Jews of Germany in the First Crusade. Christians on their way to the distant Holy Land to slaughter infidel Muslims noted that there were infidel Jews immediately at hand, and why not slaughter them first?

Unquestionably this was the most serious attack on northern European Jews, primarily in Jewish communities along the Rhine in Germany, but secondarily in other areas as far removed as Bohemia. These events have been repeatedly reported by Jewish, and a few non-Jewish, historians from the nineteenth century to the present.[9] Nevertheless, there has been considerable exaggeration about the severity of these attacks, carried out primarily by gangs of lower-class individuals and criminals released from prison on condition that they join the Crusade (the nature of which they no doubt understood but poorly) and somehow make their way to an almost mythical Holy Land.

The Jews in Germany enjoyed considerable autonomy and privileges. Bishop Rudiger of Speyer in 1084 had invited Jews to settle there to "enhance the glory" of his city, and they were protected (against the "impudence" of the rabble, as he himself said) by a wall. In 1090, the Jews of Speyer and Worms had been taken under the direct protection of the emperor, Henry IV. However, in 1096, in spite of the emperor's promise to protect the Jews of Mainz and Cologne, the rabble attacked those communities. Bishop Rudiger took the Jews into his own castle to protect them and had the hands of some of the crusaders (that is, the rabble) cut off. Nevertheless, 11 Jews died.

In neighboring Worms, no one came to the aid of the Jews; as one Hebrew source says, Christians did not wish to fight Christians to save Jews (almost identical language is found, in fact, in a Christian source). Many Jews were killed (certainly not the entire population). In Cologne and other cities, Jews took shelter in the homes of Christian neighbors. The archbishop of Cologne sent Jews also to various surrounding villages where they were protected. The archbishop of Mainz also protected the Jews, but to little avail since they were attacked. They defended themselves until overwhelmed by superior numbers. Even in Prague, where there were also attacks, the bishop protected the Jews.[10] These facts, and many others, are often forgotten by those writers who wish to blame the Church, and Christianity in general, for what they call anti-Semitism.

Nor must we accept at face value the exaggerated numbers of those killed, vague as they are, given by the late Hebrew sources. That as many as 3,000 Jews were killed (as Chazan suggests) is not believable; there could not have been that many Jews altogether in the cities mentioned. The number was no doubt in the hundreds, at most, and certainly not thousands. Many were forcibly baptized.

Very important is Chazan's statement that the record "shows no serious evidence of aggression perpetrated by the established authorities of northern Europe, either by those who did not participate in the expedition (the major governmental figures in northern Europe) or by those who took part. The extensive Hebrew reports speak of only one major baronial leader of the crusade who exploited Jewish fears in order to squeeze funds from endangered Jews."[11] For the time being, at least, both the Holy Roman Emperor (the inflated title inherited by the ruler of Germany) and the local nobles for the most part continued their favorable treatment of Jews. That would change drastically at the end of the thirteenth century.

Martyrdom   The three so-called "Hebrew chronicles," which lament the tragedies of these events, were all written many years or centuries later (one dates probably from at least the fourteenth century), although they may be based on oral tradition and perhaps some written records. The literary style of these texts has been commented upon more than once, and their veracity, while acceptable on some things, may be in doubt.

Certainly the matter-of-fact, almost casual, manner in which they report the supposed martyrdom of Jews: "each man took a sword, killed his wife and babies, and himself" does not encourage belief in the accuracy of the account. In fact, it is a sentence taken verbatim from the medieval Hebrew version of Josephus, relating the attack of the Romans at Masada and the alleged martyrdom of the surviving Jewish zealots there. This in itself has become a romantic myth of great heroic sacrifice and martyrdom.[12]

Nevertheless, there is a possibility that some Jews may have killed themselves in the attacks in Germany, although this would be a serious violation of Jewish law (to say nothing of murdering one's wife and children).[13] One would have to be very gullible, indeed, to believe that such tragic events would be reported in such a sterile and unemotional manner, instead of the usual style of lamentation replete with biblical quotations and allusions that usually characterize reporting of an actual massacre or martyrdom.

Some later rabbinical authorities, however, did permit suicide in the name of martyrdom when attacked. Thus, Isaac b. Joseph of Corbeil (d. 1280) wrote that "at the time of persecution one may give himself to death and kill himself if he fears that he cannot withstand the test." Aaron ha-Kohen of Lunel cited this and said that some argued from it that it was permitted also to kill the infants, "but there are others who prohibit it." A much later Jewish chronicler, Joseph ha-Kohen, claimed that (either at the time of Vicente Ferrer's missionary activities in Spain in the early fifteenth century, or at the Expulsion; the account is very distorted) some Jews "killed their sons and daughters" rather than convert.[14] This is not, however, confirmed in any reliable source of either period, and in fact no compulsion was used either time to convert Jews.

Martyrdom, it should be pointed out, was never a goal in itself in Jewish tradition. Talmudic law stated that only in three instances must one choose to be killed rather than transgress: idolatry, compulsive intercourse, and the order to kill another person. All of these, furthermore, must be in public (that is, in the presence of at least ten Jews) and at the command of a non-Jew, who threatens to kill the Jew if he fails to comply. True, the rabbis added that at "times of persecution" (active attacks on Jews), one should choose death rather than violate any commandment or even custom. But violating the biblical prohibition against murder and the rabbinical prohibition against suicide certainly was never a part of these considerations.[15]

However, the massacres by the crusaders in France in 1236 were far worse than those of the First Crusade in Germany (subsequent crusades saw few attacks on Jews); perhaps as many as 2,000 Jews were killed in France, if this is not another exaggerated figure. It was likely this tragedy, rather than remembrance of the then-distant events in Germany, that motivated the French rabbi's statement about martyrdom.

But martyrdom is itself a literary motif in Hebrew chronicles. The incident in the reign of Robert II with which this chapter begins was also reported with references to Jews killing themselves rather than face baptism. It should be noted, incidentally, that there would have been absolutely no legal justification for such an act, or even choosing to be killed rather than baptized, since most Jewish authorities in Christian lands agreed that Christianity is not idolatry.

Religiously, the myth of martyrdom evolved in the following centuries into a significant theme both in liturgical poetry and lamentations and in other sources such as the "chronicles" and other records of persecutions, as well as in the ascetic-mystical writings of the thirteenth-century German pietists (*hasidei Ashkenaz*).[16]

One renowned medieval rabbi wrote that when a person determines to die for the "sanctification of the name" (of God), nothing that is then done to him, neither stoning nor burning nor burial alive nor hanging "hurts him at all." He, or his disciple who wrote the account, added that normally no person can withstand the burning even of a finger, but "many deliver themselves to burning and killing for the sanctification of the name and do not cry out," for once they have made such a choice they are "promised" (by God) not to endure any pain.[17]

Vale of Tears–the Martyrdom Complex

The Jewish response to the undeniable tragedy of the attacks in Germany followed a long-familiar tradition of lamentations, invoking biblical passages and allusions, and martyrologies and so-called "chronicles," more fantasy than reality. While Jewish authorities refrained from instituting any special day of commemoration, instead combining it with the observance of Tishah B'Av, the fast day memorializing the destruction of both Temples (as in the case of the Expulsion from Spain, it was convenient, if inaccurate, to pick that day as the time of these events also), special prayers were composed. Symbolic concepts, such as the "binding of Isaac," were infused with a new meaning in reference to the martyrdom of the German Jews. Similarly, the period between Passover and Shavu'ot known as the "counting of the *omer*" (see Chapter 5 on this), during which according to tradition the students of Rabbi Aqiva died, now became a period of mourning also for the German martyrs. Interestingly, that tradition itself is part of the martyrdom myth, since according to the Talmud (*Yevamot* 62b) there was nothing heroic about the death of the students, who died at the hand of God because they hated each other, yet in the Middle Ages this became a legend of the "martyrdom" of those students.[18]

Thus began the development of the enduring martyrdom complex in Jewish self-perception that survives to the present day. This is the prevalent misconception that Jews were constantly persecuted and attacked in the Middle Ages. Not only England, France, and Germany, but even medieval Spain is included in this; for example, by writers who anachronistically (and inaccurately) refer to the "pogroms" of 1391, to say nothing of the outrageous position of some that medieval Spain was entirely anti-Semitic and even similar to the Nazis.[19] Spain, of course, was the most tolerant of all medieval countries and Jews lived there for centuries in general security and harmony with their Christian neighbors.

This tendency of careless Jewish (and now also non-Jewish) writers has aptly been termed the "lachrymose conception of Jewish history" by the late Salo Baron, the foremost Jewish historian of our time. There are encouraging indications that a few historians are beginning to get the message, as we shall see.[20]

Collective and Distorted Memory

How do we explain such misconceptions, both on the part of historians who should know better, and of the general Jewish population?[21] The answer has nothing to do with the medieval experience but rather with early modern history and the very real persecutions of Jews in eastern Europe, and general discrimination everywhere, in the nineteenth and early twentieth centuries. All contemporary Jews, with the exception of those whose origins are from North Africa or other Muslim countries, either grew up in or originate from that environment of hatred. This "collective memory" of recent persecution, to say nothing of the

Holocaust, of course, has distorted the perception of Jewish-Gentile relations throughout history as having been unrelieved hatred and suffering. The resultant "martyr complex" is one that the careful historian challenges at his or her peril.

Zionist ideology, particularly as expressed (or implicit) in the writings of the older generation of Israeli historians (Dinur, Baer, Ben-Sasson, and others), is another source of historical distortion. According to this theory, Jews can only live a normal existence in their ancestral homeland, and consequently the entire history of Jews in the Diaspora was one of persecution and intolerance.[22]

Every generation has its myths, of course, and every generation of historians seems to interpret historical events in light of the current trends of thinking. Recently, for example, the absurdities of deconstructionism, post-modernism and the overuse of terms like spaces reflect the desire to be trendy and keep up with fashionable terminology. But it is the fundamental task of the historian to analyze sources, think independently, and try to arrive at conclusions that best suit the phenomena observed. True objectivity is perhaps impossible, since we are always influenced by our times and prejudices, but at least an effort needs to be made to leave myths to the essayists and popularizers.

Far more Jews converted, under duress, in the events of 1096 than were killed. Most of these later returned to the **Conversion** Jewish people. Indeed, Henry IV and William II of England permitted Jews forcibly baptized to return to their "faith." The papacy, which constantly experienced schism in the medieval period with two and sometimes three claimants to the title, was again divided, and the strong "anti-pope" Clement III protested against the decision of the rulers. Indeed, as Chazan correctly emphasized, neither rulers nor barons took any part in, or sanctioned, the attacks on Jews. "Thus, even the turmoil associated with crusading occasioned no shift in the protective stance of the authorities and no exploitation of the volatile circumstances in the direction of anti-Jewish violence."[23] This is true as well for the later Crusades. We shall return later to the issue of Jewish conversion and its consequences.

There were isolated incidents in France and Germany through the twelfth century, but this hardly constitutes **Other Attacks** evidence of general hatred of Jews or increased persecu- **on Jews** tion.[24] In fact, precisely in the period following the attacks on German Jews in the First Crusade our most important rabbinical source, Rashi (ca. 1040–1105) provides frequent examples of continuing cordial relations between Jews and Christians, at least in France.[25]

Far more serious were the incidents in England. Jews are obligated by rabbinical law to respect the ruler or government of the country in which they live. Part of this was the tradition of greeting newly crowned rulers with celebrations and gifts. Thus, when Richard I (the "Lion-Heart") was crowned in 1189, in spite of the fact that Jews were expressly forbidden from participating in the festivities, a group of Jews brought gifts. They were driven away and a riot broke out among the people, during which several Jews were killed. There was a rumor that the king had ordered the killing of Jews, and in London they were attacked by mobs. Some were protected by taking shelter in stone houses, which nevertheless were burned, or in the Tower of London.

When Richard left at once on a crusade, more slaughter of Jews took place in other parts of the country. The most serious incident was at York, where barons were heavily indebted to Jews and took advantage of the widespread attacks to get rid of their debts. The townspeople joined in attacking the Jews, who took refuge in the castle. When troops were brought in to attack the castle, Yom Tov of Joigny, the aged scholar who was head of the community, urged martyrdom. Those who did not kill themselves (or, in fact, were killed by the rabbi) were killed the next day by the mob, under the pretext that if they emerged from the castle and were baptized they would be spared.[26]

Ironically, when Richard was captured while returning from the crusade and held for ransom by the duke of Austria, the Jews of England were taxed heavily to pay the ransom. His successor, his brother John (1199–1216), began his reign by protecting the Jews but soon imposed heavy taxes on them and in 1210 ordered the arrest of all Jews in the kingdom so that records of loans could be investigated. This was a forerunner to the continued harassment of Jews and seizure of their property, including imprisonment when they could not pay their heavy tax burden in 1240, which eventually led to the complete expulsion of Jews from the kingdom in 1290.[27]

In France, the rule of Philip II, "Augustus" (1180–1223), saw increasing demands on Jews for money, including a raid on the synagogues in 1180 when the Jews were held until they paid the exorbitant amount of 15,000 marks. Not satisfied, he seized all their property and expelled the Jews from his kingdom (the royal domain; as noted previously, a small territory around Paris). But the king missed his golden goose, the Jews, and so they were recalled in 1198. New territories were added to the royal domain in the wars with England (1202–1214), but the increased revenues did not prevent the king from once again confiscating Jewish property.[28]

The worst French kings as far as the Jews were concerned were the tyrannical "saint" Louis IX (1226–1270), venerated throughout history for his piety and still often idealized in history books, and Philip IV who expelled the Jews. It was Louis IX who, among other things, ordered the infamous burning of the Talmud in 1240 (about which more later). He also responded to the story told by one of his knights that he had beaten a Jew who allegedly spoke against the Virgin Mary, to which Louis said that one should never dispute with a Jew but rather run him through with a sword.[29] Before leaving on crusade in 1244, he also confiscated

Jewish property, both to provide money and also to encourage the Jews to convert. After returning from the crusade, he continued his campaign against Jewish money lenders, seizure of property, and increased efforts to convert the Jews by missionary activity. In 1246, the king ordered a raid on the Jews of Carcassonne, who were imprisoned. He wrote to his governor there that he should get all the money he could out of the Jews, but a month later he complained that the money thus obtained was not enough and demanded more.[30]

Often, the Jews were better off in various counties not under the control of the king. For example, in 1230 and 1252 the charters of Troyes and Provins exempted Jews from burgher control, along with clergy, noblemen, and vassals of the counts of Champagne.[31]

The defeat and capture of Louis IX in Egypt in 1250, and the refusal of the king of England to rescue him, led to a rabble of laborers and shepherds roaming the countryside and attacking the Jews, although they, of course, had nothing to do with the capture of the king.

The Shepherds' Uprising and Crusade

Worse by far was the Shepherds' Crusade of 1320. Spurred on by famine, social unrest, and poverty, the young workers and shepherds who attacked and killed many citizens and nobles continued through southern France on their way to the Holy Land, killing Jews as they went. Once again there are legendary accounts of Jews sacrificing themselves, or being killed by a fellow Jew, as martyrs. The Shepherds continued through French and into Spanish Provence, killing most of the Jews of Montclus, and even into Navarre, where the Jews were protected by the king (Jaime II). This is to be contrasted with the lack of action by Philip V of France, although the pope, John XXII, not only protested the killings but urged a counter crusade against the Shepherds. While it is too much to say that the Jewish communities of Provence were devastated, many Jews were killed and the consequences were severe.[32]

The Jews continued to suffer persecution and abuses in the royal domain of France until finally Philip IV "the Fair" (1285–1314) expelled them. There were earlier expulsions from other territories not part of the royal domain: Languedoc in 1268, Nevers in 1294, Anjou and Maine around 1289.[33]

Jews living in that part of Provence that still was part of the kingdom of Aragon-Catalonia fared much better than those in France.[34] They suffered no expulsions, a fact forgotten by many historians who include Provence in the general expulsion of 1306, but also were under the protection of Jaime I. For example, in 1252 the king protested to local officials in Montpellier who were molesting the Jews, in spite of which the local council continued its anti-Jewish activity and the king had to intervene again and guarantee the Jews his personal protection.[35] The king's intervention on the part of Jews in that province continued; for example, just to cite one important incident, in 1274 he noted that some clergy and laymen had summoned

Jews before ecclesiastical or lay courts and imposed heavy fines on them. He ordered the imprisonment and seizure of goods for the laymen involved and seizure of goods, only, for the clergy as well as the return of all fines imposed on Jews by such courts. The following year, a similar order was issued with regard to Jews in Perpignan and elsewhere.[36]

However, Spain, normally a land of safety for Jews and cordial relations with their Christian neighbors, had its own outbreak of rioting in the summer of 1391. Inspired by the exhortations of a fanatical archdeacon in Seville, already several times condemned by the king for his abuse of Jews, a mob attacked and burned local synagogues. This quickly spread to other communities in Castile and then beyond to Aragon-Catalonia and Valencia. Many Jews were robbed and homes and some synagogues destroyed, but few were killed. Many hundreds converted in hope of escaping or from fear of possible future attacks. The kings immediately intervened and many of the perpetrators were caught and put to death, and other measures were taken to restore the Jewish communities. The sense of security was, however, severely shaken and the entire Jewish community demoralized.

There were sporadic incidents of attacks, usually on individual Jews, as well as some more serious incidents during the fifteenth century, but in general Jewish-Christian relations remained as normal to the very eve of the Expulsion.

The Inquisition, which originated in Provence and then spread to Catalonia and was renewed for united Spain at the end of the fifteenth century, generally had no jurisdiction over Jews. Actual Jews, rather than converts to Christianity accused of heresy, somehow came under the jurisdiction of the inquisitors in Languedoc by the end of the thirteenth century, but the pope transferred the jurisdiction of the Jews of Toulouse and Narbonne to the bishop in order to avoid the abuses of the Inquisition (which, in spite of its original papal authorization, was often condemned by popes for abuse). In 1303, Philip III of France forbade the inquisitors to investigate alleged usury, sorcery, or other offences of Jews.[37]

EXPULSIONS

There were some temporary expulsions of Jews from certain German cities in the eleventh century, but these did not last long. The expulsion from England in 1290 has already been discussed. In France, as noted, the first expulsion was in 1182, followed by the expulsion ordered by Louis IX in 1250–1251[38] and then frequent expulsions in the fourteenth century. The "great expulsion" of 1306 was ordered by Philip IV (some Jews were briefly readmitted but then expelled again in 1311), but the Jews were readmitted by Louis X in 1315, only to be expelled again around 1359 and readmitted in 1361, followed by another expulsion in 1380 and another readmission, and the final expulsion in 1394.[39] There were also numerous expulsions from various German cities in the fourteenth century, as well as from Hungary in 1391.

A peculiarity of the relations of French rulers and the Jews remains to be explained, the cycle of expulsions and recalls. Historians have focused on the socioeconomic reasons for the various expulsions but have generally ignored the equally important question of why the Jews returned, repeatedly, to a land that obviously did not want them. There is no simple answer, but at least two possible suggestions present themselves: first, French Jews found it difficult to live elsewhere, for example Spain, because of differences of language and customs, and second, people often feel at home most in the environment in which they grew up and have lived.[40] Thus, for example, we find modern Jews who have returned to Germany or Russia, in spite of the horrendous associations those lands have for Jews.

The fifteenth century witnessed repeated expulsions of Jews in various countries on a scale never before encountered (it should be noted that, while Christian authorities may have borrowed such ideas as the notorious badge from fanatical Muslim legislation, Jews had never been expelled from any Muslim city or country, at least until the establishment of the State of Israel).

First cities and then entire regions in Germany expelled Jews throughout the century. Jews were expelled from numerous Swiss cities (they had already been expelled from Lucern in 1384), and even in tolerant Poland there was an expulsion from Warsaw in 1483 due to the fanatical missionary activity of a Dominican friar. In Piedmont, Italy, the duke expelled the Jews in 1452, recalled them, and expelled them again in 1454. There were also expulsions from various northern Italian communities. The Jews in most of Austria were expelled in 1453 and 1455, and also from several places in Bohemia. The most famous, one may say, was the great expulsion of all the Jews from Spain in 1492. The majority of the Jews had already voluntarily converted during the late fourteenth and throughout the fifteenth centuries, but the devastating moral effect of the end of the world's most important Jewish community had repercussions for centuries to come.[41]

CONVERSIONS

Conversion by Jews either to Islam or to Christianity frequently took place and was either voluntary or compulsory. There were several instances of voluntary conversion to Islam, for example, some motivated by a desire to improve social position or attain government offices and others by personal conviction. Muslims did not generally compel Jews to convert (as they did with Christians in territories conquered from them) since they were not armed enemies; however, the fanatical Almohad movement of the twelfth century did present the alternatives of conversion or expulsion or death both to Christians and Jews in North Africa and then southern Spain, which they conquered. Most Jews chose exile, but many accepted conversion.[42]

Voluntary conversions to Christianity, in the early medieval period at least, were less frequent but must have occurred. The forced baptisms of the First Crusade have already been mentioned. Most of these Jews returned to their people as soon as they had a chance, after the aforementioned permissions by the rulers. In spite of careful efforts by rabbinical scholars to distinguish between such compelled converts and apostates by choice, these and their descendants often faced discrimination in the Jewish community, about which we learn from rabbinical statements on this.[43]

St. Paul Preaching to the Jews in the Synagogue at Damascus. Byzantine mosaic, end of twelfth century. Duomo, Monreale, Italy. Bridgeman-Giraudon/Art Resource, NY.

Only in England was there a large enough number of converts that in 1232 a special *Domus conversorum* (house of converts) was built to house them in London. Many more converted when the edict of expulsion was issued in 1290. Expulsions and other persecutions of Jews, such as those detailed below, resulted in many conversions. To some degree, at least, we may view these as compulsory, since in many cases Jews accepted baptism in order hopefully to avoid torture or death.

Only in that light is it possible to consider the mass conversion of thousands of Jews in Spain as a result of the 1391 attacks. Some, indeed, were forcibly baptized but the remainder chose conversion. Not long after, at the beginning of the fifteenth century, harsh anti-Jewish legislation in Castile and the disputation at Tortosa, lasting over a year and resulting in the conversion of nearly all the rabbis present, combined with the hugely successful preaching campaign of Vicente Ferrer (who was granted sainthood for his success), resulted in the completely voluntary conversion of hundreds of thousands of Jews, literally, entire communities. All of this led to the demoralization of the remaining Jews, an almost total loss of rabbinical leadership (most rabbis converted) and the closing of *yeshivot* until near the end of the century. More conversions continued throughout the century prior to the Expulsion, and others then took place.

Indeed, the missionary campaign carried out by Dominican and Franciscan friars, which began in the thirteenth century and continued throughout the medieval period and beyond, was a constant threat to Jewish survival.[44] Jews were often compelled to listen to sermons by these friars in their synagogues or to engage in public disputations with them (in which, of course, the Christians always won). The notorious burning of cartloads of manuscripts of the Talmud in Paris in 1240, as a result of which we still have no truly critical edition of the text, was in part inspired by them, as well as, more directly, by the accusations of Nicholas Donin, a converted Jew.

Converts to other religions, particularly willful ones, were a constant threat to the welfare and indeed safety of the Jewish community. These apostates often turned in hatred against the Jews and spread false accusations against them, wrote polemics against Jewish belief, or engaged in disputations with Jews.[45]

PERSONAL SAFETY AND INSECURITY

Probably revealing only the tip of the iceberg are the many accounts of attacks on individual Jews throughout the medieval period, both in Muslim and Christian countries. Here, too, we must avoid the danger of exaggerating these events, nor can we be certain that all such attacks were caused by the Jewishness of the victims. Life in the medieval period was dangerous in general. The roads, even major ones, were notoriously

The prophet Daniel, from the prophets' window in the Augsburg cathedral. Stained glass. Around 1130. Cathedral, Augsburg, Germany. Erich Lessing/ Art Resource, NY.

unsafe, and Christian nobles or knights traveled with a retinue of protectors, as did upper-class women on the rare occasions when they traveled at all. Even in Spain, both Muslim and Christian, there were dangers on the roads. Jews were sometimes robbed and even murdered. However, so were Muslim and Christian travelers, and unless the sources specifically detail anti-Jewish motives for such attacks, care must be exercised in coming to the wrong conclusions.

Robbery, Murder and Ransom

As mentioned in Chapter 3, men who traveled on business, and particularly to distant countries, faced constant threat of robbery or worse. Jews primarily from Spain, but also some from Italy and even France, journeyed to Egypt on business and faced the dangers of storms and piracy. There were frequent shipwrecks, and sometimes a passenger would be lucky enough to survive and be rescued. If the passenger were a Jew, he might be lucky enough to be rescued by Jews or at least by sympathetic Gentiles, Muslims, or Christians, who would aid him. However, Jews would often be held for ransom.

The same was true when pirates, again either Christian or Muslim, attacked and boarded a ship. Jewish passengers would be held for ransom, either by the nearest Jewish community or by the one from which they came. So frequent were such events that Jewish communities in Muslim Spain, and presumably at least some elsewhere, had regular funds for ransom of captives (*pidyan ha-shevuim*). In cases of particular urgency, such as when a woman was held for ransom, letters would be sent to various communities and even famous Jewish scholars were involved personally in raising and transmitting such funds.[46] Even the tiny and impoverished Jewish community of Ramleh in the Land of Israel had to ransom two Jews captured by Byzantine pirates.

Not only Jews could be held for ransom; so too could stolen items of religious significance, such as Torah scrolls or phylacteries or even books.[47] In such cases, however, Jewish law made a clear distinction between people and objects. In spite of the sanctity of such objects they were not to be ransomed, lest non-Jews be further encouraged to steal such items because of the rewards.

Jews in Germany or France traveling on business, for example to the important fairs at Leipzig and elsewhere, were also in danger of attack, robbery, and murder. Nor were Jews in these countries allowed to carry weapons with which to defend themselves, and consequently they were

Burning of a Jew and his family at the stake. The Desecration of the Host, from a series of six paintings for a predella, 1465–1469. Uccello, Paolo (1397–1475). Galleria Nazionale delle Marche, Urbino, Italy. Scala/Art Resource, NY.

easy victims, in spite of the Peace Laws that allegedly guaranteed them security. It was for this reason that rabbis went to the extraordinary lengths of allowing Jewish men to dress as monks or clerics, even carrying crosses, and women to dress in men's clothing or also as clerics, when traveling, in spite of biblical and talmudic prohibitions on wearing Gentile clothing or women wearing men's clothing.

An interesting incident involved two merchants who brought wool from Cologne and were robbed on the road. The robbers then sold the wool to two other Jews, one of whom took it to Mainz and there sold it to another Jew. The original Jewish merchants meanwhile learned of this and went to Mainz to recover their wool, but the Jewish buyer there bribed the officials and courts in an effort to keep the wool. The original owners were only able to recover the price paid, minus the bribe money.[48]

A unique case involved a ship that was lost at sea off the coast, perhaps of Germany; a Jewish passenger who was rescued hired a Christian to help him save what they could from the caskets of money and personal goods that belonged to him and other Jewish passengers. At night, some other people in the area grabbed what they could from these things, and in order to force them to return the property they were required by the authorities to pass their hands through fire, known as trial by ordeal, "according to the law of the Gentiles of that place," and one of the Jews who claimed to have had his money taken by them was given the chance to prove his claim by trial by combat.[49]

There were also a small number of kidnappings of Jewish children, who were then forcibly baptized and raised as Christians. Such kidnapping of Jewish children in the name of religion continued through the centuries, with the most recent cases in the eighteenth and nineteenth centuries (reportedly also in Israel in the twentieth century). While church law officially prohibited forced baptism, once baptized, no matter under what conditions, the person must remain a Christian. The only exception to this was, as we have seen, those forcibly baptized in the events of the First Crusade who were then allowed to return to their people. Even in that case, had not the Holy Roman Emperor and the king of England sanctioned this, it is doubtful that the pope would have allowed it.

False accusations were sometimes made against Jews, either in commercial matters, such as the claim that goods offered for sale were stolen from Christians (necessitating a complicated series of laws supposedly to protect Jews, particularly in Germany), or that a loan had been repaid when it had not, and the like. More serious were allegations of crimes and, infrequently, of sorcery or magic.

Ritual Murder Accusations The most notorious of such accusations, either against individual Jews or sometimes entire communities, concerned the ritual murder and blood libel charges. These are two separate things, the first being the hysteria aroused by claims that Jews had captured and killed a Christian child (not always a boy) in some ritualistic manner, sometimes crucifixion, but also in other ways.[50] This myth has its roots also in antiquity, but the first medieval charge was in England in 1144. A dead Christian boy was found in the woods near Norwich and as in most such cases, if a body was ever actually found, at once a Jew was accused of killing him in a ritualistic manner. There was, of course, no proof of this and for years no one believed the charges until a monk took up the cause and wrote a book about it, creating the cult of little "saint" William. Further cases occurred in England and quickly spread to France and Germany, adding more "saints" to the list (curiously, only boy victims were given this distinction).

Jews were tortured in attempts to gain confessions and individual Jews or entire communities of Jews were killed, sometimes in horrible ways, but there was never proof of a single case of Jewish involvement in such cases (at times the mere disappearance of a Christian child, with no body ever found, was enough to trigger the accusation). One of the most horrendous cases was in Speyer, Germany in 1196 when the body of a Christian girl was found and in revenge the Christians dug up the corpse of the daughter of an important rabbi and hung it in the public square. When the rabbi paid a ransom to redeem his daughter's body, the mob attacked his house and those of other Jews, killing them.

The most infamous case, however, was at Trent in 1473, when the preaching of a notorious Jew hater, the Franciscan Bernard of Feltre (later made a saint), inflamed passions against the Jews. When a Christian boy who had gotten lost was found dead near the river, the Jews were of course accused. Fifteen were arrested and tortured for several days and finally burned at the stake. There was at once a movement to declare the boy, Simon, a saint, but the pope refused until at last pressured by a commission of cardinals. Contrary to the claims of some apologists, the popes did not always condemn such accusations; indeed, the famous report of Cardinal Ganginelli (later Pope Clement XIV) in the eighteenth century exonerating the Jews generally of such charges confirmed the "truthfulness" of the Simon of Trent case, who had long before been declared a "saint."

Altogether, over 150 such cases were reported, and the myth entered into the store of anti-Jewish propaganda.

Even more absurd, and dangerous, was the blood libel, also with origins in pre-Christian legend.[51] According to   **Blood Libel**
this, Jews used Christian blood (again only of children) in
various ways. The first such case was in Fulda in Germany in 1236, where five Christian boys had died and the Jews were accused not only of murdering them but of using their blood for remedies. Thirty-two Jews were slaughtered. When a delegation brought news of the incident, along with three of the corpses, to the emperor, Frederick II, his first observation was that the corpses should be buried.

This highly intelligent and educated ruler, particularly favorable to Jews, hardly was one to give credence to such a tale. He shrewdly convened an international conference, not of Jews but of converted Jews (who would be most likely to condemn their former coreligionists) to report on the reliability of such an accusation. Even these were compelled to admit that such things would be against biblical and talmudic laws. Frederick issued laws protecting the Jews from such charges, and in 1246 Pope Innocent IV also denounced such accusations, an action that was later repeated by him and other popes. In spite of this, the charges continued.

The first recorded mention of the specific charge that Jews used human blood to mix in their unleavened bread (*matzot*) for Passover is in the bull of Pope Martin V in 1422 condemning this and other such accusations. In spite of this, there were immediately such charges, particularly in Switzerland. This also continued sporadically throughout the centuries and has become well known because of the twentieth-century case in Russia against Mendel Beilis (about which books have been written, including the novel *The Fixer* by Bernard Malamud).

Poisoning Wells, Causing the Plague, and Other Crimes The plague was not something new in Europe, but the most devastating outbreaks, labeled Black Death, came in the years 1348 to 1350.[52] Spreading from the Mediterranean coast to Provence and then to Germany and other lands, hundreds of thousands fell victim.

Jews, who already had been blamed in previous centuries for murdering Christians (doctors allegedly poisoning their royal patients, which led to a general church ban on consulting Jewish physicians; although many popes had their own personal Jewish doctors, and more recently, in 1321, of poisoning wells used by Christians), were now also blamed for causing the plague. Once again Jews were tortured until they confessed, Jewish communities were attacked, and Jews were killed, not only in Germany but in the usually more tolerant French Provence. In some cities, such as in Switzerland, Jews tried to avoid persecution and burning by being baptized, but sometimes this did not save them and all were killed.

Not only traditional Jew hatred lay behind these accusations; there was also the fact that in general fewer Jews than Christians were affected by the plague, due to their better health and sanitary conditions (as mentioned elsewhere here, Jews bathed regularly, washed their hands, and carefully cleansed all utensils). The plague spread to Spain, both northern and southern, but there too proportionally far fewer Christians died than in northern Europe, and still fewer Jews (nevertheless, some important rabbis and in some cases in Toledo nearly entire families perished). Uniquely in Spain, there were no accusations that Jews were responsible, much less were there any reprisals against them.

NOTES

1. Hebrew text in A.M. Habermann, *Sefer gezeirot Ashkenaz ve-Tsarfat* (Jerusalem, 1946), 19; on the incident, see Robert Chazan, "1007–1012: Initial Crisis for Northern European Jewry," American Academy for Jewish Research. *Proceedings* 38–39 (1970–1971): 101–17. The quotation placed in the mouths of the king's advisors is, of course, a literary device by the anonymous author of the account.

2. See details in Norman Roth, *Conversos, Inquisition, and the Expulsion of the Jews from Spain* (Madison, Wisc., 1995; revised paper ed., 2002); see the index for *limpieza de sangre* (purity of blood).

3. The most extreme advocates of this view are those mentioned in note 5. Robert Chazan's, *Medieval Stereotypes and Modern Antisemitism* (Berkeley, 1997) book, is, to be sure, critical of these earlier theories, but it nevertheless concludes that modern anti-Semitism does have its medieval antecedents. His book, mostly about France and Germany (somewhat) from the eleventh through thirteenth centuries (only), of course makes no mention of the Spanish example mentioned here.

4. See, for example, the observations of Edward Flannery, *The Anguish of the Jews* (New York, 1965), 60 and n. 76. The author, a Catholic priest, has written an important and sympathetic survey of what he nevertheless calls anti-Semitism, without adhering to his own more precise categories there.

5. The best of such works attempt to chronicle events and attitudes. Examples are Peter G. J. Pulzer, *The Rise of Political Anti-Semitism in Germany and Austria* (London, 1964); Leon Poliakov, *History of anti-Semitism* (New York, 1965–1985), 4 vols. translated from the French; Amos Funkenstein, "Basic Types of Christian Anti-Jewish Polemics in the Later Middle Ages," *Viator* 2 (1971) 373–82; and most recently Chazan, *Medieval Stereotypes and Modern Antisemitism*. Each of these studies, with the possible exception of Pulzer, nevertheless has serious problems, above all the massive work of Poliakov, which suffers from the conceptual distortions noted here. An important general study is F. Lovsky, *Antisemitisme et mystere d'Israel* (Paris, 1955). Other useful works, all by non-Jewish authors, include Flannery, *The Anguish of the Jews*; Malcolm Hay, *Europe and the Jews* (New York, 1960, with preface by Walter Kaufmann); and especially Edward A. Synan, *The Popes and the Jews in the Middle Ages* (New York, London, 1965), a careful and scholarly work with translations of important texts.

6. The best discussion of this is in Synan, ibid., and see particularly there 45–46 for the oldest version (Gregory) and 229–31 for the text and translation of the earliest surviving official version. See also the older study of Solomon Grayzel, "The Papal Bull Sicut Judeis," in *Studies and Essays in Honor of Abraham A. Neuman*, ed. Meir Ben-Horin et al. (Leiden, 1962), 243–80.

7. Text and translation in Solomon Grayzel, *The Church and the Jews in the XIIIth Century* (Philadelphia, 1933), 141, bottom. On the badge, see that article in Norman Roth, ed., *Medieval Jewish Civilization: An Encyclopedia* (New York, 2003). However well-intentioned the words of the pope, the symbol (which varied from country to country) in itself was certainly often a danger to the safety and lives of Jews. Local secular authorities sometimes permitted Jews traveling to forego the wearing of it while on their journey.

8. These are distinctions that are rarely made, nevertheless, in writings on these subjects. See generally the articles "Canon Law" and "Church and the Jews" in Roth, ibid.

9. The best account, with some reservations, of the incidents connected with the 1096 Crusade is Robert Chazan, *European Jewry and the First Crusade* (Berkeley, Calif., 1987); see, for example, 66–67. Chazan has repeated the story in a series of books and articles on the same subject. There is a complete English translation of the Hebrew accounts of the First and Second Crusades by Shlomo Eidelberg, *The Jews and the Crusaders* (Madison, Wisc., 1977), and a better one in the appendix of Chazan's book. It should be mentioned that a number of items are missing from Chazan's bibliography, not only secondary studies but also some sources, and that not everyone agrees entirely with his assessment—see especially the important critique by Ivan G. Marcus in *Speculum* 64 [1989]: 685–88 and his "From Politics to Martyrdom: Shifting Paradigms in the Hebrew Narratives of the 1096 Crusade Riots," *Prooftexts* 2 (1982): 40–52, and "History, Story and Collective Memory: Narrativity in Early Ashkenazic Culture," ibid. 10 (1990):1–23, with Chazan's reply, "The Facticity of Medieval Narrative," *Association for Jewish Studies Review* 16 (1991): 31–57. (If Marcus could invent a word "narrativity," then not to be outdone Chazan invented "facticity"!).

10. See, for example, Norman Roth, "Bishops and Jews in the Middle Ages," *The Catholic Historical Review* 80 (1994): 1–17, and generally the article "Church and Jews" in Roth, *Medieval Jewish Civilization*.

11. Chazan, *Medieval Stereotypes and Modern Antisemitism*, 3. The "baronial leader" to whom he refers was Count Emicho; see his article "Emicho" (with no bibliography) in Roth, *Medieval Jewish Civilization*.

12. The best-known account and refutation of this legend is by the Israeli sociologist Nachman Ben-Yehuda, *The Masada Myth: Collective Memory and Mythmaking in Israel* (Madison, Wisc., 1995), but the question was raised already earlier by Baila R. Shargel, "The Evolution of the Masada Myth," *Judaism* 28 (1979): 357–71, and in the more significant article by Barry Schwartz, Yael Zerubavel, and Bernice M. Barnett, "The Recovery of Masada: A Study in Collective Memory," *The Sociological Quarterly* 27 (1986): 147–64, cited by Ben-Yehuda. See also Yael Zerubavel, *Recovered Roots: Collective Memory in the Making of Israeli National Tradition* (Chicago, 1995). Inevitably, of course, such work has unintentionally given comfort to the neo-Nazis and other anti-Semites.

13. Chazan accepts without question the authenticity of the story, and the general accuracy of the late Hebrew sources (against which see the aforementioned articles by Marcus.). Neither he nor any other historian has noted that this is taken from the medieval Josephus; see *Sefer Yosipon* (or *Yosifun*), ed. David Flusser (Jerusalem, 1962), 311–12, 430–31. However, the chronicles may also have been influenced by the German *Sefer hasidim*, with its emphasis on the importance of martyrdom, as suggested by Eidelberg, *Jews and the Crusaders*, 16. The Hebrew account of the massacre of Jews in France by the crusaders in 1236 also uses the exact same phrase (in Solomon Ibn Verga, *Shevet Yehudah* [Jerusalem, 1947], 148; again, not noted by historians.

14. Aaron b. Joseph ha-Kohen, *Orhot hayyim* (Jerusalem, 1981; photo reprint of earlier eds.) 2: 26. Joseph ha-Kohen, *Emeq ha-baka* (Cracow, 1895), ed. M. Letteris (actually S. D. Luzzatto), 85; German translation, *Emek habacha*, trans. M. Wiener (Leipzig, 1858), 56.

15. Jacob Katz, *Exclusiveness and Tolerance* (Oxford, 1961), tried to diminish the plain meaning of these laws (which he inadequately and incompletely discussed) in the context of his peculiar idea of a Jewish mission, which includes willingness, perhaps eagerness, to die for one's beliefs; see especially 83–85. It was not his cold rationalism that prompted Maimonides to uphold the talmudic laws on martyrdom, contrary to Katz; nor did Katz distinguish between attitudes to and persecution by Muslims and Christians. Maimonides, as is well known, forcefully rejected the claim that Muslim compulsory conversion of Jews required one to die rather than convert (see details in Norman Roth, *Jews, Visigoths & Muslims in Medieval Spain: Cooperation & Conflict* [Leiden, 1994], 117–22).

16. There is a vast literature on this movement; see briefly the article "Hasidim–Germany" by Joseph Dan, one of the leading authorities on the subject, in Roth, *Medieval Jewish Civilization*.

17. Meir b. Barukh of Rothenburg, as reported by Samson bar Tsadoq, *Sefer tashbats* (Warsaw, 1875), no. 415. Both rabbis lived in Germany in the thirteenth century. It is perhaps fortunate that Katz did not know this source or it would have added further inspiration for his mission theory (nor has it been noted by those who have written on the Crusades).

18. See Salo W. Baron, *A Social and Religious History of the Jews* (Philadelphia, New York, 1952–1983), 4: 144–45. Much more could, and should, be written on these topics. See particularly Shalom Spiegel, *The Last Trial: On the Legends and Lore of the Command to Abraham to Offer Isaac as a Sacrifice* (New York, 1967), with a translation of the Hebrew text of Ephraim of Bonn, 139–52. Although published after the first edition of Baron, this work certainly should have been added to the bibliographical notes of the subsequent editions. On the period of mourning between Passover and Shavu'ot, and problems associated with it, see Efrat Zarren-Zohar, "From Passover to Shavuot," in Paul F. Bradshaw and Lawrence A. Hoffman, eds., *Passover and Easter: The Symbolic Structure of Sacred Seasons* (Notre Dame, Ind., 1999), 71–93.

19. See on both these things Roth, *Conversos*, and especially the Afterword in the revised paper edition, which discusses the theories of Netanyahu and other extremists.

20. From a slightly different perspective, see Jeremy Cohen, "A 1086 Complex? Constructing the First Crusade in Jewish Historical Memory, Medieval and Modern," in Michael A. Signer and John Van Engen, eds., *Jews and Christians in Twelfth-Century Europe* (Notre Dame, Ind., 2001), 9–26, discussing the sources and the reactions of some nineteenth-and twentieth-century Jewish historians. Cohen makes no mention of Funkenstein and only in passing refers to Chazan.

21. In an important critique of Amos Funkenstein's theories relating to anti-Semitism, the author quoted this appropriate warning by the important medieval historian John Huizinga: "There is a great temptation to apply as a stereotype a concept once found useful to data that really require a rethinking and a new specific quantification ... the historian who is serious about presenting a living and accurate reflection of the past must be wary of using those terms, loaded as they are with feeling and ill-feeling" (David Engel, "The Concept of Antisemitism in the Historical Scholarship of Amos Funkenstein," *Jewish Social Studies* 6 [1999]: 112; article, 111–29). This certainly applies not only to Funkenstein but to all attempts to characterize medieval Christian attitudes to Jews as anti-Semitic.

22. It would require a book to treat this adequately, which hopefully will be done one day. See, for some of the more lachrymose expressions, for example by Hillel Ben-Sasson and Yitzhak Baer, quoted in Cohen, "A 1086 Complex?" 11–12, 16–17; and see Roth, *Conversos*, Afterword. Gavin Langmuir, a frequent writer on medieval (and other) anti-Semitism, admitted that his work has been primarily motivated by his concern with "European antisemitism that led directly to the Final Solution" (*History, Religion, and Antisemitism* [Berkeley, Calif., 1990], 275; cited by Engel, "The Concept of Antisemitism," 114).

23. Chazan, *Medieval Stereotypes,* 3.

24. Chazan briefly details the *eleven* incidents that occurred throughout that period, ibid., 54–57.

25. For details, see the article "Rashi" in Roth, *Medieval Jewish Civilization,* particularly 563–64 (that article generally contains information not found in other treatments of the great scholar). Note there also important statements by him concerning customs of the Christians in Germany and France; for example, the method of washing clothes. As noted in that article, his general attitude toward Christians was positive and his commentary on the Torah contains no negative statements about Christians or Christianity. The contrary claim by Katz, *Exclusiveness and Tolerance,* 24, that he did not differentiate between contemporary Christians and the idolatrous nations encountered in the Bible is false and based largely on the incorrect views cited in the above article. No medieval rabbi in Christian Europe believed, or said, that Christians were idolaters; in fact, they said the opposite (see the following chapter here).

26. This is a brief summary of the tragic events; see in detail R. B. Dobson, *The Jews of Medieval York and the Massacre of March 1190* (York, England, 1974).

27. On the history of England's Jews, see briefly the article "England" in Roth, *Medieval Jewish Civilization* and the bibliography cited there. Note especially the new information on the expulsion there, 244.

28. See William Chester Jordan's excellent book, *The French Monarchy and the Jews from Philip Augustus to the Last Capetians* (Philadelphia, 1989), and briefly his article "Philip II" in Roth, ibid. Jordan's book, extremely important and highly readable, nevertheless omits several bibliographical items, including P. Hidirgolou, "Les juifs d'apres la littérature historique latine, de Philippe Auguste a Philippe le Bel," *Revue des etudes juives* 133 (1974): 373–456. For a more general overview of the medieval period, see also Robert Chazan, *Medieval Jewry in Northern France* (Baltimore, 1973), and S. Schwarzfuchs, *Les juifs de France* (Paris, 1975), and the well-written survey by G. Nahon, "From the *Rue aux Juifs* to the *Chemin du Roy:* The Classical Age of French Jewry, 1108–1223," in Signer and Van Engen, *Jews and Christians,* 311–39.

29. This famous statement is reliably reported by the medieval chronicler Jean de Joinville, *Histoire de saint Louis* (Paris, 1872), 30. On Louis and the Jews, see also Chazan, *Medieval Jewry in Northern France,* 100–53, and especially G. Nahon, "Les ordonances de Saint Louis sur les juifs," *Les nouveaux cahiers* 6 (1970): 18–35 and the article "Louis IX" in Roth, *Medieval Jewish Civilization.*

30. Henry Charles Lea, *A History of the Inquisition of the Middle Ages* (New York, 1906) 1: 515, note. Note Pope Nicholas III's order to burn recalcitrant Jewish converts to Christianity there in 1278, and contrast that with King Philip III's protection of the same; ibid. 2: 64 and 65.

31. See the documents in Elizabeth Chapin, *Les villes des foires de Champagne des origines au debut du XIVe siècle* (Paris, 1937), 288 ff.

32. Much has been written about all these events; see briefly the article of Bat Sheva Albert, "Shepherds' Uprising" in Roth, *Medieval Jewish Civilization*.

33. For Nevers, see Jordan, *French Monarchy and the Jews*, 184–85; for Anjou and Maine see L. Lazard, "Les juifs de Tourraine," *Revue des études juives* 17 (1888): 210–34 and the more important article of L. Brunschvig, "Les juifs d'Angers et de pays angevin," ibid. 29 (1894): 229–41.

34. See the article "Provence, Spanish" in Roth, *Medieval Jewish Civilization*.

35. Salomon Kahn, "Documents inédits sur les juifs de Montpellier," *Revue des etudes juives* 19 (1889): 262 and 270–72; cf. F. Bofarull y Sans, "Jaime I el conquistador y la comunidad judía de Montpellier," *Boletin de la real academia de buenas letras de Barcelona* 5 (1909): 484–92 on the generally favorable treatment of the Jews of Montpellier by the king.

36. Jean Regne, *History of the Jews in Aragon (Catalonia), Regesta and documents 1213–1327*, ed. Yom Tov Assis (Jerusalem, 1978), nos. 596, 625.

37. Henry Charles Lea, *A History of the Inquisition of the Middle Ages*, 2: 96 and note, and 3: 449 (see also note 20 above). For the situation in Spain, see Roth, *Conversos*.

38. E.-J. Laurier et al., eds., *Ordonnances des rois de France* (Paris, 1723–1849) 1: 85; J.D. Mansi, ed. *Sacrorum Conciliorum Nova et Amplissima Collectio* (Florence, 1759;1927) 22: 882; Ibn Verga, *Shevet Yehudah* [Jerusalem, 1947], 77–78; cf. *Recueil des historiens des Gaules et de la France* (Paris, 1865) 22: 882. There is nothing about this in Jordan, *French Monarchy and the Jews*.

39. Earlier historians had referred to an expulsion in 1322, but this is erroneous; see the brilliant article of Elizabeth A.R. Brown, "Philip V, Charles IV, and the Jews of France: The Alleged Expulsion of 1322," *Speculum* 66 (1991): 294–328; see also her articles on Louis X, Philip IV, and Philip V in Roth, *Medieval Jewish Civilization*. On the expulsion of 1380, see Baron, *Social and Religious History* 11: 223 n. 40 and 10: 342–43. For a good general overview, with bibliography, of the various expulsions, see G. Nahon, "Expulsion, France" in Roth, *Medieval Jewish Civilization*. The final expulsion of 1394 was from France proper, but not the territory of Provence. In 1496, Jews were also expelled from Provence, except for Avignon and the papal territory.

40. Jordan, *French Monarchy and the Jews*, 233, speaks of a "kind of homesickness that was almost suffocating" among the Jews expelled, specifically those who went to Spain. If he knows of sources for this, he cites none, and I certainly know of none. However, as a general surmise it is probably true, but not limited to the relatively small number of French Jews who went to Spain. Other statements there by Jordan, 232–37, are seriously flawed or incorrect.

41. See "Expulsions, Other Lands" and "Expulsion, Spain," in Roth, *Medieval Jewish Civilization* and far more detail in Roth, *Conversos*. See also the article "Germany" by Friedrich Lotter in Roth, *Medieval Jewish Civilization*, 303–4 on expulsions.

42. See details in Roth, *Jews, Muslims & Visigoths*, 116 ff. and 199 ff.; see also the section on Islam in the article "Conversion by Jews," 190–92, in Roth, *Medieval Jewish Civilization*.

43. See in general the article "Conversion by Jews," in Roth, ibid.

44. In spite of much criticism, Jeremy Cohen, *The Friars and the Jews: The Evolution of Medieval Anti-Judaism* (Ithaca, N.Y., 1982) remains widely quoted. Some of the worst errors and omissions of Cohen's book are pointed out in my review in *Jewish Quarterly Review* 74 (1985): 321–26. Contrary to his claim (16), for example, there were only one or two Dominican friars in the late fifteenth century who advocated expelling, certainly not killing, Jews. The aim of their missionary campaign was the conversion of Jews; see the more balanced treatment by Robert Chazan, *Daggers of Faith. Thirteenth-Century Missionizing and Jewish Response* (Berkeley, Calif., 1989). See also the details in the article "Dominicans and Franciscans" in Roth, *Medieval Jewish Civilization.*

45. See "Disputations" in Roth, *Medieval Jewish Civilization.*

46. See examples of such incidents in Roth, *Jews, Visigoths & Muslims,* 197–99.

47. For example, a Jew in Orleans agreed to keep for a Christian some containers containing money that the Christian had borrowed on interest from another Jew. However, the containers were seized by city officials (for some unspecified reason), and the Christian therefore took a Bible codex and other property from the Jew that was worth twice the amount he had left with him. Nevertheless, even in Paris, where he went to sell the Bible, no Jew would buy it because of the law discouraging such a practice; responsum of Rashi in *Teshuvot hokhmei Sarfat ve-Lotir,* ed. Joel Müller (Vienna, 1881), No. 29.

48. Meir b. Barukh of Rothenburg, *She'elot u-teshuvot,* ed. Moses Bloch (Budapest, 1895), No. 828. Incredibly, Meir decided that the purchaser in Mainz could legitimately deduct his expenses for the bribe from the money he had to repay the original owners.

49. Rashi, *Teshuvot hokhmei Sarfat ve-Lotir,* No. 97.

50. See the article "Ritual Murder," with bibliography, in Roth, *Medieval Jewish Civilization.* Less accurate accounts are to be found in virtually every general history of the Jews.

51. See "Blood Libel" in Roth, ibid., with bibliography and information not found elsewhere.

52. See the lengthy article "Black Death," with bibliography, in Roth, ibid. No mention is made of Spain, about which I plan to write elsewhere.

RECOMMENDED READING

Baron, Salo W. *A Social and Religious History of the Jews.* Philadelphia, New York, 1952–83), 4: 89 ff.

Flannery, Edward H. *The Anguish of the Jews* (New York, 1965).

Parkes, James. *The Jew in the Medieval Community* (New York, 1976), chapters 3 and 4.

Signer, Michael A., and John Van Engen, eds., *Jews and Christians in Twelfth-Century Europe* (Notre Dame, 2001).

10

RELATIONS BETWEEN JEWS AND GENTILES: LIVING WITH, IF NOT LOVING, YOUR NEIGHBOR

We have seen in the last chapter some of the many dangers that confronted Jews in their personal lives and as a community, and a survey–however brief and incomplete–of some of the persecutions of Jews and attacks against them in the medieval period. This, however, was not the whole picture, and to end on a more positive note let us consider the good as well as the bad of daily relations between Jews and Gentiles, both Muslims and Christians.

JEWS AND MUSLIMS: A SHARED CULTURE

It is no wonder that Jews adjusted so easily and completely to life in lands conquered by the Muslims, first in their ancient homes of Babylon (now Iraq), and the whole of the former Persian Empire, and in the Land of Israel itself, then in Syria, Egypt, North Africa, Sicily, and Spain (not forgetting Yemen, where Jews had lived since pre-Muslim days). Jews shared with Muslims the previously discussed fact of being a civilization rather than just a religion.[1] Arabic is a Semitic language, similar in many respects to Hebrew. In fact, there had been Jewish poets living in pre-Muslim Arabia, whose Arabic poetry had contributed to the development of that language and as part of the classical tradition was thus venerated along with the *Qur'an* for the mythical perfection of Arabic.

Islam had borrowed much of its customs, laws, and beliefs from Jewish traditions, however imperfectly understood (and despite the vitriolic anti-Jewish, and anti-Christian, polemic of the *Qur'an*); thus, Jews and Muslims shared a common understanding of many aspects of daily life. Jews prayed three times a day, Muslims five. Both required washing before prayer and at other times. Hospitality was an important part of the legal tradition of both, and the concept of what we call charity was defined by nearly the same word in Hebrew (*tsedaqah*) and in Arabic (*tsadaqa*); however the Jewish idea, and to some degree also in Islam, is not doing some extraordinary good deed but rather setting right that which is out of order; in other words, doing what is expected and necessary to provide food, clothing, and shelter for those in need, and also to help them find a job if that is needed. Indeed, talmudic law requires that if a person has fallen on hard times he or she must be restored to the standard of living to which the person was accustomed.

Muslims borrowed from Jewish law also the notion of certain food that is permissible as opposed to that which is not. Unlike the Jews, however, they made no prohibition on mixing meat and dairy products, and only pork is absolutely forbidden. Ritual slaughter of animals is required, as in Jewish law, and in the Middle Ages several questions arose in different Jewish communities in the Muslim world (Spain, North Africa) about the permissibility of slaughtering animals for Muslims. Even in Christian Spain in the thirteenth century, when Muslims continued to live among Christians and Jews, there were such cases of Jews slaughtering meat for Muslims. This was allowed also by Muslim law, except for a fanatic judge in Seville in the twelfth century who prohibited it.

Circumcision is required in both Jewish and Muslim law for males (at eight days after birth for Jews, but at varying times from a few days old until age 13 in Muslim practice). Muslim law does not require, but considers praiseworthy, also the circumcision of females. Notwithstanding the differences, the practice of circumcision was another major factor that differentiated both Muslims and Jews from the uncircumcised Christians. There can be no doubt, incidentally, as to the essentially anti-Semitic intent of many of the current advocates of not circumcising male babies, as a look at their online materials makes apparent.

There are numerous other similarities. Both the mosque and the synagogue are unadorned by human images or statues and both were primarily intended for study and only secondarily for prayer. Therefore, we hear of Jews in the medieval period who prayed in mosques (in one case in Tunisia a funeral was held in the mosque for a Jew who every week had prayed there). Both had a system of law that covered all aspects of life and was constantly evolving in response to changing needs. Education was equally important to both cultures, at least in the medieval period.

Jews quickly learned Arabic in the new Muslim countries, and by the ninth and early tenth centuries were renowned as physicians, mathematicians, doctors, and astronomers, all writing in Arabic.[2] One of the greatest contributions of medieval Muslim culture, of course, was the translation of numerous Greek scientific, mathematical, philosophical, and medical treatises, along with others from ancient Egypt, Babylonia, Persia, and India. This vast body of knowledge, in addition to the growing number of original works in Arabic, presented Jews with a whole new world of science and philosophy, to which they now also eagerly contributed. The normal educational curriculum of a medieval Muslim or Jewish boy living in Muslim lands far exceeded the accomplishments of students and their professors at the most outstanding universities of the world today. This was particularly true of Muslim Spain, of course, but while deterioration had already set in by the eleventh century it had also been true in Iraq and much of the former Persian Empire (not just modern Iran, but extending to India).

Thus, there was a common intellectual discourse and understanding between Jew and Muslim. Both valued the same knowledge, had studied with the same teachers, often together, both were able to write and extemporize Arabic verse (the Jew also Hebrew verse). There were, of course, significant cultural differences. The Muslims, except for some of the more heretical philosophers, venerated the *Qur'an* as God's final and perfect revelation, while the Jew did the same for the Torah. The insistence on the perfection of Arabic, and that it was the only language in which poetry had been or could be written, aroused a reaction not only among native Persians but also among Jews in Muslim Spain. The result of this was that Jews were motivated to study the Bible and to discover the grammar of the Hebrew language and at the same time to begin writing Hebrew secular poetry, which soon outshone the Arabic model.[3]

Some rare instances of real tolerance and understanding, as we would consider it, also existed. For example, in Damascus in the thirteenth century, a Muslim Sufi (mystical) scholar, Abu Ali Ibn Hud al-Mursi, born in Murcia (Spain), son of the conqueror and governor of Murcia, was arrested for wandering drunk in the Jewish quarter. He blamed the Jews for having made him drunk. The source for this account further reports that "under his guidance the Jews were wont to occupy themselves with the study of the *Kitab al-dalalat:* this is a work upon the principles of their religion by *Ra'is* Musa." The reference is to the *Guide of the Perplexed* by Moses b. Maimon. This Ibn Hud was apparently one of those Muslims who found value in Islam, Judaism, and Christianity, as he is reported to have valued all of them, and even faced the rising sun and crossed himself.[4]

Jewish scholars in Muslim Spain, in spite of the general polemical attitude against Islam, nevertheless did not hesitate to cite Muslim writings, proverbs, poetry, and even verses from the *Qur'an*.[5] Every Jewish boy, particularly in Muslim Spain and to some extent also in other Muslim lands, learned both Arabic and Hebrew, the Bible and the *Qur'an*, and many continued their education with Muslim scholars, just as Muslim boys did. Thus, they were thoroughly familiar with Muslim culture.

Most Muslims were less well acquainted with Jewish culture, but some scholars had a significant amount of knowledge of the Hebrew Bible and some even of parts of the Talmud and other rabbinical traditions. Of course, some of these gained their knowledge secondhand by discussions with Jews, just as did some Christian scholars. However, there are examples of Muslim scholars who read Hebrew and the Bible.[6] Just as Jews did not hesitate to cite Muslim traditions and writings, so many Muslims throughout the centuries repeated traditions learned orally from Jews or that they found in other written sources. Indeed, a tradition (*hadith*) attributed to Muhammad said "narrate (traditions) concerning the Children of Israel, and there is nothing objectionable in that." Later Muslim scholars made similar statements.[7]

Jews and Muslims in Daily Life

Medieval Jews never assimilated into any culture. The choices were either to remain a Jew or to convert. While some Jews, indeed, converted to Islam of their own free will in the early medieval period, most remained loyal to their own people and traditions.[8] However, the Jews in the Muslim world were acculturated in that they not only shared the aforementioned cultural outlook but also daily customs and way of life. These included such things as housing, clothing, and food, among others.

Living in primarily warm climates, it was natural that houses should be constructed to be as cool as possible, particularly for the unbearable summer months, and take advantage of open spaces and windows. Both Jews and Muslims lived in such houses, with high ceilings and usually of two stories, the upper one containing chambers for sleeping. Further comfort was added by marble floors and walls for the more affluent and open courtyards with fountains and gardens. Houses often had several such courtyards, in fact, and the fountains also served to cool the atmosphere, sometimes with channels carrying water into the interior of the house.

Clothing was also designed for comfort as well as style. Cool fine linen cloth, usually imported, was the preferred material, although in the winter heavier cotton or brocade might be used. Muslim men, not women, wore veils, often a part of the turban that extended to cover the lower portion of the face. There was no distinction in clothing worn by Jews from that of Muslims until the eleventh century in Egypt when certain restrictions were imposed. This was more strictly adhered to by the fanatic Almohads in the twelfth century, as noted elsewhere here.

With the exception of dietary restrictions, animals slaughtered according to Jewish law, the strict separation of dairy from meat products, and other things, Jews ate the same kinds of food as did Muslims. Both had a fondness for every imaginable kind of vegetable and fruit, the cultivation of which the Jews largely learned from their Muslim neighbors, although, also as previously mentioned, Jews had always been involved in agriculture and may have been responsible for such things as the introduction of olives to Spain. It is unfortunate that we do not have medieval Jewish cookbooks, as we do Arabic ones, but some information may be gleaned from other sources, such as the previously mentioned medical books of Maimonides.

Jews and Muslims frequently were partners in commercial activities, both temporarily and on a more permanent basis, as evidenced particularly in the Genizah documents studied by Goitein and others.[9] I have not found evidence of any such relationships between Jews and Muslims in Spain, but the sources are of course far more limited.[10] Jews and Muslims of course frequently bought goods and produce from each other. The Jewish markets in Muslim Spain, for example, particularly in cities such as Lucena, which, it was claimed, was totally Jewish, attracted Muslim merchants on a regular basis.

Another aspect of financial contact was the lending or borrowing of money. While again there are few references to this in Muslim Spain, there are many in Spain after the Christian reconquest, particularly in Aragonese towns and cities where a substantial Muslim population continued to reside.

On a social level, there was constant contact between Muslims and Jews. The wine parties or banquets that were a frequent part of Muslim life are the most prominent example of this. Again, particularly in Muslim Spain, Jews frequented such parties hosted by Muslims, and at least in the case of Samuel Ibn Naghrillah, the eleventh-century prime minister and commander-in-chief of the Muslim kingdom of Granada, Muslims often visited him. At wine parties, which often lasted throughout the night, wine was drunk to the accompaniment of song and dance (either boys or girls or both) and poetry was recited and often extemporized, of course in Arabic. Jews had their own parties of this kind as well. Many Hebrew poems describe such things, and give evidence of the amorous attachments of Jews for Muslim girls and boys, and Arabic poetry similarly refers to Jewish boys, at least.

Sexual relations took place, in spite of the theoretical prohibitions both of Jewish and Muslim law. Such activities were sanctioned and in fact participated in by the outstanding Jewish and Muslim poets, as well as more average people. The public baths frequently provided opportunity for such contacts as well (Jews were not prohibited from using these, together with Muslims, except in the reign of the fanatic Almohad rulers; in Christian Spain, separate days were set aside for the use of baths by Christians and Jews and Muslims).

Not all was sweetness and light, of course, in the relations between Muslims and Jews. The careful historian must **Negative** avoid such extremes as recently represented by the claims of **Attitudes** one writer that medieval Islam was more tolerant of Judaism and Jews than was Christianity, and that of another that medieval Jews preferred living under Christianity rather than Islam.[11] It would require a lengthy article to correct all the misconceptions of these two positions, but some brief remarks are necessary. Comparing the attitudes toward, and treatment of, Jews between two vast cultures such as this requires more than a brief book (nor is this the first such effort). But medieval

Christendom, to use Cohen's phrase, included more than Germany, with passing references to France (like Cohen, Robert Chazan, as noted in the previous chapter, considered only Germany and some references to France in his book). Neither Spain nor Italy, England, the Byzantine Empire, or central and eastern Europe are mentioned.

Not only is it incorrect to claim, particularly on the basis of such limited evidence, that Jews were excluded from medieval Christian society, but the whole concept of a more tolerant Islam falls apart in light of such things as the persecution in Egypt (including Syria-Palestine) under al-Hakam II in the eleventh century or the far worse persecution suffered under the Almohads in the twelfth century, which included slaughter of entire communities and forced conversion of many Jews and Christians.[12]

In truth, the attitudes both of Muslims and Christians with regard to Jews were complex and need to be considered on different levels: the official position of theologians or lawyers, religious authorities, and rulers; the attitudes as expressed in chronicles and other writings, including polemics; and to the extent possible the popular level of daily relations between people. As I have elsewhere dealt at length with Jewish and Muslim polemic, and topics such as the charges that Jews fabricated the Torah, which were made both by Muslims and, to a lesser extent, Christians, I shall not repeat that here except to add a few details.[13]

One of the themes common in Christian anti-Jewish polemic from the letters of Paul through the medieval period and beyond was that the Christians are the "true Israel," the real heirs of Abraham. At least some Muslims shared similar ideas about Islam. Thus, the famous Persian Muslim historian al-Tabari (d. 923) in a work on the *Qur'an* commented (on II .135–140):

The meaning of the verse is: Say, O Muhammad to those Jews and Christians who quarrel with you about God, having hidden away the proof they have that Abraham and those whom We named together with him [Ishmael, Isaac, Jacob and his twelve sons] were Muslims, and having pretended they (*scil.,* Abraham and his descendants) were Jews or Christians, and having thus lied.... (etc.)

The statement concludes with a warning to Jews and Christians not to rely on the merit of their ancestors; for reward and punishment depends on each individual, and not on ancestral merit.[14]

But the attitudes expressed in official sources varied widely. For example, Ibn Sai'd of Toledo (1029–1070), an important religious judge, wrote a history of the nations in which he demonstrated considerable knowledge and appreciation of Jews, and of individual Jewish scholars in Spain, some of whom he knew personally. He expressed admiration for Jewish knowledge of the sciences and intercalation of the calendar in particular and added: "This people is the house [source] of prophecy and of the prophetic message [written scripture] of mankind, and the majority of the prophets—the blessings and peace of Allah upon them."[15] But another famous Muslim scholar of Spanish origin, the great historian Ibn Khaldun (1332–1406) was not so admiring of the Jews. In his discussion of the important Muslim concept of "group feeling" and false claims to noble descent and the like, he observed:

The Israelites are the most firmly misled in this delusion. They originally had one of the greatest "houses" in the world, first, because of the great number of prophets and messengers born among their ancestors, extending from Abraham to Moses.... Then they were divested of all that, and they suffered humiliation and indigence. They were destined to live as exiles on earth. For thousands of years they knew only enslavement and unbelief [or, in one text, "subservience to unbelief"]. Still the delusion of (nobility) has not left them. They can be found saying: "He is an Aaronite [descendant of Aaron];" "He is a descendant of Joshua;" "He is one of Caleb's progeny;" "He is from the tribe of Judah." This in spite of the fact that their group feeling has disappeared and that for many long years they have been exposed to humiliation.[16]

He also wrote: "One may look at the Jews and the bad character they have acquired, such that they are described in every region and period as having the quality of *khurj*, which, according to well-known technical terminology means 'insincerity and trickery.'"[17] However, he was by no means entirely against the Jews, for he later noted that the Jews in the Land of Israel became expert in the crafts related to food, clothing, "and all the other parts of (domestic) economy, so much so that these things, as a rule, can still be learned from them to this day."[18]

In addition to the militant anti-Jewish and Christian polemic found in Islam, there was also a subcategory, the minority opinion of general religious skepticism. For example, Abu'l-Allah al-Ma'arri of Syria (973–1058), a blind grammarian, expressed skeptical views in his great poetic work *Luzumiyyat,* as well as other writings; for example:

> They all err—Moslems, Christians, Jews and Magians;
> Two make Humanity's universal sect:
> One, man intelligent without religion,
> And one, religion without intellect.

In other words, to explicate this rather awkward translation, two things only are universally to be found among people: those who are intelligent without religion and those who believe in a religion but without intelligence.[19] But even the skeptic was particularly antagonistic to Jewish traditions, as in the following:

> The Jews went astray: their Torah is an invention
> of the doctors [meaning scholars] and rabbis
> Who pretend to have derived it from one [a prophet] like

themselves; then traced it further back to the Almighty.
Whenever you discomfit a man who argues for his religion,
he hands over its keys [the task of defending it]
to the traditions [by which it is attested]

On the popular level, where often there are few sources from which
to draw significant conclusions, in addition to the previously discussed
examples of daily contact between Muslims and Jews, such things as the
evidence of amulets, talismans, and other magical incantations utilizing
Hebrew names of God and the mystical Jewish formulae for their invoking of guardian angels (all carefully transliterated in Arabic script) are
evidence of some substantial reliance upon Jewish superstitions among
ordinary Muslim people.[20]

As for the notion that Jews preferred living under Christianity rather
than Islam, there are sources that clearly contradict this; for example, an
apocalypse, written apparently in 750, purporting to be the visions of
Simon bar Yohai, in which God reveals to him that the Muslim kingdom
will rule over the Jews after "Edom" (the Christians), to which the rabbi
complains that they are just as bad as the Christians, but he is told that
they were only brought to save the Jews *from* the Christians.[21]

The attitude of the more pious Jews was expressed by Bahya b. Asher
of Zaragoza at the end of the thirteenth century, who in his commentary
on Deuteronomy 30.7 explained "your enemies" as Ishmael (the Muslims)
and "those who hate you" as Esau (the Christians). An enemy, he further
explains, is worse than a hater since he has "eternal enmity in his heart."
Esau is bad enough, but the Muslims are "more difficult" to the Jews than
the Christians, and hence it was said "[better] under [the rule] of Edom,
but not under Ishmael." Generally, he considered that the present exile,
under domination both of Muslims and Christians, was the worst ever
faced by Jews.[22] But Bahya, who had been a student of the renowned
Solomon Ibn Adret in Barcelona, was raised and lived in Christian Spain.
True, there was a substantial Muslim population in Zaragoza, but there is
nothing in any of the sources to indicate bad relations between them and
the Jews; on the contrary.

As a corrective to the exaggerated statements of both theories are the
countless harsh polemics against both Islam and Christianity. The latter
have been discussed generally by numerous scholars over the centuries,
whereas the former are certainly less known but no less severe.[23]

In point of fact, the attitude of rabbis and Jewish authorities toward
Muslims and Christians depended largely on where the writer lived. Those
such as Maimonides and others in Muslim countries vigorously denied
that Muslims were in any way to be considered idolaters in terms of the
talmudic law prohibiting business relations or other contacts with such
(on certain days, before and after their holidays), whereas Christians definitely were.[24] Scholars living in Christian lands, such as Rashi and nearly

all European rabbis, just as vigorously asserted that Christians were not idolaters.[25]

Jews owed a great deal to Muslim civilization. From it derived their own knowledge of and substantial contribu-   Conclusions
tions to science, medicine, philosophy, poetry, and literature, among other things. Daily life, in terms of comfortable clothing and housing, the quality and variety of food, health and sanitary standards, was unquestionably far superior to that of Jews living in Christian Europe (with the possible exception of Italy in the late medieval period). Generally, Jews and Muslims understood each other and got along well, but it would be wrong to speak of tolerance in modern terms. Jews were always second-class citizens, at best, under Islam (in fact, of course, they were not citizens at all, since they did not have equal rights in any area). However, they generally did not suffer undue discrimination, until the fanatical laws imposed by al-Hakam II in the early eleventh century or the far worse Almohads in the following century.

But, while avoiding the exaggerated claims that Islam was by nature far more tolerant of Jews than was Christianity, neither is it true that Jews preferred living under Christians rather than Muslims. We must not be misled by the few obviously polemical statements made in some religious writings. Jews in Christian lands, of course, had no choice (some, it is true, migrated to Muslim countries, but the difficulties of learning Arabic and adjusting to a completely different culture were enormous). As for Jews in Muslim lands, we do not hear of any significant move to Christian countries except during the Almohad persecution, when many Jews in Muslim Spain fled north to Christian cities. The average Jew did quite well under Muslim rule, and many became wealthy and rose to high positions in the government.

JEWS AND CHRISTIANS: COEXISTENCE

One of the chief differences between Jewish-Muslim and Jewish-Christian relations is that of shared culture, as we have seen. Islam, like Judaism (as mentioned elsewhere here, an incorrect term), was a civilization, whereas Christianity was and is a religion. The only shared cultural heritage is the Bible.[26] Yet, as we shall see, the understanding of that was usually completely different for Christians and Jews.

The fundamental doctrines of Christian theology were unintelligible to Jews. With the exception of some Spanish scholars, primarily in the fourteenth and fifteenth centuries, Jews had no knowledge of the complexities of that theology (anyway, few could read Latin, in which theological works were written). Such things as the incarnation of God as man, the virgin birth, and the resurrection of Jesus were completely beyond comprehension. Jewish polemics in many countries focused on these, as well as other Christian beliefs, and offered often very strong arguments against them. The doctrine of the Trinity was the most misunderstood. To the Jew, it seemed that this simply means there are three gods, and thus a denial of the one true God. This did not, of course, make Christians idolaters (indeed, the Talmud already stated that association of other powers with God on the part of Gentiles is not included in that category), but it seriously misunderstood the intricate nature of the doctrine, which does not mean that there are three gods but that God is manifest in three distinct but united presences.[27]

From the Christian side, Jews were a problem. On the one hand, they were "witnesses to the truth" of the Christian scriptures, a peculiar notion that originated with St. Augustine (354–430). For this reason, Christians decided to keep Jews alive and not kill them.[28] From the other side, Jews were heretics who denied the basic principles of the Christian faith and whose very existence was a constant challenge to Christianity. Within canon (church) law, Jews were dealt with under the category of heretics. The whole history of Christianity had been one of conflict with heresy within its own ranks. As one noted scholar has observed, "a chief reason for the existence of heresy lies in the nature of Christianity itself ... the Christians' interest in abstract truth led them to try to define it in a system of orthodoxy, and since no definition of truth ever goes unchallenged, the inevitable companion of orthodoxy is dissent."[29] It was, indeed, the same fanatic zeal for persecution of heresy that produced the Dominican Order, the Inquisition, and the persecution of Jews.

All of this, and more, produced an unending stream of Christian polemic throughout the Middle Ages. Most of this was directed against Judaism rather than Jews, but there were certainly examples of the latter as well. Just as with the question of Muslim attitudes to Jews, so also with Christian we must distinguish official positions from popular feelings. The former includes the polemics, the attitudes of popes and theologians, canon law, and church councils. As all of this has been dealt with more or less adequately elsewhere, it will not be discussed here.[30]

However, even in official circles it was not all darkness. Bernard of Clairvaux, as is well known, came to the defense of Jews in the Second Crusade, although he was certainly not entirely friendly towards Jews. The important defense of the Jewish status quo issued by every pope, sometimes several times by each, has already been mentioned in the previous chapter. Particularly notable are the strong words of rebuke against the attack on Jews in France in the Crusade of 1236: "[they] plot impious designs against the Jews and pay no heed to the fact that the proof of the Christian faith comes, as it were, from their archives".... He then condemned the hypocritical claim used to justify the torture and killing of Jews because they refused baptism, saying that they "are not to be compelled to the grace of baptism unless they want it voluntarily."[31] This was in accord with canon law and was an important protection against attempts to forcibly convert Jews.

An important Spanish monk of the late eighth century, Beatus of Liebana (who probably never met a Jew in his life), broke with a long Christian tradition of referring to the "synagogue of Satan," which had led in the earlier centuries to burnings of synagogues and prohibitions on rebuilding destroyed synagogues, in declaring that the expression in the book of Revelation does not refer to actual Jews but to heretical Christians, "they who are called Jews but are not."[32]

The hostile attitudes of Christians to Jews, and physical assaults on them, have been discussed in the previous chapter (to which much more could be added). **Positive Relations** Bad as the record is, it is also true that these incidents **between** took place sporadically, sometimes separated by hundreds **Christians** of years. On the whole, medieval Jews did not **and Jews** consider that their life with the Christians was intolerable or that they were constantly persecuted. Had they done so, there was a very simple solution: leave the country. Nor can we say, but to go where? For even if it were to be argued, incorrectly, that all of Christian Europe was hostile to the Jews, they could certainly have gone to Muslim lands. In fact, all of Europe was not antagonistic, and with the exception of Jews expelled from England or (several times) France, very few Jews actually moved to Spain, for instance, which certainly was more tolerant than other countries, or even to the papal territory in central Italy where Jews were not persecuted.

In medieval Germany, in the very time of the First Crusade (or slightly before or after), Rashi testifies to the close relationships that were common between Christians and Jews. They jointly owned ovens for baking. Jews frequently employed Christian laborers, had their horses shoed by Christian blacksmiths, borrowed food for their animals, and had their clothes washed and repaired by Christians.[33] Jews borrowed money from Christians, as well as lending to them (so also, frequently, in medieval Spain). Jews gave gifts to Christians, particularly on Purim.[34]

Few medieval Jews (except in Rome) ever saw a pope, and even fewer ever saw a theologian, but many of them dealt frequently with the local archbishop or bishop, many of whom, everywhere in Europe, were on friendly terms with Jews and were respected by them. In Spain, particularly, there were archbishops and bishops who were protective of Jews and counted Jews among their personal friends.[35]

As stated more than once here, there were no ghettos in the Middle Ages. Jews and Christians lived as neighbors, quite often literally next door to each other (only in the later medieval period were there some attempts to separate Jews in special quarters, or areas, within a city). Furthermore, their Christian neighbors were mostly illiterate, except possibly in Spain, and therefore had no knowledge of all the official anti-Jewish polemic. It is quite easy to understand, under these circumstances, why *on the whole* Jews and Christians got along quite well together. In the daily routine of work, raising and feeding children, worrying about the crops, they had far more in common than in the things that separated them.

NOTES

1. For details of much of what follows here, see Norman Roth, "*Dhimma:* Jews and Muslims in the Early Medieval Period," in Ian Richard Netton, ed., *Studies in Honour of Clifford Edmund Bosworth* (Leiden, 2000) 1: 238–66. It is unfortunate that there is no good book on the subject of general relations between Jews and Muslims in the Middle Ages.

2. See some examples and details, with bibliographical references, in Roth, ibid., 256–64, with much new information.

3. See Norman Roth, "Jewish Reactions to the Arabiyya and the Renaissance of Hebrew in Spain," *Journal of Semitic Studies* 31 (1976): 145–58. Time and fate permitting, I plan a study and anthology of translations of some of this poetry.

4. Ignaz Goldziher, note in *Jewish Quarterly Review* 4 (1894): 218–20.

5. See examples in Norman Roth, *Jews, Visigoths & Muslims in Medieval Spain: Cooperation & Conflict* (Leiden, 1994), 177–79, to which other examples could be added.

6. See Roth, "*Dhimma* in Early Islam," 263–64, and especially on Ibn Hazm and his extensive knowledge not only of the Hebrew Bible but of talmudic and other traditions, in Roth, *Jews, Visigoths & Muslims,* 224. Hava Lazarus-Yafeh, *Intertwined Worlds: Medieval Islam and Bible Criticism* (Princeton, N.J., 1992), a little book not without some value, has her own agenda; the reply to her unwarranted criticism of my statement about Ibn Hazm will be in the Spanish translation of my book. See also Roth, "Muslim Knowledge of the Hebrew Bible and Jewish Traditions in the Middle Ages," *Maghreb Review* 16 (1991): 74–83.

7. See "*Dhimma* in Early Islam," 262–63.

8. See the section on conversion to Islam, 190–92, in the article "Conversion by Jews" in Norman Roth, ed., *Medieval Jewish Civilization: An Encyclopedia* (New York, 2003).

9. See, for example, S. D. Goitein, *Mediterranean Society: The Jewish Communities of the Arab World as Portrayed in the Documents of the Cairo Geniza* (Berkeley, Calif., Los Angeles, London, 1967–1993), 1: 173 and 2, ch. 8.

10. On Jews in commerce generally in Muslim Spain, see Roth, *Jews, Visigoths & Muslims,* 145 ff. (a revised Spanish translation of that work is in preparation).

11. The first is the view of Mark R. Cohen, a distinguished scholar and expert in Jewish life in medieval Egypt, in his book, *Under Cross and Crescent: The Jews in the Middle Ages* (Princeton, N.J., 1994), and the second that of Bernard Septimus, "Under Edom and Not under Ishmael—the Fate of a Saying" (in Hebrew), in *Zion (Tsiyon)* 47 (1982): 103–11. Far more than Cohen's thesis, rightly criticized by various scholars, that of Septimus has curiously become the popular view (no doubt because of the obvious implications for current Israeli-Arab relations). It is, nevertheless, no less inaccurate than Cohen. One of the best of the critical reviews of Cohen's book is Joel Kraemer in *Journal of Religion,* 77 (1997): 449–54. On some of the sources overlooked by Septimus, see Roth, *Jews, Visigoths & Muslims,* 316, notes 32 and 35.

12. For details, primarily relating to Spain, of course, see Roth, *Jews, Visigoths & Muslims,* 116 ff. There I have provided for the first time a translation of Abraham

Ibn Ezra's eulogy on the destruction and conversion of Jewish communities (I now believe that poem was written while he was in France, however, which explains some incorrect information).

13. See Roth, ibid., all of ch. 7 and the notes; see also Roth, "Forgery and Abrogation of the Torah: A Theme in Muslim and Christian Polemic in Spain," *American Academy for Jewish Research. Proceedings* 54 (1987): 203–36 and "Polemic in the Hebrew Religious Poetry of Medieval Spain," *Journal of Semitic Studies* 34 (1989): 153–77.

14. Translated by M. Schwarz, "'Aquisition' (*Kasb*) in Early Kalam," in S. M. Stern, et al., eds., *Islamic Philosophy and the Classical Tradition* (Oxford, 1972), 364–65. Schwarz's punctuation here (colon) is erroneous, giving the impression that the "lie" is the quotation from the *Qur'an* that follows. The "lie" is the statement just made; that is, that the patriarchs were "Jews or Christians."

15. Quoted in Roth, *Jews, Visigoths & Muslims,* 180, and see the discussion of sources in note 60 there.

16. Ibn Khaldun, *Muqqadimah,* trans. Franz Rosenthal (New York, 1958) 1: 275.

17. Ibid. 3: 306; on the difficulty of this word, see Rosenthal's note there.

18. Ibid.2: 287–88 (not "Syria," as Rosenthal translated, here and elsewhere; the Arabic word *al-Sham* includes both lands, but in the context obviously the Land of Israel is meant.

19. Ma'arri, *Luzumiyyat* II. 201.21; trans. R.A. Nicholson, *Studies in Islamic Poetry* (Cambridge, 1921; reprinted 1969), 167; On other polemical writings of his, see I. U. Kratchkovsky, *Among Arabic Manuscripts* (Leiden, 1953), 21 ff. Nicholson was absolutely right in seeing in this writer's apparent anti-Jewish polemic a veiled skeptical attack on Islam; for example: "Follow Reason and do what it deems good, for it gathers the honey of counsel, and accept not a commandment from the Torah, for verily the truth is hidden from it." (I. 394.8; trans. ibid., 168).

20. See Ignaz Goldziher, "Hebraische Elemente in muhammedanischen Zaubersprüchen," *Zeitschrift der deutschen morgenlandischen Gesellschaft* 48 (1894): 358–60; reprinted in his *Gesammelte Schriften* (Hildesheim, 1967) 3: 348–50.

21. Judah Even-Shmuel, ed., *Midrashei geulah* (Jerusalem, 1954), 187.

22. See the complete quotations and discussion in *Jews, Visigoths & Muslims,* 211–13.

23. For an overview of the former, see the article "Polemics, anti-Christian" in Roth, *Medieval Jewish Civilization,* with bibliography. There is no survey, or even study, of anti-Muslim polemic; however, many examples will be found in Roth, *Jews, Visigoths & Muslims,* ch. 7, as previously mentioned.

24. See Roth, *Jews, Visigoths & Muslims.*

25. See the article "Christian-Jewish Relations" in Roth, *Medieval Jewish Civilization,* 151–52, on this.

26. The tendency today is to refer to the "Hebrew Bible," as if there were another kind (all others are translations, of course), probably to avoid the polemical term "Old Testament." The Catholic Church, however, correctly emphasized that only the Hebrew scriptures are of divine origin (either "revealed," the Torah, or "inspired," the Prophets) and the "New Testament" derives its authority from them.

27. In Latin, *persona;* actually a legal term that does not mean "persons" but that reflects the Greek term "hypostasis." See the important discussion by Henry Osborn Taylor, *The Emergence of Christian Culture in the West* (New York, 1958). There is, of course, a vast literature on Christian theology; for the medieval

period perhaps the best general survey is Jaroslav Pelikan, *The Christian Tradition: A History of the Development of Doctrine* (Chicago, 1971–1978), the first three of five volumes. See also specifically Richard Cross, *The Metaphysics of the Incarnation: Thomas Aquinas to Duns Scotus* (Oxford, 2002).

28. Augustine, *City of God*, Book 18, ch. 46 (see the quotation and discussion in the article "Church and the Jews" in Roth, *Medieval Jewish Civilization*, 163). See also the thirteenth-century theologian Alexander of Hales, quoted in Robert Chazan, *Church, State and Jew in the Middle Ages* (New York, 1980), 45 (the glossator to whom he refers is Augustine, commentary on Psalm 59. 10–12) and St. Bernard of Clairvaux, ibid., 103.

29. Jeffrey Burton Russell, *Dissent and Reform in the Early Middle Ages* (Berkeley, Calif., 1965), 2. This is an excellent book, though it betrays a strong bias against the heresies, which the author condemns more than describes.

30. See, for example, all of the articles listed under "Christian-Jewish Relations" in Roth, *Medieval Jewish Civilization*, ix. Unfortunately, there is no general survey of Christian anti-Jewish polemic, nor was it possible to have an article on that in the aforementioned encyclopedia.

31. Text and translation in Solomon Grayzel, *The Church and the Jews in the XIIIth Century* (Philadelphia, 1933), 226–27.

32. *Beati in Apocalipsin*, ed. Henry A. Sanders (Rome, 1930), 175 (II. 2 .7).

33. *Sefer ha-orah*, by Rashi or his students (Lemberg, 1905, photo reprint 1966), part 2: 41, 53, 54, 56.

34. *Teshuvot hokhmei Sarfat ve-Lotir*, ed. Joel Müller (Vienna, 1881), 86; Abraham b. Natan of Lunel, *Sefer ha-manhig*, ed. Yitzhak Raphael (Jerusalem, 1978) 1: 248, notes to line 35 citing numerous statements in Rashi on gifts to Gentiles.

35. See Roth, "Bishops and Jews in the Middle Ages," *The Catholic Historical Review* 80 (1994): 1–17, and the index to Norman Roth, *Conversos, Inquisition, and the Expulsion of the Jews from Spain* (Madison, Wisc., 1995; revised paper ed., 2002).

RECOMMENDED READING

Baron, Salo W. *A Social and Religious History of the Jews.* Philadelphia, New York, 1952–1983, 9.

Chazan, Robert, ed. *Church, State and Jew in the Middle Ages.* New York, 1980.

Roth, Norman. *Jews, Visigoths & Muslims in Medieval Spain. Cooperation & Conflict.* Leiden, 1994.

GLOSSARY

Gaon (pl. *geonim*)   rabbinical head of the academies in Baghdad, or in the Land of Israel.

Genizah   "hidden" (Hebrew); place where worn manuscripts and books, usually of sacred writings, were kept rather than destroying them; primarily, it refers to the famous collection found in Cairo that includes all kinds of writings, Hebrew and Arabic, from the medieval period.

midrash (pl. *midrashim*)   homiletic interpretation of the Bible, individual works of various titles composed from the fourth century C.E. through the early medieval period.

Mishnah   collection of the basic laws, which, interpreting biblical commandments, became the foundation for the Talmud; traditionally said to have been compiled by Rabbi Judah "the Prince" ca. 200 C.E.

Qaraites   heretical Jewish sect that emerged in the eighth century and rejected all rabbinical laws and interpretation of the Bible, claiming to follow the Bible literally; continued to be important throughout the Middle Ages but declined afterwards.

Talmud   multivolume collection of laws, records of discussions by the rabbis, stories and homiletic interpretation of the Bible; there are actually two, the more famous "Babylonian" Talmud and the "Palestinian," or Jerusalem, Talmud, which has only survived in an incomplete form.

yeshivah (pl. *yeshivot*)   academy in which boys and young men studied the Talmud and Jewish law. *Yeshivot* were located in all countries in the medieval (and modern) period.

BIBLIOGRAPHY

SELECTED SOURCES

Abraham b. Isaac. *Sefer ha-eshkol*, ed. Hanoch Albeck. Jerusalem, 1928. 2 vols.
Abraham b. Natan of Lunel. *Sefer ha-manhig*, ed. Yitzhak Raphael. Jerusalem, 1978.
    2 vols.
Benjamin of Tudela. *Itinerary*, ed. and trans. M. Adler. London, 1907.
Ibn Ezra peirushei ha-Torah, ed. A. Weiser. Jerusalem, 1976.
Ibn Khaldun. *Muqqadimah*, trans. Franz Rosenthal. New York, 1958.
Isaac al-Fasi. *She'elot u-teshuvot*. Livorno, 1781; reprinted Warsaw, 1884, No. 73.
Isaac b. Sheshet. *She'elot u-teshuvot*. Vilna, 1878; with notes; photo reprint Jerusalem,
    s.a. 1967.
Jacob b. Meir. *Sefer ha-yashar* (responsa). Berlin, 1898.
Jacob b. Moses Mölln (or Molin). *Sefer Mahari"l*, ed. Shlomo Spitzer. Jerusalem,
    1989.
Judah ha-Levy, *Selected Poems*, trans. Nina Salaman. Philadelphia, 1928.
Judah Minz. *He la-khem zera le-tsedakah (She'elot u-teshuvot)*. Fürth, 1766.
Judah b. Samuel. *"he-Hasid," Sefer hasidim*. Berlin, 1893.
Kitab al-muhadara wa'l-mudhakra, ed. and trans. Montserrat Abumalham Mas.
    Madrid, 1986.
Lilio de medecina, first published in Seville in 1495; critical edition by John Cull and
    Brian Dutton. Madison, Wisc., 1991.
Ma'arri, *Luzumiyyat* II. 201.21, trans. R.A. Nicholson, *Studies in Islamic Poetry*.
    Cambridge, 1921; reprinted 1969.
Meir b. Barukh of Rothenburg. *She'elot u-teshuvot*, ed. Moses Bloch. Budapest, 1895.
————. *She'elot u-teshuvot*. Prague, 1608.
Moses b. Maimon. *A Maimonides Reader*, ed. Isadore Twersky. Philadelphia, 1972.

———. *Mishneh Torah* (available in numerous editions).

———. *Mishnah im peirush … Neziqin.* Jerusalem, 1963, Hebrew text translated according to the Arabic by Joseph Kafi.

———. *Qovets teshuvot ha-Rambam.* Leipzig, 1859; photo reprint Westmead, England, 1969.

———. *Treatise on Asthma,* trans. S. Munter. Philadelphia, 1963.

Moses Maimonides' Two Treatises on the Regimen of Health, trans. A. Bar-Sela, H. E. Hoff, and Elias Faris. Philadelphia, 1964.

Moses b. Nahman. *Hidushey ha-Ramban, Shabbat, Eruvin, Megilah,* ed. Moses Herschler. Jerusalem, 1973.

"Rabenu Tam." See Jacob b. Meir.

Sefer ha-orah, by Rashi or his students. Lemberg, 1905, photo reprint 1966.

Rashi, *Teshuvot hokhmei Sarfat ve-Lotir,* ed. Joel Müller. Vienna, 1881.

Samson bar Tsadoq, *Sefer tashbats.* Warsaw, 1875.

Teshuvot hokhmei Sarfat ve-Lotir, ed. Joel Müller. Vienna, 1881.

Tosafot (additional commentaries; by French rabbis) in standard editions of the Talmud.

SECONDARY LITERATURE

Abrahams, Israel, ed. and trans. *Hebrew Ethical Wills.* Philadelphia, 1948.

Abulafia, Anna Sapir. *Disputational Literature and the Rise of Anti-Judaism in the West.* Brookfield, Vt., 1998; important collection of her articles.

Adler, Morris. *The World of the Talmud.* Philadelphia, 1968.

Alexander, Tamar. "Folklore." In Roth, ed., *Medieval Jewish Civilization: An Encyclopedia.* New York, 2003.

Azaceta, J. M., ed. *Cancionero de Juan Fernandez de Ixar.* Madrid, 1956.

Baer, Yitzhak (Fritz). *A History of the Jews in Christian Spain,* abridged trans. by Louis Schoffman. Philadelphia, 1966. 2 vols.

Bareket, Elinoar. "Fustat" (Egypt). In Roth, ed., *Medieval Jewish Civilization: An Encyclopedia.* New York, 2003.

Baron, Salo, W. "The Jewish Factor in Medieval Civilization." American Academy for Jewish Research. *Proceedings* 12 (1942): 1–42.

———. *A Social and Religious History of the Jews.* Philadelphia, New York, 1952–1983, especially vols. 1–4, 9, 10.

Baskin, Judith R. "Jewish Women in the Middle Ages." In Baskin, ed., *Jewish Women in Historical Perspective.* Detroit, 1991, 94–114.

———. "Marriage." In Roth, ed., *Medieval Jewish Civilization: An Encyclopedia.* New York, 2003.

Ben-Yehuda, Nachman. *The Masada Myth: Collective Memory and Mythmaking In Israel.* Madison, Wisc., 1995.

Berliner, Abraham. *Hayei ha-yehudim be-Ashkenaz.* Warsaw, 1900; photo reprint Jerusalem [?], 1969.

Bofarull y Sans, F. "Jaime I el conquistador y la comunidad judía de Montpellier." *Boletin de la real academia de buenas letras de Barcelona* 5 (1909): 484–92.

Bowman, Steven. "Byzantium." In Roth, ed., *Medieval Jewish Civilization: An Encyclopedia.* New York, 2003.

———. *The Jews of Byzantium, 1204–1453.* Tuscaloosa, Ala., 1985.

Brody, Robert. *The Geonim of Babylonia and the Shaping of Medieval Jewish Culture.* New Haven, Conn., London. 1998.

———. "Geonim." In Roth, ed., *Medieval Jewish Civilization: An Encyclopedia.* New York, 2003.

Brown, Elizabeth A. R. "Philip V, Charles IV, and the Jews of France: The Alleged Expulsion of 1322." *Speculum* 66 (1991): 294–328.

Bullough, Vern L. "The Development of the Medical University at Montpellier to the End of the Fourteenth Century." *Bulletin of the History of Medicine* 30 (1956): 508–23.

Calders. T., trans. *El principe I el Monjo.* Sabadell, 1987.

Chapin, Elizabeth. *Les villes des foires de Champagne des origines au debut du XIVe siècle.* Paris, 1937.

Chazan, Robert. "1007–1012: Initial Crisis for Northern European Jewry." American Academy for Jewish Research. *Proceedings* 38–39 (1970–1971): 101–17.

Chazan, Robert, ed. *Church, State and Jew in the Middle Ages.* New York, 1980.

Chazan, Robert. "Crusades." In Roth, ed., *Medieval Jewish Civilization: An Encyclopedia.* New York, 2003.

———. *Daggers of Faith. Thirteenth-Century Missionizing and Jewish Response.* Berkeley, Calif., 1989.

———. *European Jewry and the First Crusade.* Berkeley, Calif., 1987.

———. "The Facticity of Medieval Narrative." *Association for Jewish Studies Review* 16 (1991): 31–57.

———. *Medieval Jewry in Northern France.* Baltimore, 1973.

———. *Medieval Stereotypes and Modern Antisemitism.* Berkeley, Calif., 1997.

Cohen, Arthur. *Everyman's Talmud.* New York, 1948.

Cohen, Jeremy. "A 1086 Complex? Constructing the First Crusade in Jewish Historical Memory, Medieval and Modern." In Michael A. Signer and John Van Engen, eds., *Jews and Christians in Twelfth- Century Europe.* Notre Dame, Ind., 2001, 9–26.

———. *The Friars and the Jews: The Evolution of Medieval Anti-Judaism.* Ithaca, N.Y., 1982.

Cohen, Mark R. "Egypt." In Roth, ed., *Medieval Jewish Civilization. An Encyclopedia.* New York, 2003.

———. "Islam and Jews." In Roth, ed., *Medieval Jewish Civilization. An Encyclopedia.* New York, 2003.

———. *Jewish Self-Government in Medieval Egypt: The Origins of the Office of Head of the Jews, ca. 1065–1126.* Princeton, N.J., 1980.

———. *Under Cross and Crescent. The Jews in the Middle Ages.* Princeton, N.J., 1994.

Corriente, F., and A. Saenz Badillos, eds. *Poesia estrofica.* Madrid, 1991.

Cross, Richard. *The Metaphysics of the Incarnation: Thomas Aquinas to Duns Scotus.* Oxford, 2002.

Davidson, I., ed., and I. Zangwill, trans. *Selected Religious Poems* of Ibn Gabirol. Philadelphia, 1923; reprinted New York and Philadelphia, 1973 (paper ed.).

Dobson, R. B. *The Jews of Medieval York and the Massacre of March 1190.* York, England, 1974.

Duran, Simon b. Semah. *Sefer ha-tashbetz.* Lemberg, 1891; photo reprint Tel Aviv, s.a.

Elon, Menahem. *Jewish Law: History, Sources, Principles.* Philadelphia, 1994. 4 vols., translated from Hebrew.

Engel, David. "The Concept of Antisemitism in the Historical Scholarship of Amos Funkenstein." *Jewish Social Studies* 6 (1999): 111–29.

Epstein, Morris, ed. and trans. *Tales of Sendebar*. Philadelphia, 1967.

Even-Shmuel, Judah, ed. *Midrashei geulah*. Jerusalem, 1954.

Falk, Zeev W. *Jewish Matrimonial Law in the Middle Ages*. Oxford, 1966.

Ferber, Stanley. "Micrography: A Jewish Art Form." *Journal of Jewish Art* 3–4 (1977): 12–24.

Finkelstein, Louis. *Jewish Self-Government in the Middle Ages*. New York, 1964.

Fischel, Walter. *Jews in the Economic and Political Life of Medieval Islam*. 1937; reprinted New York, 1969.

Flannery, Edward H. *The Anguish of the Jews*. New York, 1965.

Flusser, David, ed. *Sefer Yosipon* (or *Yosifun*). Jerusalem, 1962.

Forteza-Rey, Maria, trans. *Libro de los Entremientos*. Madrid, 1983.

Frenkel, Miriam. "Adolescence in Jewish Medieval Society under Islam." *Continuity and Change* 16 (2001): 263–81.

Friedenwald, Harry. *The Jews and Medicine*. Baltimore, 1944; reprinted New York, 1967. 2 vols.

Friedhaber, Zvi. "The *Tanzhaus* in the life of Ashkenazi Jewry during the Middle Ages." (In Hebrew). *Jerusalem Studies in Jewish Folklore* 7 (1984): 49–60.

Friedman, Mordechai A. "Marriage as an Institution: Jewry under Islam." in David Kraemer, ed., *The Jewish Family: Metaphor and Memory*. New York, Oxford, 1989, 33–34.

———. "Polygyny in Jewish Tradition and Practice: New Sources from the Cairo Geniza." American Academy for Jewish Research. *Proceedings* 49 (1982): 33–68.

Funkenstein, Amos. "Basic Types of Christian Anti-Jewish Polemics in the Later Middle Ages." *Viator* 2 (1971) 373–82.

Goitein, S.D. "A Jewish Business Woman of the Eleventh Century." In Abraham A. Neuman and Solomon Zeitlin, eds., *The Seventy-Fifth Anniversary Volume of the Jewish Quarterly Review* (Philadelphia, 1967), 225–42.

———. *A Mediterranean Society: The Jewish Communities of the Arab World as Portrayed in the Documents of the Cairo Geniza* (Berkeley, Calif., Los Angeles, London, 1967–1993). 6 vols.

———. *Seder ha-hinukh bi-mei ha-geonim*. Jerusalem, 1962. In Hebrew.

———. "Three Trousseaux of Jewish Brides from the Fatimid Period." *AJS* (Association for Jewish Studies) *Review* 2 (1977):77–110.

Golb, Norman. *The Jews in Medieval Normandy: A Social and Intellectual History*. New York, 1998.

———. *Les Juifs de Rouen au Moyen Age: portrait d'une culture oubliée*. Rouen, 1985.

Goldziher, Ignaz. *Gesammelte Schriften*. Hildesheim, 1967.

———. "Hebraische Elemente in muhammedanischen Zauberspruchen." *Zeitschrift der deutschen morgenlandischen Gesellschaft* 48 (1894): 358–60.

———. Note in *Jewish Quarterly Review* 4 (1894): 218–20.

Gollancz, Hermann, trans. *Tophet and Eden*. London, 1921.

Grayzel, Solomon, ed. and trans. *The Church and the Jews in the Thirteenth Century*. Vol. 1. (Philadelphia, 1933); Vol. 2, ed. with additional notes Kenneth Stow (New York, 1989).

Grayzel, Solomon. "The Papal Bull Sicut Judeis." In *Studies and Essays in Honor of Abraham A. Neuman*, ed. Meir Ben-Horin et al. Leiden, 1962, 243–80.

Guttmann, Joseph. *Hebrew Manuscript Painting.* New York, 1978.
Joseph Gutmann, "Jewish Medieval Marriage Customs in Art: Creativity and Adaptation" In David Kraemer, ed., *The Jewish Family: Metaphor and Memory.* New York, Oxford, 1989.
Habermann, A. M. *Sefer gezeirot Ashkenaz ve-Tsarfat.* Jerusalem, 1946.
Hadas, Moses, trans. *The Book of Delight* (sic). New York, 1932.
———. *Fables of a Jewish Aesop.* New York, 1967.
ha-Kohen, Aaron b. Joseph. *Orhot hayyim.* Jerusalem, 1981; photo reprint of earlier editions.
ha-Kohen, Joseph. *Emeq ha-baka.* Cracow, 1895, ed. M. Letteris (actually S. D. Luzzatto).
Halkin, Abraham S., ed. and trans.(modern Hebrew). *Sefer ha-iyunim ve-ha-diyunim (Kitab al-muhadara wa'l-mudhakra).* Jerusalem, 1975.
Hallamish, Moshe. *An Introduction to the Kabbalah.* Albany, N.Y., 1999.
Haxen, Ulf. *Kings and Citizens.* New York, 1983.
Hay, Malcolm. *Europe and the Jews.* New York, 1960, with preface by Walter Kaufmann.
Herford, R. Travers. *The Ethics of the Talmud: Sayings of the Fathers.* New York, 1945.
Hidirgolou, P. "Les juifs d'apres la littérature historique latine, de Philippe Auguste a Philippe le Bel." *Revue des etudes juives* 133 (1974): 373–456.
Hirschfeld, Hartwig, trans. *The Kuzar.* London, 1905.
Ibn Verga, Salomon. *Shevet Yehudah.* Jerusalem, 1947.
Idel, Moshe. *Kabbalah: New Perspectives.* New Haven, Conn., 1988.
Jackson, Bernard S. *Jewish Law in Legal History and the Modern World.* Leiden, 1980.
Jarden, Dov, ed. *Mahberot* (sic). Jerusalem, 1957; reprinted 1984.
Joinville, Jean de. *Histoire de saint Louis.* Paris, 1872.
Jones, Alan, ed. *Romance Kharjas in Andalusian Arabic Muwassah Poetry.* London, 1988.
Jordan, William Chester. "French Law, Jews in." In Norman Roth, ed., *Medieval Jewish Civilization: An Encyclopedia.* New York, 2003.
———. *The French Monarchy and the Jews.* Philadelphia, 1989.
———. *Women and Credit in Pre-Industrial and Developing Societies.* Philadelphia, 1993.
Kahn, Salomon. "Documents inédits sur les juifs de Montpellier." *Revue des etudes juives* 19 (1889): 262 and 270–72.
Kanarfogel, Ephraim. "Charity." In Roth, ed., *Medieval Jewish Civilization: An Encyclopedia.* New York, 2003.
———. *Jewish Education and Society in the High Middle Ages.* Detroit, 1991.
Katz, Jacob. *Exclusiveness and Tolerance.* Oxford, 1961.
Kibre, Pearl. *The Nations in Medieval Universities.* Cambridge, Mass., 1948.
Kiener, Ronald C., trans. *The Early Kabbalah.* New York, 1986.
Kisch, Guido, "The Jews' Function in the Mediaeval Evolution of Economic Life." *Historia Judaica* 6 (1944): 1–12.
———. *The Jews in Medieval Germany.* Chicago, 1949.
———. "Nationalism and Race in Mediaeval Law." *Seminar* (Catholic University School of Canon Law) 1 (1943): 48–73.
Kraemer, David, ed., *The Jewish Family: Metaphor and Memory.* New York, Oxford, 1989.
Kratchkovsky, I. U. *Among Arabic Manuscripts.* Leiden, 1953.

Ladner, G, "The Concepts of Ecclesia and Christianitas." *Sacerdozio e regno da Gregorio VII a Bonifacio VIII.* Rome, 1954.

Langerman, Y. Tzvi. *The Jews and the Sciences in the Middle Ages.* Aldershot, 1999.

Langmuir, Gavin. "European Antisemitism That Led Directly to the Final Solution" in *History, Religion, and Antisemitism.* Berkeley, Calif., 1990,

Lazar, Moshé. *Poema de Yosef, Joseph and His Brethren. Three Ladino Versions.* Culver City, Calif., 1990.

———. *The Sephardic Tradition.* New York, 1972.

Lazard, L. "Les juifs de Tourraine." *Revue des études juives* 17 (1888): 210–34.

Lazarus-Yafeh, Hava. *Intertwined Worlds: Medieval Islam and Bible Criticism.* Princeton, N.J., 1992.

Laurier, E.-J., et al, eds. *Ordonnances des rois de France.* Paris, 1723–1849.

Leviant, Curt, ed. and trans. *King Artus, a Hebrew Arthurian Romance of 1279.* New York, 1969.

Lewis, Bernard, trans. and annotated. *The Kingly Crown.* London, 1961.

Lewis, E. "Organic Tendencies in Medieval Political Thought." *American Political Science Review* 32 (1938): 849–76.

Lea, Henry Charles. *A History of the Inquisition of the Middle Ages.* New York, 1906.

Leibowitz, J.O. "Abraham Caslari's Hebrew Ms. 'Pestilential Fevers'." *Korot* 4 (1968): 69–72 (English), 517–20 (Hebrew).

Lieber, Elinor. "Asaf's 'Book of Medicines': a Hebrew Encyclopedia of Greek and Jewish Medicine." *Dumbarton Oaks Papers* 38 (1984): 233–49.

Llubera, Ignasi, trans. from Hebrew. *Llibre d'Ensenyaments Delictables.* Barcelona, 1931.

Lopez, Robert S. "Byzantine law in the seventh century." *Byzantion* 16 (1944): 445–61.

——— and Irving W. Raymond, eds. *Medieval Trade in the Mediterranean World.* New York, London, 1968.

Lotter, Friedrich. "Cologne." In Norman Roth, ed., *Medieval Jewish Civilization: An Encyclopedia.* New York, 2003.

———. "Frankfurt." In Norman Roth, ed., *Medieval Jewish Civilization: An Encyclopedia.* New York, 2003.

———. "German Law, Jews in." In Norman Roth, ed., *Medieval Jewish Civilization: An Encyclopedia.* New York, 2003.

———. "Germany." In Norman Roth, ed., *Medieval Jewish Civilization: An Encyclopedia.* New York, 2003.

Mann, Vivian B., ed. *Gardens and Ghettos.* Berkeley, Calif., 1989.

Mansi, J.D. ed. *Sacrorum Conciliorum Nova et Amplissima Collectio.* Florence, 1759–1927.

Marcus, Ivan G. "From Politics to Martyrdom: Shifting Paradigms in the Hebrew Narratives of the 1096 Crusade Riots." *Prooftexts* 2 (1982): 40–52.

———. "History, Story and Collective Memory: Narrativity in Early Ashkenazic Culture." *Prooftexts* 10 (1990): 1–23.

Melzer, Aviv. *Asaph the Physician—the Man and His Book.* Unpublished dissertation, Madison, University of Wisconsin, 1971; available on microfilm, Ann Arbor Microfilms, 1972.

Milano, Attilio. *Storia degli ebrei in Italia.* Turin, 1963.

Montefiore, C.G., and H. Loewe. *A Rabbinic Anthology.* Philadelphia, 1960.

Muntner, Suessman. *Mavo le-sefer Asaf ha-rofe.* Jerusalem, 1957.

Nahon, G. "Les ordonances de Saint Louis sur les juifs." *Le nouveaux cahiers* 6 (1970).

———. "From the *Rue aux Juifs* to the *Chemin du Roy:* The Classical Age of French Jewry, 1108–1223." In Michael A. Signer and John Van Engen, *Jews and Christians in Twelfth-Century Europe.* Notre Dame, Ind., 2001, 311–39.

Narkiss, Bezalel. *Hebrew Illuminated Manuscripts.* Jerusalem, 1969.

Oelsner, Toni. "Wilhelm Roscher's Theory of the Economic and Social Position of the Jews in the Middle Ages." *YIVO Annual* 2 (1958): 183–212.

———. "The Place of Jews in Economic History as Viewed by German Scholars." *Year Book of the Leo Baeck Institute* 7 (1962): 183–212.

Parkes, James. *The Jew in the Medieval Community.* New York, 1976.

Pelikan, Jaroslav. *The Christian Tradition: A History of the Development of Doctrine.* Chicago, 1971–1978.

Perry, T. A. , trans. *The Moral Proverbs of Santob de Carrión.* Princeton, N.J., 1992.

———. *Proverbios morales.* Madison, Wisc., 1986.

Poliakov, Leon. *History of Anti-Semitism.* New York, 1965–1985. 4 vols. translated from the French.

Post, Gaines. *Studies in Medieval Legal Thought.* Princeton, N.J., 1964.

Pulzer, Peter G.J. *The Rise of Political Anti-Semitism in Germany and Austria.* London, 1964.

Rabinowitz, Louis. *The Social Life of the Jews of Northern France in the XII-XIV Centuries.* New York, 1972; second edition.

Regne, Jean, ed., *History of the Jews in Aragon, Regesta and Documents 1213–1327,* ed. Yom Tov Assis. Jerusalem, 1978.

Reichert, Victor E., trans. *The Tahkemoni.* Jerusalem, 1965, 1973.

Rodriguez, Carlos del Valle, trans. *Las Asambleas de los Sabios (Tahkemoni).* Murcia, 1988.

———. *El Divan Poetica.* Madrid, 1988.

Roscher, Wilhelm. "The Status of the Jews in the Middle Ages Considered from the Standpoint of Commercial Policy," trans. Solomon Grayzel in *Historia Judaica* 6 (1944): 19–20.

Rosner, Fred. *Medicine in the Mishneh Torah of Maimonides.* New York, 1984.

Roth, Cecil. *A History of the Jews in England.* Oxford, 1964; third edition.

———. *The History of the Jews of Italy.* Philadelphia, 1946.

Roth, Norman. "*Am Yisrael*: Jews or Judaism?" *Judaism* 37 (1988): 199–209.

———. "Bishops and Jews in the Middle Ages." *The Catholic Historical Review* 80 (1994): 1–17.

———. "Christian-Jewish Relations." In Norman Roth, ed., *Medieval Jewish Civilization: An Encyclopedia.* New York, 2003.

———. "Church and Jews." In Norman Roth, ed., *Medieval Jewish Civilization: An Encyclopedia.* New York, 2003.

———. "Clothing." In Norman Roth, ed., *Medieval Jewish Civilization: An Encyclopedia.* New York, 2003.

———. "Commerce." In Norman Roth, ed., *Medieval Jewish Civilization: An Encyclopedia.* New York, 2003.

———. *Conversos, Inquisition, and the Expulsion of the Jews from Spain.* Madison, Wis., 1995; revised paper ed., 2002.

———. "'Deal Gently with the Young Man'–Love of Boys in Medieval Hebrew Poetry of Spain." *Speculum* 57 (1982): 20–51.

————. "*Dhimma:* Jews and Muslims in the Early Medieval Period." In Ian Richard Netton, ed., *Studies in Honour of Clifford Edmund Bosworth.* Leiden, 2000, 1: 238–66.

————. "Education." In Norman Roth, ed., *Medieval Jewish Civilization: An Encyclopedia.* New York, 2003.

————. "Food." In Norman Roth, ed., *Medieval Jewish Civilization: An Encyclopedia.* New York, 2003.

————. "Forgery and Abrogation of the Torah: A Theme in Muslim and Christian Polemic in Spain." American Academy for Jewish Research. *Proceedings* 54 (1987): 203–36.

————. "Jewish and Muslim Physicians of Ali Ibn Tashufin." *Korot. The Israel Journal of the History of Medicine and Science* 10 (1993–1994): 83–91.

————. "Jewish Reactions to the Arabiyya and the Renaissance of Hebrew in Spain." *Journal of Semitic Studies* 31 (1976): 145–58.

————. *Jews, Visigoths & Muslims in Medieval Spain: Cooperation & Conflict.* Leiden, 1994.

————. "Languages, Used by Jews." In Norman Roth, ed., *Medieval Jewish Civilization: An Encyclopedia.* New York, 2003.

————. *Maimonides: Essays and Texts.* Madison, Wis., 1985.

————. "Medicine." In Norman Roth, ed., *Medieval Jewish Civilization: An Encyclopedia.* New York, 2003.

————, "Muslim Knowledge of the Hebrew Bible and Jewish Traditions in the Middle Ages." *Maghreb Review* 16 (1991): 74–83.

————. "A Note on Research into Jewish Sexuality in the Medieval Period." In Vern L. Bullough and James A. Brundage, eds., *Handbook of Medieval Sexuality.* New York, 1996, 309–17.

————. "Polemic in the Hebrew Religious Poetry of Medieval Spain." *Journal of Semitic Studies* 34 (1989): 153–77.

————. Review of Jeremy Cohen, *The Friars and the Jews: The Evolution of Medieval Anti-Judaism, Jewish Quarterly Review* 74 (1985): 321–26.

————. "Science and Mathematics." In Norman Roth, ed., *Medieval Jewish Civilization: An Encyclopedia.* New York, 2003.

————. "The 'Wiles of Women' Motif in the Medieval Hebrew Literature of Spain." *Hebrew Annual Review* 2 (1978): 145–65.

Roth, Norman, co-ed. (and author of various articles). In Michael E. Gerli, ed., *Medieval Iberia: An Encyclopedia.* New York, 2003.

Roth, Norman, ed. *Medieval Jewish Civilization: An Encyclopedia.* New York, 2003.

Rubens, Alfred. *A History of Jewish Costume.* New York, 1967.

Russell, Jeffrey Burton. *Dissent and Reform in the Early Middle Ages.* Berkeley, Calif., 1965.

Sanders, Henry A., ed. *Beati in Apocalipsin.* Rome, 1930.

Saperstein, Marc. *Jewish Preaching, 1200–1800.* New Haven, Conn., 1989.

Scholem, Scholem. *Kabbalah.* New York, 1974.

Schwartz, Barry, Yael Zerubavel, and Bernice M. Barnett, "The Recovery of Masada: A Study in Collective Memory." *The Sociological Quarterly* 27(1986): 147–64.

Schwarz, M. "'Aquisition' (*Kasb*) in Early Kalam." In S. M. Stern, et al., eds., *Islamic Philosophy and the Classical Tradition.* Oxford, 1972, 364–65.

Schwarzfuchs, S. *Les juifs de France.* Paris, 1975.

Septimus, Bernard. "Under Edom and Not under Ishmael—The Fate of a Saying." (In Hebrew.) *Zion (Tsiyon)* 47 (1982): 103–11.

Sharf, Andrew. *Byzantine Jewry from Justinian to the Fourth Crusade.* New York, 1971.

Shargel, Baila R. "The Evolution of the Masada Myth" *Judaism* 28 (1979): 357–71.

Shatzmiller, Joseph. "An Aspect of Social Life of Provençal Jews." *AJS* (Association for Jewish Studies) *Review* 2 (1977): 228–30, with texts, 242–47.

———. *Jews, Medicine, and Medieval Society.* Berkeley, Calif., 1994.

Shepard, Sanford, ed. *Proverbios morales.* Madrid, 1985.

Signer, Michael A., and John Van Engen, eds., *Jews and Christians in Twelfth-Century Europe.* Notre Dame, Ind., 2001.

Smalley, Beryl, *The Study of the Bible in the Middle Ages.* Notre Dame, Ind., 1964 edition; reprinted 1970.

Sola-Sole, Joseph, ed. *Corpus de poesia mozarabe.* Barcelona, 1973.

Solis-Cohen, Solomon, trans. Moses Ibn Ezra(h), *Selected Poems.* Philadelphia, 1945.

Spiegel, Shalom. *The Last Trial: On the Legends and Lore of the Command to Abraham to Offer Isaac as a Sacrifice.* New York, 1967.

Starr, Joshua. *Jews of the Byzantine Empire.* Athens, 1939.

Stephenson, Carl. *Borough and Town.* Cambridge, 1933.

Synan, Edward A. *The Popes and the Jews in the Middle Ages.* New York, 1965.

Taitz, Emily. "Champagne." In Norman Roth, ed., *Medieval Jewish Civilization: An Encyclopedia.* New York, 2003.

———. *The Jews of Medieval France: The Community of Champagne.* Westport, Conn., 1994.

Taylor, Henry Osborn. *The Emergence of Christian Culture in the West.* New York, 1958.

Urbach, Ephraim. *Ba'aley ha-tosafot.* Jerusalem, 1968.

Vernet, Juan. "Un antiguo tratado sobre el calendario judío en las 'Tabulas probatae'." *Sefarad* 14 (1954): 59–78.

Vetulani, Adam. "The Jews in Medieval Poland." *Jewish Journal of Sociology* 4 (1962): 274–94.

Wettinger, Godfrey. "Late Medieval Juadeo-Arabic Poetry in Vatican Ms. 411: Links with Maltese and Sicilian Arabic." *Journal of Maltese Studies* 13 (1979): 1–16.

Wiener, M. *Emek habacha.* Leipzig, 1858.

Zarren-Zohar, Efrat. "From Passover to Shavuot." In Paul F. Bradshaw and Lawrence A. Hoffman, eds., *Passover and Easter: The Symbolic Structure of Sacred Seasons.* Notre Dame, Ind., 1999.

Zerubavel, Yael. *Recovered Roots: Collective Memory in the Making of Israeli National Tradition.* Chicago, 1995.

Zunz, Leopold. *Zur Geschichte und Literatur.* Berlin, 1895; photo reprint Hildesheim, 1976.

INDEX

About the Author

NORMAN ROTH is Professor of Jewish History, Hebrew literature, and Jewish Studies at the University of Wisconsin, Madison. Over his long and productive career he has written and edited many books, including *Maimonides: Essays and Texts* (1985), *Jews, Visigoths, and Muslims in Medieval Spain* (1994), *Conversos, Inquisition, and the Expulsion of the Jews from Spain* (1995), and *Medieval Jewish Civilization: An Encyclopedia* (2003).